Words on Fire

The Douglass Series on women's lives and the meaning of gender

*Elizabeth Gurley Flynn, in Sheriff Merning's office in Minnesota, taken while she was
organizing iron miners of the Mesabi Range, 1916*

Words on Fire

The Life and Writing
of Elizabeth Gurley Flynn
by Rosalyn Fraad Baxandall

Rutgers University Press, New Brunswick and London

Cover illustration of Elizabeth Gurley Flynn agitating during the Paterson Strike, 1913, courtesy of the Library of Congress. The photograph on page 185 of NYCP members leaving the Federal Court House after being indicted under the Smith Act, July 1951, courtesy of The New York Times. *All other photographs in this book are courtesy of the Tamiment Institute Library, New York University.*

Library of Congress Cataloging-in-Publication Data

Flynn, Elizabeth Gurley.
  Words on fire.

  (The Douglass series on women's lives and the meaning of gender)
  Includes index.
   1. Women and socialism.   2. Women—Social conditions.   3. Women—Poetry.
4. Communism—United States.   5. Communists—United States—Biography.
6. Flynn, Elizabeth Gurley.   I. Baxandall, Rosalyn Fraad, 1939–   .   II. Title.
III. Series.
HX546.F55   1987   335 .0088042   86-31325
ISBN 0-8135-1240-9
ISBN 0-8135-1241-7 (pbk.)

British Cataloging-in-Publication data available

Contents

Acknowledgments

Words on Fire has taken far too long to write. The project began in the early 1970s, when Meredith Tax and I discovered Elizabeth Gurley Flynn's papers at the American Institute of Marxist Studies (AIMS), a dingy, three-room library and office in New York City, presided over by Herbert Aptheker, the author of many books on slavery and black rebellions. The search for these papers grew out of our interest in radical women's history.

My original women's liberation group, New York Radical Women (1967–1969), the first feminist group in New York City and the most inspiring and exciting group I have ever been part of, was the spark igniting my original interest in women's history. Kathy Amatniek Sarachild was the group's leader, although there was no formal acknowledgment of her role. She was the most daring and honest, and later helped me with the Flynn manuscript, sending me clippings and generally pushing me to refine and redefine my ideas. She also assisted in editing the conclusion. Carol Hanisch, Anne Forer, Marion Davidson, Cindy Cisler, Irene Pesilikis, Peggy Dobbins, Judith Thibault, and Judith Duffet raised my feminist and class consciousness and helped provide a feminist vision of the world and focus for my life. Pam Allen, Shulamith Firestone, Anne Koedt, Pat Mainardi, Jenny Gardiner, Marilyn Lowen, Joanne Hoit, Helen Kritzler, Ruth Glass, and Ellen Willis added new ideas and opened up new horizons.

When the feminist movement got going in the 1960s, we thought, rather euphorically and naïvely, that after a few years both society's institutions and human consciousness would change to accommodate women's equal participation on the job, in government, and in personal relations. Unfortunately, change was painfully slow and often beyond our control, and the women's liberation movement grew more moderate as it gained wider recognition.

Perplexed at the conservative turn the movement was taking in the early 1970s, a few radical feminist activists decided to study women's history, looking for insights into their situation. The task of this group of feminist socialists, called the Great Atlantic Patchwork Quilt, was the exploration of the radical roots of earlier women's struggles. The women in that group, especially Sarah Eisenstein and Meredith Tax, encouraged me to work on Elizabeth Gurley Flynn.[1]

As a red diaper baby I felt a great deal of family loyalty to the Communist party, even though I knew about the horrors of Stalinism and the Party's failure to come to grips with the American reality. I was brought up in the McCarthy years, and my parents were too fearful to freely discuss their politics. However, they dedicated themselves to socialism, to struggles for peace, community control, and freedom; they were humanitarians. They set an example of a communist life of struggle and community. The bits of communist theory and history I caught were enough to spark my interest. Learning about Flynn and American communism was my way of learning about my past.

Finding the Flynn papers was easy. But it has taken almost fifteen years of badgering, howling, and having others nudge and kick to make the papers available to the public. When Meredith Tax and I first tracked down these papers in 1971, they were stuffed into six rusty file drawers. Nobody, except Audrey Olmstead, who had written a thesis on Flynn's oratory, had ever looked at these papers.[2] The collection contained remarkable items—letters, poems, photos, a button collection and Wobbly souvenirs, flags, announcement cards, and posters.

Many of the papers crumbled in my hands. They needed to be microfilmed and preserved. The Communist party claimed not to have the funds to restore and catalog the papers. However, after I arranged for first the Labadie Collection at the University of Michigan and then the University of Wisconsin's Historical Society to do the microfilming, it became apparent that the real issue was not money but control over the Flynn papers.

As I hounded the Communist party to raise money for microfilming and cataloging, the Party became suspicious and forbade access to the files. I was never formally notified of this decision or their reasons for it. Finally, after I met with the Woman's Committee of the Party and several people intervened on my behalf, I was again granted permission to use the Flynn papers.

When I next saw the papers I decided to xerox anything that the Communist party might consider embarrassing, for example, Flynn's love poems, her criticisms of the Party, and some letters. I began tracking down Flynn's relatives and friends and learned from her will that all her personal papers had been left to her nephew, Peter Martin, who has given me permission to reprint them here, but that the Party had never allowed him to take them.

Meanwhile, Herbert Aptheker and AIMS moved to the West Coast, and the Flynn papers were transferred to Communist party headquarters on West Twenty-Third Street in New York City. The Communist party claimed the papers were lost in this move. However, the moving men were positive the files had arrived safely at Party headquarters. It took years of organized pressure to get the Party to locate the Flynn papers.

Sometime in 1983 Dorothy Swanson, the chief librarian at the Tamiment Library, New York University, heard that the Communist party had found a file drawer of Flynn's papers and would donate them to the Tamiment. What was found, however, were only official notebooks and clippings of her *Daily Worker* columns, and none of her IWW material, poems, letters, notebooks, or manuscripts. I located my list of all the Flynn materials and asked people to pressure the Communist party to find the rest of the papers. In the beginning of 1985 the Party located most of the Flynn papers. One of the stories was that the files were found among some garbage about to be thrown out. Still missing from the papers, however, are items about Flynn's years in Oregon, when she was recuperating from ill health and living with lesbian Marie Equi, and her criticism of the Communist party. Fortunately, earlier I had xeroxed copies of much of this material.

Again with Meredith Tax's encouragement I decided to put together a collection of Flynn's writing on women. James Allen of the Communist party's International Publishers contacted me and suggested I publish a book of Flynn's writings. Allen was a well-informed, conscientious editor; he was extremely helpful and made constructive criticisms. All was going smoothly until Allen resigned from International Publishers; his successor stalled indefinitely and finally lost the manuscript.[3]

One of the great pleasures in working on this book has been meeting and chatting with Flynn's relatives, friends, and colleagues. Many were most helpful, such as Steve Nelson, Dorothy Healy, Peggy Dennis, Al Richmond, Annette Rubinstein, John Gates, Martha Stone, Evelyn Weiner, Virginia Gardiner, Vera Buch Weisbord, Lester Rodney, Joe Starobin, Yuri Suhl, Gurley Turner, Sam D'Arcy, Abe McGill, and Grace and Manny Granich. All have left the Party, but continue to fight against American imperialism and for a nuclear-free world. Their militance and continued optimism have been inspiring. Of the people I interviewed, several have become friends: Charlotte Todes Stern, Martha Stone, Roberta Bobba, Peter Martin, and Steve Nelson. Most Party members refused to talk to me; many did not openly object but were just never available. There were exceptions: Arthur and Pearl Zipser were generous with their knowledge and material. Gil Green, Jim Tormey, and Art and Ester Shields spoke to me, and I talked to William Weinstone, who was quite ill, on the phone. Claude Lightfoot and Jack Kling gave permission for me to read their letters to Flynn that the FBI had copied. Herbert Aptheker often answered my many questions while he was at the AIMS office. I also interviewed George Charney, Dorothy and Al Blumberg, Ann Timpkins Burlak, Oakley Johnson, and the owners of John and Mary's Restaurant, where Flynn hung out.

Most of Flynn's relatives have been helpful, especially Roberta Bobba and Peter Martin. Frances Onipede wrote from Nigeria and answered my questions. Betty Mallard and Marge Franz talked to me on the phone, and Yuri Suhl and Selma Dubrin gave me photographs. Robert Kempner sent me lists of books to read and had a sign made for my car, "Honk If You Know Elizabeth Gurley Flynn.

In the course of the project I met people researching friends of Flynn's, and they shared their work with me and sent me material: Dee Garrison, who was writing a biography of Mary Heaton Vorse;[4] Peter Carlson, who wrote a biography of Big Bill Haywood;[5] Neil Basen, an inveterate researcher who was writing a biography of Kate Richards O'Hare; Nuncio Pericone, who was writing a biography of Carlo Tresca; Nancy Krieger, who wrote an article on Marie Equi and has become a close friend;[6] and Charlot Holzkamper, who wrote a paper on Elizabeth Gurley Flynn.

Many librarians have been extremely helpful, especially Dione

Miles at the Wagner Archives at Wayne State University; she herself is knowledgeable about the IWW. Dorothy Swanson, Ethel Lobman, Debra Bernhardt, Robert Shaffer, and Peter Filardo of the Tamiment have helped a great deal. Martha Foley, an archivist at the Tamiment, is in the process of cataloging the Flynn papers and is doing a devoted, meticulous job. My present editor at Rutgers University Press, Marlie Wasserman, gave me intelligent advice, that was often painful to hear. Kathryn Gohl, the copyeditor, improved the book a great deal. My agent, Charlotte Sheedy, and her assistant, Regula Noetzle, helped as well.

While I grew discouraged over the many setbacks, John McDermott, with whom I taught, carried on. He put the articles on women I had collected in a bound file in the Old Westbury library. Clary Perez now of Ponca, Arkansas, and Rachel Geise of North Truro, Massachusetts, typed out many of Flynn's newspaper articles.

More time passed and Linda Gordon encouraged me to write an article on Flynn for *Radical America*.[7] Paul and Mary Jo Buhle, Jim Green, and Lee Baxandall helped with this effort, editing and giving general guidance.

The people in American Studies at the State University of New York at Old Westbury have been extremely supportive, especially John McDermott, John Ehrenreich, Naomi Rosenthal, Laura Schwartz, and Maria Spiccattie, the secretary who typed several versions of the manuscript and mailed and xeroxed for me. Elaine Goodman typed the Introduction. Carol Niles faithfully xeroxed all too much on her lunch hours. Paul Lauter and Florence Howe were also encouraging at the beginning. My dearest friends, Elizabeth Ewen, Wini Breines, and Linda Gordon, have all listened to my obsession with Flynn and have helped in editing, overall conception, and hand holding. Elizabeth Ewen, who is both a close friend and colleague, has helped in visible and invisible ways on an almost daily basis throughout the long process. Stuart Ewen came up with the title, and encouraged me to swim and relax. Obie Bing, Steve Bronner, Richard Elman, and Jonathan Ree have all been there when I needed them. Paul Breines helped me edit the introduction and generally had faith in the project. Steve Bronner encouraged me to learn more about the Comintern, and Jonathan Ree asked me all the hard questions. Sheila Rowbotham and Jean McCrindle shared my interest in the old Left and went over an early version of the introduction. Lee Baxandall inspired me by example and when we were together put in many hours typing, editing, and listening. Even after we separated I could still call on him occasionally to discuss the trials and tribulations of this work.

Ed Greer, my lawyer and friend, fought the FBI with cunning and patience to obtain Flynn's files through the Freedom of Information Act. A short-lived CP study group (1984–1985)— Meredith Tax, David Paskin, Josh Freeman, and Mark Naison— gave me new ideas and encouragement. Harriet Fraad, my sister and friend, provided psychological counseling, support, and some help with strengthening my perceptions. Obie Bing provided tender loving care, tolerated my Flynn fever, and helped make daily life calm. My sweet son Phineas Reed Baxandall insisted that I learn how to use a word processor, which ultimately made the task possible. He also provided hours of joy and relaxation. I hope he will inherit a better world.

Words on Fire does not include all of Elizabeth Gurley Flynn's writings on women. It does, however, contain samples of her writings and speeches on women from every period of her life, and all the major themes and issues Flynn addressed are represented.

Flynn was best known as a speaker and columnist. The majority of her talks were not recorded, except by the FBI, and those recordings were often inaccurate. Most of Flynn's writing was published in the *Daily Worker*; she hammered out two or three columns a week. However, she was also an inveterate letter writer, sometimes, especially when she was traveling, writing as many as six letters a day. Her letters and poems, to which almost no one was privy, and which she kept in a bound diary, express her vulnerable, sensitive side, witnessed by only a few of her closest friends.

While all Flynn's letters and poems relating to women are not included in this collection, I have tracked down as many as possible from manuscript collections, friends, foes, and FBI files. Flynn wrote an autobiography of the first half of her life, *Rebel Girl*, which is still in print, therefore, no selections have been excerpted from it.

As an aid to the reader, I've quietly corrected some of Flynn's unorthodox punctuation and spelling.

Introduction

I feel very proud of my life
yet humble in the living of it.
Elizabeth Gurley Flynn, August 6, 1955

Elizabeth Gurley Flynn (1890–1964) led a long, illustrious, and stormy life. She was a key organizer of East Coast labor strikes, a leader of free speech battles, and a major figure in labor defense. Celebrated in song (Joe Hill, the Wobbly songwriter, wrote *The Rebel Girl* for her), she was cheered by thousands whom she inspired in a militant, melodious tone to fight for decent wages and a share of life's glories. Flynn was one of the great orators of her era, an era that spanned the violent labor strife of the early 1900s, the repression and Red Scare of the World War I period, the depression of the 1930s, the left-wing militance of the World War II period, the jailings of the McCarthy years, and the beginnings of the 1960s activism. She wrote a weekly newspaper column for twenty-six years, as well as political pamphlets, an autobiography, and a jail memoir. Beloved and worshiped by left-wing radicals, she inspired hundreds with her verve and warmth, yet conservatives vilified her as a she-devil, jailed her, and tried to prevent her from agitating. One of the founders of the American Civil Liberties Union, she ran for Congress and was the first female chairman of the Communist Party of the United States of America.

FORMATIVE YEARS

Elizabeth Gurley Flynn launched her dazzling career as orator and defender of women by winning a gold medal in her grammar school debating society for urging that women be given the vote.

At this time women had not yet gained the right to vote in New York, her home state, nor in many states for that matter. At fifteen, Flynn insisted in public speeches that freedom for women was impossible under capitalism. She argued that the government should financially support children so that women could bear them without dependence on men. A daily press headline in response to her rousing first public address, "What Socialism Will Do for Women," read: "Mere Child Talks Bitterly of Life."[1] Theodore Dreiser was so impressed by this speech that he wrote a magazine article about her dark Irish loveliness, calling her an East Side Joan of Arc (in fact, she lived in the Bronx). The popular left-wing poet of the period, Adolf Wolff, also compared her to Joan of Arc in his poem entitled "Elizabeth Gurley Flynn."

> She too a vision had and voices heard.
> She heard the groans of slaving, starving workers:
> She had a vision of their liberation.
> She too shall live an ever-shining glory,
> In human history, in human hearts—
> An even brighter glory than Jeanne d'Arc.[2]

Flynn was first arrested when she was sixteen, along with her father, for blocking traffic and speaking without a permit, but the fear of incarceration never prevented her from addressing a crowd. She was arrested ten times in all. A newspaper described the first occasion: "The crowd listened to the talk of the men, but when the pretty girl began they whooped and cheered so much that ten policemen were sent from the West 30th Street Station."[3] The subsequent trial ended with the case dismissed and her lawyer proclaiming Elizabeth Gurley Flynn the "coming Socialist woman orator of America."

Elizabeth Gurley Flynn continued to make public speeches throughout her life, "one a day, two a day, and during the big Passaic textile strike in 1926, ten a day." The *New Yorker* critic likened her to the Greek mythological brass-lunged giants. The less literary *Los Angeles Times* merely called her a "Clear and Present Danger," noting that "Most Bloodthirsty of Agitators Are [the] She Dogs of Anarchy."[4]

Elizabeth Gurley Flynn was a prodigy. The strong character of her parents and the poverty of her Irish-American working-class family contributed to this development.

The conditions in the textile towns of New Hampshire and Massachusetts made a profound impression on me as a little girl . . . huge gray mills, like prisons, barracks like company boarding houses, long hours, low pay, long periods of slack. . . . I saw lard instead of butter on neighbors' tables, children without underwear in cold New England winters, a girl scalped by an unguarded machine in a mill across the street from our school. We heard her terrible screaming. I saw an old man weeping as they put him in a lock up as a tramp. . . . I saw my mother humiliated by unpaid grocery bills, the landlord standing at the door demanding his rent. More than once the gas was turned off and we studied by the light of the oil lamp.[5]

Flynn's family loomed large. They were a primary influence throughout her life. Her mother's relatives were educated land-owning peasants from the same stock as George Bernard Shaw; her father's folks were poor, but militant fighters for the Fenian cause. Her parents were dirt poor and certainly had their share of hard times. But poverty never dampened their spirits, and both remained energetic and alert. Her mother died in 1938 and her father in 1943.

Mama, as her mother, Annie Gurley, was warmly called by her children, was the saint and center of the Flynn family, beloved by all. Annie Gurley was a modest, forceful, cultured, and accomplished woman. She contributed to her daughter's intellectual development by reading aloud from Irish history and poetry, from Swift, Yeats, Burns, Byron, Elizabeth Barrett Browning, and Greek mythology. Her interests were political as well as literary. She was a member of the Irish Feminist Club and went out of her way on foot to hear Susan B. Anthony and other early suffragists speak. She was a strong advocate and supporter of equality for women. All four of her children were delivered by female doctors, much to the consternation of the Flynn in-laws and neighbors. Elizabeth was named after one of these doctors, Elizabeth Kent.

Mama, who had aristocratic tastes, kept the Flynns respectable by sewing all their clothes. She was a skilled tailor and refused to be called a seamstress. The female physician who delivered Bina, the youngest Flynn, ordered a pants suit from Annie Gurley, but the doctor required a police permit before she could wear it on the street, as it was unlawful to wear the clothes of the opposite sex at that time.[6]

Flynn wrote many newspaper columns about her mother, especially around Saint Patrick's Day, her mother's birthday.

She was a patient and devoted mother [but] she did not consider the home a career for women. . . . Mama was interested in politics, which few women were in those days. She did not talk about material success, but wanted her girls to get an education and do something worthwhile. . . . Even when we were little children, we knew our mother was different from others in our neighborhood. She read a great deal, and began to collect a small library which we have today—Mama's books, we call them. . . . She went to lectures, and attended night school to improve her handwriting. . . . Our mother was a Socialist early in her lifetime.[7]

Thomas Flynn, Elizabeth's father, was a quarry worker in New Hampshire when Elizabeth was born. He had previously attended Dartmouth College and worked as a civil engineer. Papa, as Thomas Flynn was called, was a math whiz. He wrote a math text and sent his Dartmouth professors unresolvable problems that he had managed to master, as well as writing a great deal of flowery poetry to such figures as Eugene Debs and Emma Goldman.[8] A highly political man, Thomas Flynn belonged to the Knights of Labor, the Anti-Imperialist League, the Socialist Labor party, and the Socialist party. He ran for city engineer in 1896, in Manchester, New Hampshire, and for the New York State Assembly in 1920, in South Bronx, on the Socialist party ticket, getting more votes in New York City than the Republican candidate. He was defeated in Manchester, New Hampshire, because he was Irish.

Elizabeth, the most beautiful and political of the daughters, was the apple of the father's eye, and Thomas took her along to socialist meetings when he spoke. Most writers credit him with Elizabeth's political development. Yet as Elizabeth's younger sister Kathie said: "It burns me up how people talk about Pop as if we never had a mother. He was belligerent and vociferous, while Mama was quiet and composed. In plain English, Pop talked loud and long while Mama got things done. The notion that we got all our progressive views from him is erroneous."[9] Thomas's contributions to the family were political rather than economic. He disliked working, rationalizing that his labor would only make some greedy capitalist richer. His favorite book was *The Right to Be Lazy* by Marx's son-in-law, Paul Lafargue.[10]

Elizabeth maintained close family ties all her life, and much of the time she lived with her parents. After her mother's death she lived with a younger sister and lifelong best friend, Kathie, who was a schoolteacher and served as Elizabeth's secretary. New York City was Elizabeth's home base owing to her family, but she loved the West and the industrial heartland and would have preferred to live there. "If it were not for my mother, I doubt if I'd ever go near New York City. It is a nerve wracking place for me and too Jewish for me."[11] She traveled across the United States several times a year throughout her life, and every time she left New York City she felt as if she got "a blood transfusion."[12]

Although the Flynns were colorful, they were not atypical of many European, self-educated, immigrant poor who made their way to the teeming American city slums at the turn of the century. Certainly the Flynns were a close-knit clan, and they provided Lizzie, as they called her, with a socialist set of values as well as with an intellectual curiosity and foundation. She could not have become a political activist without their emotional and financial sustenance.

In the nineteenth century, the expression *red diaper baby* had not yet been invented; if it had been, Elizabeth Gurley Flynn would have been called a red-and-green diaper baby—red for radicalism and green for the Emerald Isle of her ancestors, Ireland. Her mother's first language was Gaelic; her youngest sister, Sabina, called Bina, was a member of the Irish players; and all the Flynn girls had the Irish gift of gab. Her dad never spoke the word *England* without adding, "God damn her."[13]

Many of the heroes of the Irish freedom movement—James Larkin, Tom Mann, James Connolly—stayed at the Flynn Bronx cold-water flat. They were impressed by Elizabeth's intelligence and militance and proudly encouraged her. James Connolly, the Irish revolutionary who was later executed by the British for his leading role in the Easter Uprising of 1916, wrote to a friend, inquiring about the infamous Elizabeth and wondering whether she was the run-of-the-mill conceited child prodigy or something special. The friend, John Matheson, responded:

The Belle Flynn is alright. Like you I have a distrust of prodigies. But Lizzie is entirely free from the stereotyping characteristic. In fact the really wonderful thing about her is her readiness [with] which she evinces a desire to learn and to abandon her former opinions—when proven untenable. She started out a pure utopian, but she now laughs at her former theories. Had she stuck to her first set of opinions, she would have continued a persona grata with the Socialist Party crowd, which commands the biggest

purse and biggest audience, but her advocacy of straight revolutionary socialism and industrial unionism alienated them.[14]

Outside of Irish revolutionaries and her immediate family, a
major radicalizing influence was Elizabeth's high school sweetheart
Fred Robinson, the son of Dr. William Robinson, the well-known
anarchist and birth control advocate. Fred encouraged her to read
the utopian socialist William Morris's *News from Nowhere* and introduced her to many anarchists. Among them was Emma Goldman,
who disappointed the young Elizabeth because she was such an
unglamorous, stout, small woman in a flat hat. However, when
Elizabeth heard Goldman speak she changed her mind; despite
her adolescent concerns about appearance, Flynn delighted in
Goldman's ideas.[15] Her father was disturbed about these dangerous anarchist influences and insisted that his daughter counteract
them with Marx and Engels's diatribe against utopian socialism,
Socialism Scientific and Utopian. Her anarchist connections continued, however, and her lover of fourteen years (1912–1926)
would be the Italian anarchist Carlo Tresca.

Despite her immersion in anarchist ideas, Flynn claimed that
her reason for becoming a socialist was a change in her family's
economic circumstances: her father, in spite of winning a lawsuit
against his employer, was not paid for two years of contracted
labor.

> During two consecutive winters we suffered from the misery and crushing,
> but sometimes revolutionizing poverty. I became ill, lost six months from
> school and had time to read, think and reflect carefully. I had theories:
> here was a condition that did not coincide with my theories; the theories
> had to go. I began to see the hypocrisy and dishonesty surrounding me
> and became an iconoclast and a utopian of an anarchist trend. As I studied
> the evolution of society, of class struggle and economic factors and their
> power over our lives, I demanded principles more practical and organized
> or scientific and yet revolutionary. I became and am now a class conscious
> Marxist socialist. My economic conditions had changed and in many cases,
> my ideas changed in rapid order.[16]

In spite of Flynn's claim that she was a scientific socialist, none of
her early writings reflect the class, materialistic, or dialectic analysis necessary for Marxist theory. All of her early pieces were origi-

nally written for high school assignments, many of them for the debating club, although she delivered them at the Harlem and West Side Socialist Club, the New York City Unity Club, Socialist Sunday schools, on street corners at the West Orange, New Jersey, Temple of Honor Hall, and Irvington's city hall.[17] By her midteens she was a seasoned soapbox stomper.

If her family, its grinding poverty, and the encounters with Irish revolutionaries influenced Flynn's thought, so did the long hours spent with books. In high school she read Friedrich Engels's *Origin of the Family, Private Property, and the State,* Mary Wollstonecraft's *Vindication of the Rights of Women,* August Bebel's *Women and Socialism,* and Peter Kropotkin's *Appeal to the Young,* which, she said, "helped to catapult me into socialist activities." Her sister Kathie described her at this time as "deadly serious . . . she seldom laughed or even smiled. . . . Later we [Kathie and Elizabeth] agreed that poverty is bound to make older children super-serious."[18]

IWW ORGANIZER

Both the Chicago founding of the Industrial Workers of the World (IWW) in 1905 and the revolutionary upsurge in Russia that same year had a profound effect on Flynn's development. She heard about the IWW from James Connolly, who took a special interest in her political development. Gurley, as she was called by IWW mates, joined the militant working-class "one big union" in 1906 as a member of the mixed Local No. 179 in New York City. Women and juniors (both categories applied to her as she was only sixteen) were exempt from the otherwise strict requirement that membership was for wage earners only. She chose not to join the Socialist party since her parents and professors as well as lawyers, doctors, ministers, and middle-aged and older people were all members. "We felt it was rather stodgy," she explained, and "we felt a desire to have something more militant, more progressive and more youthful, and we flocked into the new organization, the IWW."[19]

The Wobblies, as they were familiarly known, stood as a militant romantic reproach to the moderate, cautious American Federation of Labor (AFL) and the increasingly tame Socialist party. They were the wildest, wooliest, most joyous radical group to strike fear into the hearts of the American bourgeoisie. One Big Union of all workers organized by industry rather than craft was their motto. Their strident militance is summed up in the preamble to their constitution, which began: "The working class and the employing class have nothing in common. There can be no peace as long as hunger and want are found among millions of working people and the few who make up the employing class, have all the good things in life."

In 1907 Flynn, age seventeen, was elected a delegate to the IWW convention. On the way back from Chicago she made a speaking tour for the Wobblies, and was surprised when she was compensated with two weeks' salary. "I remember it quite vividly because they gave me a twenty dollar gold piece after paying my railroad fare and lodging and I was so thrilled at such a big amount of money. But when I got home the family rent of eighteen dollars was due, so I rapidly returned to normalcy of purse and pride."[20]

Many of the Wobbly membership were itinerant hobos and single, foreign-born males, but Gurley felt as safe among them "as if in God's pocket." There were few female Wobbly organizers, but more than in any other labor union of its time. More innovative and open, the IWW was also less rigid in its ideas about woman's place. This is not to say the Wobblies were free of male supremacy. Their general attitude toward women was classic and simple: "There were good women like their mothers and bad women [prostitutes] who fleeced them on pay day."

An IWW song sung with great sentiment reflects this attitude. It describes:

> One little girl, fair as a pearl,
> Who worked every day in a laundry,

The song goes on to explain how she was lured into the red-light district. The refrain is:

> Who is to blame, you know his name,
> It's the boss who pays starvation wages.[21]

When the heroic Wobbly hobo married, he usually referred to his wife as the "ball and chain."[22] Gurley became the IWW female ideal. She was Delacroix's Liberty—young, sexy, yet hardy and statuesque. The Wobs, who could be quite macho and crude, treated her both as an elegant lady, lace-curtain Irish, and as one of the boys. She drank, joked, talked dirty, and basked in their admiration. She was described as "the saint in our house," when she was spoken of. It was in "hushed reverence," a Wobbly reminisced. Those who knew her in her youth described her with "flaming red hair," "auburn hair," others "pitch black locks." Some people said "she belted out her message"; others said she was "soft spoken." [23] She became a secular IWW saint, a mythic hero. People found in her whatever they themselves were seeking.

Gurley did not accept all the Wobbly attitudes and practices toward women, nor did she think them unchangeable, but she agreed with the basic IWW tenet that the problems of women cannot be separated from the problems of the working class and women therefore should not organize separately. In that context, she wrote articles and gave fiery orations on how members of the One Big Union should in thought and action become more sensitive to women's needs, recruit more females into the organization, and eradicate the male chauvinism that prevented the women from actively participating. Her saintly status, however, led her to identify with male leaders and removed her from the consciousness of ordinary women. Some female Wobblies drew strength and courage from Gurley; others were awed and felt intimidated by her talents and stature.

Unlike other labor organizations, the IWW organized telephone operators in Portland, Indianapolis, Chicago, and Seattle, and domestics in Denver, as well as thousands of textile workers in the mills of Bridgeport, Connecticut; Minersville, Pennsylvania; Lawrence, Massachusetts; and Paterson, New Jersey. [24] Unlike other unions, the Wobblies welcomed all wage workers regardless of their sex, color, creed, nationality, or politics. Much of their literature and propaganda was addressed to "Working Men and Women." Gurley was the soul of the IWW movement, an outstanding speaker and agitator.

> Her lithe little figure, her flaming red tie, her beautiful oval face with the broad clear brow and mischievous eyes: these were seen on a make shift rostrum, and wherever she went she drew people, held them as ponderous philosophers and thumping haranguers of the labor movement were unable to. [25]

As a public speaker she was considered in a class with William Jennings Bryan and Billy Sunday. She once told a reporter after being jailed, "I agitate a listener. I know how to get the power out of my diaphragm instead of my vocal chords and I'm happy to be free to give capitalism hell."[26]

From Big Bill Haywood, the one-eyed executive secretary of the IWW and former cowboy and miner, she learned to speak simply to the immigrant masses and to distrust interpreters, as many of them were government agents and provocateurs who exaggerated freely in order to provoke violence. Haywood advised Gurley "to speak to immigrants as one would speak to children." Other socialist and labor groups either ignored the immigrants or addressed them in heavy, theoretical tones. "The key," Haywood said, "was in speaking in short clipped sentence fragments and in using only the simplest words. Eight fingers for an eight hour day, a fist for unity, a few fingers for the offerings of management, many for the wages demanded by strikers."[27]

Being a skilled speaker in the early 1900s was equivalent to being a movie star, a media hero today. Before the advent of radio and television, all mass communication depended on either the printed word or unaided spoken words. For radicals these two modes were closely associated, for the main source of sales of their literature was at open-air meetings. To stop the meetings would have reduced a movement to impotence. Therefore, in the early 1900s a considerable portion of the activity of the IWW was directed toward the defense and extension of the right to hold outdoor meetings. Those rights, the rights of assembly and free speech, were guaranteed by the Constitution.

However, the attitude of "respectable society," the business leaders and politicians, toward the IWW was that its members were noisy loafers with an innate indisposition toward work and that therefore the "noise" these agitators made was not free speech as protected by the Constitution. As with many other radical, progressive issues in United States history, new laws were passed and old laws rediscovered, resurrected, or reinterpreted—and sometimes vigilante violence was promoted—to effectively deny the IWW the right to speak, publish, assemble, organize, or use the United States mails.

Speaking in the streets was a necessary way of reaching masses.

Street life was busy and rich. Peddlars sold food and clothes on the street, and as most people had no telephones and few could read, information was passed on through the peddlars. Tenements were small, and people spent a lot of time in the street. Many got an education simply by attending the university of the streets. Some open-air talks went on for hours, with considerable give and take from the audience. To be a speaker who could communicate with a street crowd was to have a tremendous source of power and popularity. Much of Flynn's prominence came from this ability to touch and move a crowd, first on street corners and later in mass strike meetings.[28]

During the Paterson silk strike of 1913, Gurley addressed one of the first street mass meetings, and after her talk, 25,000 silk workers left their jobs. The police chief locked Gurley up for causing chaos and turmoil and told her that she could go free only if she left town for good. She chose jail. Her speeches took the audience (in many places, two-thirds non-English-speaking) to the precipice of every human emotion and left them ready to fight. Even unions hostile to the IWW, like the United Mine Workers, enlisted Flynn to speak to their members.

The life of a "jawsmith," as IWW speakers and agitators were called, had a powerful appeal for Gurley, who had spent most of her life in the slums of the South Bronx and Manchester, New Hampshire. School seemed insignificant after a taste of travel, the romance of meeting new people, and learning through action. So, at seventeen and an *A* student, Flynn quit high school to follow what turned out to be a lifetime of traveling, agitating, organizing, and writing. "I fell in love with my country—its rivers, prairies, forests, mountains, cities and people. . . , I had a sensation of excitement, which I never lost no matter how many trips I took over the spacious bosom of my country."[29]

Having put school behind, Flynn tried her wings as an organizer, first in Paterson and then on the Mesabi iron mountain range in Minnesota. While at the IWW convention in Chicago, she had met Jack Archibald Jones, a Wobbly organizer from Bovey, Minnesota, who had spent ten years in prison on arson charges. He wrote to her urging her to join him on the Mesabi Range, which she did. They married and moved first to Chicago, where he shoveled snow, then to Ontario, and then back to Missoula. As the noted IWW leader Vincent St. John remarked, and Flynn later concurred, "Elizabeth fell in love with the West and the miners, and she married the first one she met."[30]

Their life together was hectic and brief: two years and three months. Most of the time they saw little of each other. Gurley was busy writing and organizing and was arrested in Missoula, Montana, and Spokane, Washington, while agitating for free speech. In Spokane she became the sixth editor of the IWW newspaper, *Industrial Solidarity,* the previous five having been jailed. She delayed her arrest by chaining herself to a lamppost while she spoke to a crowd. Once in jail, she charged the sheriff with using the women's section of the jail as a brothel, with the police soliciting customers.[31] Jack Jones in this period was employed to dig a railroad tunnel near Duluth. He too was in jail for part of their marriage—the first time just ten days after the ceremony—on charges of attempting to dynamite the residence of a mine official. Like other Wobblies at this time, Gurley too advocated sabotage against the ruling class. In fact her most controversial piece of writing, a pamphlet titled *Sabotage,* is a defense of workers' right to use sabotage.

Gurley and Jack had two children. The first was born prematurely and died within a few hours, probably due to the strenuous life and harsh conditions Gurley endured while pregnant (jail, inadequate housing and nutrition, and little sleep). Therefore when she again became pregnant, Jones demanded that she settle down to domesticity. Although this was a normal enough expectation for the time, it seemed odd coming from Jack Jones, who had not previously shown enough marital concern to have visited her in jail or come to her two jury trials. Fellow Wobblies guessed that Jones worried she might be drifting away from him and having affairs with other men. Both seemed likely. By the time the second child was born, "the love had died," and Flynn was impatient and bored with Jones; as she said, "I was high-spirited and headstrong and was not ready to attempt to adjust to another person."[32] She had kept her name throughout, and had given it to Fred, their son.[33]

Other accounts of Jack Jones indicate that he was an erratic and difficult person to live with. He remained a Wobbly until 1911, when he joined William Z. Foster's Syndicalist League. Foster was a leader in the steel strike of 1919 and a national executive in the

Communist party later. Also Jack Jones became a member of the AFL painter's union in Chicago. In 1920 he gave notice of divorce from Flynn on grounds of desertion and then remarried. For his honeymoon, he and his bride planned to navigate Lake Michigan in a boat he had built, but a terrible storm came up on the lake and the bride was drowned.[34] In later years Jones, described as a master showman in a lumber jacket, with unkempt hair and a thin dreamer's face, became the proprietor of the Dill Pickle, a radicals' nightclub and theater that was the "center of corn belt bohemia" on the north side of Chicago and edited a mimeographed sheet called the *Dil Pickler,* consisting of luscious bits of gossip, items of poetry, and drawings mainly by Jones himself.[35]

Jack Jones never left much of a mark on Gurley's emotional life. Her niece and nephew told a story of walking down Forty-second Street with her and running into him. They all chatted, and when the two asked Flynn his name, as they had not been introduced, Flynn said rather sheepishly, "I forgot."[36]

Against most of her IWW friends' advice, but with her mother's support, Flynn returned to the Bronx. Her mother took over the care of Fred Flynn (or Buster, as Elizabeth called the baby) so that she could resume her work as a Wobbly jawsmith. In fact these were the most fruitful, dramatic years of Flynn's life. She was young, energetic, and beautiful; possibilities appeared infinite. There was an active suffrage movement and Socialist party, and the political climate was receptive to radicals. Although Flynn believed that cross-class collaboration was destructive because the working class could only help themselves through industrial organizations of their own, she nevertheless gained support and reinforcement from middle- and upper-class organizations and individuals. In fact, the suffragists paved the way for Flynn by preparing the public for forceful women. Flynn, while often cynical, defined herself in reference to these bourgeois women. Although she attacked them for obscuring and mediating class conflict, she also relied on their contacts to raise money for IWW strikes and defense funds.

However, unlike many of the male Wobbly leadership such as Big Bill Haywood, Flynn was never dazzled by the Greenwich Village bohemian and artistic set. They invited her to their saloons and soirees, but she preferred the company of militant immigrant

workers and rough and tough frontiersmen. Flynn's closest female friend, Mary Heaton Vorse, a well-known labor journalist,
was middle class. Flynn was regularly in touch with the wealthy
Mary Dreier of the Women's Trade Union League and the well-off
Inez Haynes Irwin of the Woman's party. She spoke at the Heterodoxy Club, a "club for unorthodox women," which met in Greenwich Village from 1912 to the early 1940s, and saved their invitations. In the Heterodoxy Club album Flynn referred to her
membership as "an experience of unbroken delight, . . . a glimpse
of women of the future, big spirited, intellectually alert, devoid of
old 'femininity' which has been replaced by a wonderful free ma-
sonry of women."[37] So, although she criticized bourgeois women
in her speeches and writing, in fact she benefited from them socially and intellectually.

During this IWW period, Flynn wrote some of her most fiery
and original work for the IWW and Socialist party press; this work
reveals a traditional socialist rather than feminist consciousness.
However, in comparison to other Wobbly women such as Lucy Parsons, the Chicago free speech and labor agitator, and Mother Jones,
the miner's angel, Flynn was far more concerned with women's issues. Many of her speeches discussed such topics as the Woman
Question, the Rights of Women, Women before and under Christi-
anity, Women and Labor, Women in Modern Industry, Political
Rights of Women, Labor Legislation for Women, Women and
Unionism, Women and Education, Equality and the Home, Marriage and Divorce, Love—Free and Otherwise, the Problem of
Prostitution, Birth Control, the Modern Family, Sex Differences
and Antagonisms, Women in Art and Literature, Women and Science, and Small Families.[38] It was important that socialist and
working-class men heard their feisty heroine speaking about topics
usually reserved only for female audiences.

Speaking and writing were only a small part of Flynn's daily
duties. When there was action, Flynn was sure to be there. She
helped organize women and girls on strike at the Coombe Garment Company of Minersville, Pennsylvania (1911), fought alongside the 25,000 Lawrence textile workers (1912) who victoriously
resisted a pay cut of thirty cents a week (the cost of five loaves of
bread), and battled the police with the Paterson silk weavers and
ribbon makers who endured five months of police brutality, ar-

rests, and near starvation (1913). She marched with the New York City hotel and restaurant workers, with the unemployed (1914), and with the miners of the Mesabi Range (1916). She participated in the Passaic textile strike (1926) when workers withstood gassing and clubs, ice-cold drenchings, injunctions, and jailings for thirteen months.

The workers in places such as Lawrence, Paterson, and Passaic were often low-paid women and children, usually immigrants, and their working conditions were horrendous. They worked ten or more hours daily, six days a week, in mills that were dirty, noisy, unventilated, and unsafe. A medical observer said of conditions in Lawrence: "a considerable number of boys and girls die within the first two or three years after beginning work . . . thirty out of every hundred of all men and women who work in the mill die before or by the time they are twenty five years of age."[39] In Paterson, several wage scales would be applied for the same work in the same shop: one girl might receive a weekly wage of $1.42 after forty-two weeks of work, while another might receive a weekly wage of $1.85 after thirty-two weeks. Often girls aged fourteen to seventeen received only half their weekly wage (after fines); the remainder was withheld until the end of the year, when it would be paid out if the girl was still employed.[40]

Not only did women constitute more than one-half the work force out on strike in these epic confrontations, they often provided the leadership on the picketline. The Lawrence police were ordered to strike women on the arms and breasts and men on the heads. They killed one striker, Anna La Pizza. Several newspaper reports at the time blamed the extreme militancy not on the IWW but on "unruly and undisciplined female elements." "Just as soon as women disregard constituted authority by catching and tearing officers' coats," bemoaned a Massachusetts judge, "why then you have the foundation for all that follows." The leader of this feminine mob was Flynn, described by the Lawrence press as a "reincarnation of the militant and maddened woman who led the march of the Commune from Paris to Versailles."[41]

The Lawrence strike united not only women and men of forty-five nationalities, but also unemployed women, housewives, mill workers, shop clerks, wives of grocery store owners, and some teachers and midwives. These women often branched out from the long parades and pickets and organized themselves into endless human chains by linking arms and encouraging others in the area to join in. They wove through the neighborhoods and business sections jeering, hooting, and hissing. One Lawrence reporter noted that they would rush out, as if on cue, and attack police, militia, unsympathetic priests, nuns, and city officials by booing loudly. Sometimes women hid scissors in their long cloaks, and when the troopers tried to arrest or separate them they would draw out their domestic sabers and cut the backs of soldiers' uniforms. At other times they would cut suspenders or collectively strip scabs.[42] By creating scenes, noise, and commotion, they confused officers and camouflaged the identity of individual attackers.

Flynn and the IWW learned from these militant women, and in turn the women were inspired by the IWW and Flynn. The IWW understood that women were key to winning strikes, and special efforts were made to reach them. Women's meetings were held in Lawrence and Paterson, where Flynn spoke of the unique oppression facing women workers and workingmen's wives:

> The women worked in the mills for lower pay and in addition had all the housework and care of the children. The old-world attitude of man as "lord and master" was strong. At the end of the day's work—or, now of strike duty—the man went home and sat at ease while his wife did all the work preparing the meal, cleaning the house, etc. There was considerable male opposition to women going to meetings and marching on the picket line. We resolutely set out to combat these notions. The women wanted to picket. They were strikers as well as wives and were valiant fighters. We knew that to leave them at home alone, isolated from the strike activity, a prey to worry, affected by the complaints of trades people, landlords, priests and ministers, was dangerous to the strike. We brought several Socialist women in as speakers and a girl organizer, Pearl McGill, who helped organize the button workers of Muscatine, Iowa. The A.F. of L. revoked her credentials for coming to Lawrence. . . . We talked especially to the women about the high cost of living here—how they had been fooled when they first came here, when they figured the dollars in their home money. They thought they were rich till they had to pay rent, buy groceries, clothes and shoes. Then they knew they were poor. We pointed out that the mill owners did not live in Lawrence, they did not spend their money in the local stores.[43]

No group remained outside politics for Flynn. If young girls were sometimes hard to reach, then imaginative appeals had to be made to involve them. During the Paterson silk strike, Flynn urged them to boycott a policemen's ball:

> There will be two balls in Paterson tomorrow night, the policeman's and the workingmen's. The policemen have done everything in their power to break this strike, and I don't believe a woman in the working class wants to put her hand in the bloody hand of a policeman. If you want to dance tomorrow night, dance with the man before you. I will ask the girls to do another thing: Don't only stay away from the policeman's ball, but picket the armory. Don't let any girls go in to dance if you can help it. I think the right minded girls will join in your protest against police brutality.[44]

In the Passaic woolen, silk, and dye strike, Victory Playgrounds were set up to free women for strike activity and to educate the children, who were organized in Pioneer groups and taught songs, and English.[45] Passaic was one of the three cities in the United States with the highest illiteracy rate, and employers resisted the efforts of the Board of Education to teach English to the workers' children. The women strikers and wives at Passaic organized into groups that met weekly, called Working Women's Councils. The Women's Council discussed conditions in the factories—such as the fact that many Passaic women worked nights, which was illegal in New Jersey—as well as problems with maternity, child care, and housework. These groups survived as mutual help organizations well after the strike was lost.

Many of the women who participated in the Lawrence, Paterson, and Passaic strikes—both workers and intellectuals—were radicalized by the experience. Although they had yet to win the vote in the United States, women had the vote in all IWW strike decisions. And Flynn symbolized the leadership women could exercise. As Mary Heaton Vorse reported:

> When Elizabeth Gurley Flynn spoke, the excitement of the crowd became a visible thing. She stood there, young, with her Irish blue eyes, her face magnolia white and her cloud of black hair, the picture of a youthful revolutionary girl leader. She stirred them, lifted them up in her appeal for solidarity. Then at the end of the meeting, they sang. It was as though a spurt of flame had gone through the audience, something stirring and powerful, a feeling which has made the liberation of people possible, something beautiful and strong had swept through the people and welded them together, singing.[46]

Vorse elsewhere recalled her first meeting with Flynn during this Lawrence confrontation:

> I walked with Bill Haywood into a quick lunch restaurant. "There's Gurley," he said. She was sitting at a lunch counter on a mushroom stool, and it was if she were the spirit of this strike that had so much hope and so much beauty. . . . There was ceaseless work for her that winter. Speaking, sitting with the strike committee, going to visit the prisoners in jail and endlessly raising money. Speaking, speaking, speaking, taking trains only to run back to the town that was ramparted by prison-like mills before which soldiers with fixed bayonets paced all day long. . . . Every strike meeting was memorable—the morning meetings, in a building quite a way from the center of things, owned by someone sympathetic to the strikers, the only place they were permitted to assemble. The soup kitchen was out here and her groceries were also distributed and the striking women came from far and near. They would wait around for a word with Gurley or with Bill. In the midst of this excitement Elizabeth moved calm and tranquil. For off the platform she is a very quiet person. It was as though she reserved her tremendous energy for speaking.[47]

Children were a central consideration in any strike. Many of the Lawrence children worked in the mills, and others attended public or Catholic schools. Flynn and Haywood organized special schools for the children during the strike, to resist the instruction they were getting in school, which was

> directed at driving a wedge between the school children and the striking parents. Often children in such towns become ashamed of their foreign-born, foreign-speaking parents, their old country ways, their accents, their foreign newspapers, and now it was their strike and mass picketing. . . . Some teachers called the strikers lazy, said they should go back to work or "back to where they came from." We attempted to counteract all this at our children's meetings. . . . The parents were pathetically grateful to us as their children began to show real respect for them and their struggles.[48]

The parents suffered at seeing their children hungry, in danger of assault by the police, or left at home unsupervised. The Italians in Lawrence proposed that the strikers' children be sent to the homes of sympathetic friends in nearby towns, as was the custom during earlier strikes in Italy, France, and Belgium. The majority of strikers were gratified to have their children looked after and voted for the exodus. Gurley was placed in charge of what came to be called the Lawrence Children's Crusade. She arranged the transportation, and she placed children aged four to fourteen in suitable (that is, only left-wing) homes. "Publicity seekers" such as the wealthy Mrs. O. H. P. Belmont were turned down as not having the interests of the strikers' children at heart.[49]

The exodus of the children eased the strikers' burden while it also drew enormous sympathy for their cause. On one occasion, as the children assembled at the Lawrence railroad station, the police sought to block them from boarding the cars that would carry them to Philadelphia. An observer from the Philadelphia Women's Committee later testified that the policemen

> closed in on us with their clubs, beating right and left with no thought of the children who then were in desperate danger of being trampled to death. The mothers and the children were thus hurled in a mass and bodily dragged to a military truck and even clubbed, irrespective of the cries of the panic-stricken mothers and children.[50]

This act of police brutality became the turning point in the strike. Newspaper editorials, and liberal and establishment spokesmen and women focused national attention on Lawrence and a congressional investigation began. Funds for the strikers poured in from every corner of the country. The American Woolen Company was compelled to accede to every point of the strikers' demands. As a result, wages went up throughout the New England textile industry.

Flynn was one of the best reporters on the activities of women and children during the Lawrence strike. The chapter on Lawrence in her autobiography, *Rebel Girl,* remains the fullest, most accurate, dramatic, detailed account of the heroic acts of the female Lawrence strikers and supporters. Without that chapter, women's participation in Lawrence would be buried and forgotten.

Other strikes Flynn participated in had less glorious outcomes. Paterson and Passaic were lost, and these failures were hard on Flynn. Speaking, agitating, and fund-raising were grueling work and began to wear her down. Fatigue, burnout, and overexhaustion are the diseases of the jawsmith trade. The life of an organizer was taxing, but male agitators found rest and resuscitation in their families' bosoms. Gurley's home life at this time was not a haven from the heartless world. Money was always scarce. Her young son complained that his mother was not around enough; her love life was turbulent as well.

HER GREAT LOVE

Flynn's romantic life was never peaceful. During the years of militant IWW activity and then of labor defense work, Flynn maintained a stormy relationship with Carlo Tresca. She met this flamboyant Italian anarchist on May Day 1912 while involved in Lawrence defense work. She lived with him for thirteen years; he was the great passion of her life. They worked together in the textile battles of Little Falls, New York; Chicago, Illinois; New Bedford, Massachusetts; Passaic, New Jersey; in the iron workers' strike on the Mesabi Range; in the waiters' strike in New York City; and in many unemployed and antimilitarist demonstrations. On New Year's Eve 1913, during the waiters' strike, they stood outside New York's most elegant hotels, picketing with the waiters and whispering to those who crossed the picket line, "Look out for sabotage as you go in, examine your food carefully." Gurley and Tresca kept many guests away, but they were arrested and accused of "placing foreign substances in food to render it unpalatable, breaking crockery, dipping table forks in crude oil, using stink pots in dining rooms and introducing bed bugs in first class hotels."[51] In organizing restaurant workers they advocated an end to tipping, and invented a form of sabotage that benefited the customer and was contrary to employers' instructions. Wine waiters instructed to dilute wines were to refrain from doing so; cooks given margarine to use in products sold as butter-baked goods were to use so much margarine that the product became as expensive as if butter had been used.[52] Gurley and Tresca's romance was the talk of the town, and pictures of them often appeared in the evening newspapers. Tresca introduced Gurley to the tightly knit Italian anarchist community, and she presented him to the liberal bohemian set.

Tresca was from a comfortable landowning family in Sulmona, northern Italy. He was on his way to becoming one of the leaders of the Socialist party in Italy when, in 1904, due to radical agitation, he was forced into exile rather than face a jail term. In Italy Tresca edited *Il Germe* (*The Seed*), a revolutionary paper, and was secretary of the railroad workers union. In the United States

Tresca centered his activity on the Italian community.[53] He was a rousing speaker and effective organizer, and he edited the anarchist papers *Il Proletario* and *Il Martello*, and *La Plebe*, the official organ of the Italian U.S. Socialist Federation. Tresca cared little about improving his rough English. In Italian he was eloquent, bold, and fearless. It was said that his first word in English was *guilty*. For organizing Italian iron miners in the Mesabi Range and for shouting "Viva Socialismo" in a cop's face he was jailed; for carrying birth control advertising in his newspaper, he was sent to the Atlanta Federal Penitentiary. He made many enemies both personal and political, was arrested thirty-six times, and had his throat cut by a hired assassin; he was bombed, kidnapped, and shot four times.

Tresca was petulant, individualistic, strong-willed, and difficult to work with. Tall, dark and handsome, with pale blue eyes, dimples and sensuous lips, Tresca usually wore a broad-brimmed Stetson hat and flowing tie and was quite the womanizer. His commitment to unfaithfulness caused Gurley much pain and turmoil. As she stated in her autobiography: "Carlo had a roving eye that roved in my direction in Lawrence and now, some ten years later was roving elsewhere." Tresca was aware of this quality. He explained to Max Eastman, the editor of *The Masses*, "I like one woman, an' then time pass an' I like another. I make many good frien'ship with women because I always say ver' frank: 'Don't trus' me. My character ver' emotional. I have gran' an' real passion now, but when dat gone, I gone too.'"[54]

Tresca was a committed revolutionary but he resented Flynn's total immersion in political activities, often trying to get her to spend more time in his company. Carlo, Flynn wrote,

> was shocked and amazed that I would even consider leaving him after he had been in jail since July. "But you are out now," I protested, "and all these men are in jail." I felt I was right, hard as it was to go. . . . Carlo was so angry that he did not write to me for six weeks after I arrived in Seattle. . . . I suffered a great deal from loneliness and worry.[55]

Although Gurley adored him, she never put him before her work. Although he admired the fact that she was a power in her own right, he also required more attention than she could spare. Many of their Italian friends encouraged her to make him the center of

her life. Carlo assumed responsibility for Fred, her son, who related to him as a father; he helped pay rent and expenses and
offered Flynn money after they split up, which she did not accept.

Tresca lived with the Flynn family in the southeast Bronx, and
while Elizabeth was away organizing, he had a long secret love affair with Bina, the youngest of Elizabeth's sisters and an actress in
Eugene O'Neill's Provincetown Players. In fact a son, Peter Martin,
was born of this affair on January 6, 1923.[56] This incident caused
the entire Flynn family great strain. The event was kept from
Elizabeth until 1926 and entirely from Annie, Elizabeth's mother,
who had recently discovered that Thomas, her husband, had another wife and daughter, Evelyn, born in 1900 in Boston. Annie
threw Thomas out of the house, and Bina took her son Peter to
Miami, Arizona, where she lived with Romolo Bobba, a former
Wobbly, who had become an organizer for the Mine, Mill, and
Smelters Union. Bina and Romolo had two girls together, Jane
and Roberta, and Bina worked as an editor of *Rancho Romance* and
wrote travel stories for magazines. She was a facile writer, made
good money, and bought her father a house in an artists' colony in
Sherman, Connecticut, where Hart Crane, Allen Tate, and Malcolm
Cowley lived. Bina and Elizabeth did not speak for nine or ten
years, but finally made up. The family had an unconventional
bohemian streak, and a great range of unorthodox behavior was
tolerated. Thomas Flynn lived in Sherman until his death, supported by Evelyn Felton, his Boston daughter, who inherited money
from an old man she had befriended.[57]

Flynn continued to love Tresca, although they quarreled constantly over political and personal matters. Elizabeth was used
to working in organizations and compromising; Carluccio, little
Carlo, as he was affectionately called, worked alone and bullied
brazenly until he got his way. He was an anarcho-syndicalist; she
was in the process of becoming a Leninist, with a strong belief in
democratic centralism and industrial unionism. They broke up in
1926. The split might have come sooner, were it not for their common work on the defense of the Italian anarchists Sacco and Vanzetti. Flynn mobilized her oratorial and organizing powers in their
defense, speaking in every town that offered her a forum. Vanzetti
even expressed concern about her health when she visited him in
Charlestown prison. "Elizabetta you must be tired of talking about

us." Vanzetti was amused when Flynn confided that to keep the story fresh, she varied it. "Sometimes I start with your youth and work forwards, sometimes with the present and work backwards, sometimes in the middle and go both ways."[58]

LABOR DEFENSE

The Sacco and Vanzetti case was only one of the defense campaigns Elizabeth Gurley Flynn organized. For Flynn, who had once hoped to become a constitutional lawyer, strike-organizing activity blended seamlessly into labor-movement defense work.[59] Indeed the two are interdependent as long as labor defense is not conceived in purely legalistic terms. Flynn thought that a labor defense should be a renewed labor offensive, and in this field she was altogether a pioneer. With the help of the IWW, the Socialist party, and some independent American Federation of Labor unions, in 1914 she put together the first united front defense group, the Workers Defense Union. It included "honest" liberals such as Lincoln Steffens and renowned lawyers willing to fight alongside such radicals as Emma Goldman and Mary Heaton Vorse.

Flynn was an old hand at defense strategy. She had participated in the first free speech fight in Missoula, Montana (1908), and in the dramatic, prolonged free speech battle in Spokane, Washington (1909–1910). Many IWW leaders opposed these attempts to put the Bill of Rights into practice, and felt this was "fighting the Bull [police] and not the boss," depleting meager Wobbly resources.[60] Flynn disagreed, and saw defense work not as a drain but as a necessary base for further organizing. Flynn found that the rights to free speech and assembly were glittering generalities and idle boasts when applied to Wobbly labor organizing. In fact in order to fight the boss, that is, to warn unsuspecting Wobblies of unfair labor practices, the IWW had to engage first in a free speech battle.

In Missoula and Spokane an ordinance was passed forbidding the IWW (but not the Salvation Army) from holding outdoor meetings. Since the streets were the IWW recruiting halls, where the Wobblies carried the message of industrial unionism to the unorganized and distributed newspapers, leaflets, and pamphlets, to forbid the Wobblies from speaking outside was to deny them the right to organize. The firebrand Flynn was at the hub of these successful free speech fights, getting herself arrested, singing loudly in jail, protesting the jail conditions, and writing articles about her experiences in the IWW newspaper *Solidarity* and in the Socialist theoretical journal *International Socialist Review.*

Flynn organized the defense committees and directed the strategy for the major twentieth-century battles over political rights for the working-class movements and immigrants: Joe Ettor and Arturo Giovannitti, the Lawrence strike leaders; Joe Hill, the IWW songwriter bard; Tom Mooney and Warren Billings, two socialists falsely accused of throwing a bomb during a Preparedness Day parade in San Francisco in 1916; and Nicola Sacco and Bartolomeo Vanzetti, with whom she was closely associated for seven years, having been the first non-Italian to understand the injustice of the case against them and to bring it before the English-language public.

Much of Flynn's defense work was undertaken for the rank and file as well as for the leaders. She came to it through her involvement with the Workers Defense Union during 1918–1924, the International Labor Defense League during 1918–1926, and the Garland Fund during 1925–1926. Both in Europe and America the socialist ranks had split over whether to support World War I. U.S. militant feminists and socialists opposed entry, whereas British suffragists supported participation. The U.S. government tried many women actively opposed to the war on charges of conspiracy or espionage (Dr. Eva Harding, Louise Oliverau, Jeanette Rankin, Myra Danton, Margaret Davies, Dr. Elizabeth Bauer, Flora Foreman, Elizabeth Ford, Dr. Marie Equi, Anita Whitney, Kate Richards O'Hare, Emma Goldman, and Rose Pastor Stokes), and Flynn helped defend them. She gave long hours under dreary conditions, raising funds for prisoners' families, visiting jails, writing publicity, lining up lawyers and speakers in several languages, gaining union and liberal support. She always had a sense that people are politics and never saw legal issues sealed off from everyday life. She said she felt as imprisoned as those she defended.

> It is hard to re-create a picture of the long years of intense brutal reaction which lasted from 1917–1927. . . . It seemed then like a hideous nightmare amidst the hum and horror of it all, working day and night in a de-

fense office. . . . I lived in the Bronx, came down early to our office (on 14th Street), and stayed late or spoke at night. I saw little of my family, my child or husband. I recall Christmas snow, with Isaac, the attorney who represented the Russian deportees and realizing suddenly that I should be home, filling my child's stockings instead of attending a meeting.[61]

Art Shields, a labor reporter, described the "small back room in the Rand School" where Flynn worked tirelessly as "a fascinating place" where he would come after

my bread and butter work was done. For here I would meet some of the most fascinating men and women. . . . Mother Bloor, the Defense Union's field organizer would drop in, Vincent St. John, the organizing genius of the IWW . . . was there everyday at Elizabeth's right hand while out on bail from Leavenworth Penitentiary. The towering form of Jim Larkin, the famous Irish leader . . . would fill the little door. And an Indian political leader from the Office of Friends of Freedom for India in the same building might enter for legal advice.[62]

After the Russian Revolution in 1917, the United States government panicked, and in an effort to prevent a similar upheaval here, tried to eradicate all traces of revolutionary activity. Progressives were censured and hunted down. To continue protest was to risk prison. Many who had joined the Left in the early 1900s drifted back to the mainstream. As the government prosecuted radicals, defense work became more vital, but there were fewer supporters available to mount the defense campaigns. Many radical groups were forced to disband for lack of funds or dwindling membership. Some former activists who opposed World War I or war in general on philosophical and religious grounds, rather than the system that produced it, abandoned the Left for its support of revolution. The arty Greenwich Village set decided radicalism was no longer trendy and deserted the sinking red ship for greener, more lucrative shores. The educated and monied were tired by the tensions and stress and impatient to pick up the pieces of their disrupted lives; they retreated temporarily or permanently into private life. But most working-class activists, like Flynn, did not have the option to return to careers or resume affluent lives. They could fight or betray the cause. Very few Wobblies became informers. Many left political agitation and joined the working class. Raising

money and mass support was therefore arduous and often un-
rewarding during this postwar period. But Flynn, the stalwart,
lifetime revolutionary, managed on a meager budget and with less
sleep to fight the good fight.

Flynn's work increased as the paranoia about bolshevism and
immigrant radicals culminated in the Palmer Raids (named after
Attorney General Mitchell Palmer) in 1920. These repressive mea-
sures tore ten thousand immigrants from their homes and families. Whole Russian and Italian communities were routed out of
bed by police and soldiers, who arrived on horseback and clubbed
the prisoners into submission. Henrietta Rodman, a teacher and
Greenwich Village bohemian, turned her group, the Feminist Alliance, over to Flynn as a support committee for Palmer Raid victims.
The number of deportees, foreign-born socialist and anarchist opponents of war, mounted. The files of the Workers Defense Union
were filled with hopeless appeals from hundreds of political prisoners, melancholy testament to government indifference, squalid
prison conditions, as well as political repression. Flynn made re-
peated complaints to the Department of Immigration and finally
got a response from the commissioner of Ellis Island, Mr. Howe,
who said that the vermin and filth in the jails were caused by
"people whose methods of living and surroundings have not been
up to the standards of Americans."[63]

Two examples of Flynn's unremitting labors for working people
are the cases of Mollie Steimer and Jennie Boddo. A twenty-
year-old Russian-born waist maker, Mollie Steimer, was given a
fifteen-year sentence for violation of the Espionage Act merely
for distributing leaflets protesting U.S. military intervention in
Bolshevik-governed Russia. Flynn worked hard and obtained a review of the Steimer case by the U.S. Supreme Court, which, however, upheld the conviction. The Steimer family required relief
money because the only brother had died of influenza and the father of shock shortly after Mollie's conviction, leaving the mother
and four younger children penniless. Flynn then organized petitions and letters to Pres. Woodrow Wilson and Attorney General
Palmer asking for the young woman's pardon. Many speakers
eventually made the Mollie Steimer case a public concern; Flynn,
with others whose conscience was stirred, paid calls at the Jefferson
City penitentiary in Missouri. The convicted woman appeared to

maintain optimistic spirits for she wrote letters about feeling joy at the worldwide awakening of the working people; meanwhile she also directed attention to the plight of her fellow prisoners. She declared she should not be lionized or pitied as an especially appealing or youthful prisoner. "I want justice, but not pity," Flynn's client-militant wrote, "either work for the release of all or none."[64] Amnesty finally was granted by the federal authorities in 1921, with the provision that the "anarchist" Steimer leave the country.

A less exhausting defense was needed for Jennie Boddo, convicted in 1919 of the minor crime of affixing IWW stickers to the trees and buildings of New Brunswick, New Jersey. A female lawyer, Rose Weiss, was found to go to New Brunswick, and the charges were dropped.

The Workers Defense Union also defended blacks. It mounted a propaganda and protest campaign against the Ku Klux Klan, which was on the rise in the wake of World War I and unemployment. In fact thousands of Klan members in robes marched in front of the Capitol in Washington, D.C. On June 9, 1921, the WDU organized a meeting in Harlem, and five hundred people came to discuss the Tulsa massacre, where several blacks had been killed for occupying oil lands.[65]

Flynn was accustomed to antiracist activity because the IWW was the only labor organization of the time to fight for black equality. The Wobblies had special pamphlets appealing to "Colored Men and Women" in "lumber and turpentine camps, in fields of cane and tobacco, in mills and mines of Dixie," and on the waterfront in Louisiana.[66] Flynn and Carlo Tresca formed a Chinese branch of the IWW and Flynn herself took several cases of Chinese restaurant workers who were being deported because of so-called attacks on restaurant owners." In fact the name *Wobbly* came about because of the way the Chinese-born members pronounced the letters *IWW*.[67]

Elizabeth Gurley Flynn also got an opportunity to work on her own behalf. In 1917 she was the only female among 166 Wobblies indicted for antiwar propaganda. In 1917, without consulting her, the IWW published *Sabotage*, a pamphlet she had written specifically for the Paterson strike, long before World War I, in three languages, Italian, Lithuanian, and Hungarian. The U.S. government charged her with violating the Espionage Act; the expected sentence was forty years and a $4,000 fine. Flynn had no money for a lawyer or defense and refused to turn herself in, as the majority of the Wobblies did. Her defense strategy, a minority point of view, was that each defendant should move for a severance, that is, request a separate trial and thus, through a nationwide series of pretrial proceedings, stymie the prosecution. Unlike Flynn, most of the Wobblies felt they lacked the influential friends and supporters necessary to do this. Furthermore, the IWW lacked financial and legal resources to conduct a battery of individual cases, and most Wobblies wanted to stand together as a matter of principle.[68]

Flynn moved for severance; she even wrote a special plea, as a humble and obscure citizen who has struggled for democracy and "as one idealist to another," to President Wilson, appealing to him to intervene in "this flagrant injustice and to clear these unjust charges." She stated, "I have not taken part in any strikes or other IWW affairs since long before the War was declared, due to violent disagreements which arose within the organization last December. I have engaged in no anti-war agitation of any character." Had Flynn parted company from the IWW by April 17, 1917, when war was declared, or was she maneuvering to get off? In her letter to President Wilson she also claimed that "for seven years I have supported my child, and helped educate two sisters (one of whom is now a teacher) and a brother, who is eligible to the draft. This is, of course, only what other women are doing and has been a labor of love, but it is rather incompatible with the popular conception of a 'labor agitator.'"[69] Clearly this is an expansion of the truth. In the August 25, 1917, issue of *Solidarity,* the official Wobbly newspaper, she stated,

> A weird rumor that I am opposed to all strikes during war time and so stated in Minnesota recently and that I was therefore "discharged" or dropped from the IWW has been given widespread publicity in the capitalist press and gained credence in many quarters. Will you kindly allow me the space to brand this as an absolute falsehood? I am a member of the IWW at this writing and never stated otherwise anywhere. . . . I would not have my friends believe me a quitter in a crisis. We have enough "slackers" in the class war already.

Unlike many of the Wobs, she wanted to win, even if it meant lying and pulling strings rather than being martyred and jailed to maintain an abstract purity. However, in fighting other defense battles she had recommended the principled political path rather than the pragmatic victory. Bill Haywood, executive secretary of the IWW, was overly confident. He saw the indictment as a gaudy balloon supported by hot air and unable to stand up in court. The thousand crimes ballyhooed in the press, he felt, boiled down to one alleged offense, counseling an estimated ten thousand draft-age Wobblies to refuse to register for World War I. Haywood knew that the IWW had never taken an official position on registration.[70] Haywood, like Flynn, cultivated liberal contacts, whereas most Wobs shunned relationships with the enemy class, even intellectuals or artists. Perhaps Haywood counted on his rich and famous friends to come to the IWW's aid.

Flynn was much less cocky and did not share Haywood's optimism. To her these were troubled times for the Wobblies, who were painted in the press as disloyal saboteurs on the German payroll. If the Wobblies were judged as a group rather than as individuals, they would be seen as members of an unruly terrorist conspiracy. Her strategy proved successful; by 1922 charges against her, and those against Tresca and Ettor who followed her strategy, were dropped.[71] The other Wobblies went to jail for several years, and political repression snowballed.

Haywood, sick, burnt out by a life of agitation and long unjust trials, fled to the Soviet Union, escaping the trial he had asked others to face. Flynn felt this was cowardly, unforgivable, irresponsible behavior on the part of a leader. In fact this decision of Haywood's so bothered her that she began to doubt her youthful decision to join the IWW. Disillusioned by Haywood and her fellow Wobs, Flynn vowed never again to trust her theoretical judgments; she decided her talent was merely agitation and carrying out others' orders, rather than making strategy herself.[72]

Did Flynn overreact to Haywood's desertion? Her liberal friends had written to President Wilson asking for her pardon, and she had written a sob story to the president containing only partial truths. Flynn's own behavior was hardly above reproach. Was the leader of the IWW's betrayal sufficient cause to make her doubt her intellectual authority? Besides, her strategy had proved successful. She was free while most of her comrades sat in jail. Defense agitation is a line of work calling for patience and nurturing.

Was she worn down and burned out? Did she finally need some tender loving care herself? Perhaps she was facing a midlife crisis. The general repressive climate, false prosperity that in ten years would culminate in the country's worst depression, lack of labor militance, and twenty years of hard work had taken its toll. It is hard to be a labor agitator without a labor movement, and the IWW was no longer a threat or even a movement.

Flynn's agitational and defense work was nonetheless recognized. A testimonial dinner in 1926 marking her first twenty years in the labor movement brought out a Who's Who of the American Left and labor movement. William Green, president of the American Federation of Labor, sent greetings, as did the Chicago Federation of Labor, Eugene Debs, who ran for president five times, and Sidney Hillman, president of the Amalgamated Clothing Workers. Bartolomeo Vanzetti on this occasion wrote from death row, "As I sit in my cell here I drink a toast to you. I drink water only in my tin cup but it is heartfelt, heartfelt, because I know, dear Elizabeth, that you, people like you, will bring the great day of human liberty." More than 172 liberal celebrities sponsored the dinner, including Jane Addams, Helen Keller, Floyd Dell, Roger Baldwin, Freda Kirchway, Scott Nearing, and Arthur Garfield Hays.[73] So many and diverse personalities turned out to fête her because Flynn's friendship network spanned numerous circles—labor, liberals, bohemians, and feminists.

REST IN PORTLAND, OREGON, 1926–1936

Although her hard work was appreciated, these were tough times for Flynn both politically and emotionally. Upset by Tresca's unfaithfulness, worried that she found so little time to spend with her son, overworked by the continual pressure of speaking and organizing, and depressed by the splintered and decimated Left, Flynn suffered a mental and physical collapse in 1926. Her best friend, Mary Heaton Vorse, the well-known journalist, came to New York City from Provincetown to console and comfort her. Vorse wrote that Gurley spent days sobbing: "you can see her terrific will crashing against circumstance, and her talking like some girl, a jealous pitifully unbalanced creature."[74] Finally the family and work tensions had broken her spirit.

The immediate medical reason for her collapse was an enlarged heart and a severe infection of the teeth. Flynn spent most of the next ten years recuperating mentally and physically. She lived at the Portland, Oregon, home of the well-to-do Dr. Marie Equi, an abortionist and dispenser of (illegal) birth control information, who was a friend from the early IWW days. Flynn made occasional trips east to visit her family and to speak, but most of the time she stayed put in Portland. At first it primarily was a matter of her own recovery; after 1930 she also nursed Equi, who became ill with a heart attack, a painful scalp infection, and the aftereffects of pneumonia which she contracted during her ten-month imprisonment at San Quentin in 1920–1921, under the wartime Anti-Espionage Acts still being invoked to suppress progressive activity. After spending time in prison Equi became active in prison reform, recommending more outdoor life for prisoners and efforts to make them self-supporting after release.[75] Equi was an outspoken, open lesbian, and it seems plausible that she and Gurley had a love affair during this time. In fact the Flynn family was so disturbed about their relationship that both her sisters Bina and Kathie came to Portland to try to tear her away. But it was not lesbianism that bothered her family as much as it was that Flynn seemed imprisoned by Equi and unable to make a jail break.[76] Margaret Sanger, the noted birth control activist describes her as

> Marie Equi, M.D., a rebellious soul—generous, kind, brave, but so radical in her thinking that she was almost an outcast in Portland. Upon arrival, she captures every well-known woman who comes to Portland. Her reputation is or was lesbian but to me she was like a crushed flower which had braved the storms and winds of terror and needed tenderness and love. She was living with a younger woman in Portland and had adopted a child—I liked Marie always.[77]

Marie Equi could not join the IWW because she was not a wage earner, but she was associated with it informally. She led the cannery strike in Portland in 1914, and in July 1917 she was arrested for spurning the American flag and charged with shouting "dirty contemptible scum" to parading soldiers and comparing them unfavorably to clean, open fighters of the IWW. Equi also advised the Wobblies to follow the example of the Irish revolutionaries, who struck the British Empire when their masters were weak and preoccupied. She charged the ruling class in the United States with owning the army and navy and said that American working-men in the trenches of France fought their German fellow workers reluctantly.[78]

Although from a working-class background, Equi was like Tresca in that she was imperious, and she was feared and hated in the Northwest because of her outspoken criticism of politicians, industrialists, and so-called civic leaders. She usually got her way because as a doctor who performed illegal abortions for many of Portland's ruling class, she believed she was untouchable and could afford to be outrageous and provocative. Her jail sentence, however, proved her vulnerability. Equi's wartime trial was marred by slurs on her character and sexual proclivities; the prosecuting attorney called her "unsexed," and when she insisted on an apology, he said he meant "unwomanly."[79]

How involved was Flynn in the support networks of prominent lesbian career women such as Anna Howard Shaw, the suffrage leader, and Marie Equi? It is difficult to discern. However, when Flynn was sick and needed care, she turned to a woman. In bad times, it was this lesbian sororial community that nurtured and revived her.[80]

Writing about Equi and her life in Portland, Flynn said,

> She was not the easiest person in the world to get along with, she had a high temper from her Irish-Italian origin, but she had a brilliant mind, a progressive spirit, had been in prison for her opposition to World War I, and I admired her a great deal. I knew I needed to rest, to get well, to stay quietly in one place, slow down, think things out as to my future direction. The cleaning, laundry and other household chores were done for us. Much of our food she ordered from fancy groceries and restaurants. I read a great deal—history, science, the classics, medical books, even the Bible.[81]

These were difficult years in a nation beset with depression and in Elizabeth Gurley Flynn's life, but they proved to be years of self-education and personal growth. "I learned in Oregon," she reminisced many years later, that "one can have economic security, leisure, rest and yet be frightfully unhappy." On the other hand, the time of collapse and renewal provided "a tonic lesson that no one is indispensable."[82] While imprisoned in 1955, Flynn wrote to her sister Kathie:

> It seems amazing now that I could have been sick so long then—there were so much fewer medicines than there are now—nature had to take her course. It was a much more painful period than even the present, for you and me. You had the load of the family and the depression and I did not know if I would ever be really well again.[83]

REENTRY

At last, on Independence Day 1937, Flynn returned to the East against the advice of Dr. Marie Equi, who warned Flynn that she could not live more than two years if she left. Equi might have insisted that Flynn stay in Portland because rest was the prescribed nineteenth-century cure for depression. Complete quiet and isolation had similarly been recommended for Charlotte Perkins Gilman and Jane Addams. However, for the activists Gilman, Addams, and Flynn, return to activity rather than calm seemed the final cure. Equi might also have wanted to hold Flynn in Portland because she loved her.

Flynn's brother's suicide finally provided the excuse to break away. Elizabeth said: "The immediate reason that brought me home is that my dear brother Tom died suddenly in January. He was 42 years old, had always lived at home and it was a terrible shock to my mother. She is quite frail now and weak, so I am glad to be home with her and able to do for her a while at least."[84]

Thomas Flynn, the only son and youngest of the Flynn brood, was rather a lost soul, silent, handsome, cool, and an alcoholic. He was mediocre and low key, low in energy, and dwarfed by his parents and sisters. Daily life overwhelmed him. His suicide note read: "There are too many buttons to button. I am through." He worked as an optician who ground glass during the week and on weekends ran and was part owner of an unsuccessful movie house in Sheepshead Bay, Brooklyn. He never married as "he never found a woman as good as his mother."[85]

Flynn also was anxious to return east to see her son. Her ten-year absence was hardest on Fred, who had always resented his mother's lack of attention and finally punished her by cutting off

communication altogether. Buster, as the family called Fred, resembled Tom, Elizabeth's brother, in that he was lost in the high-
powered Flynn household and never established his own sense of
self apart from his family. Fred asked his mother why she bothered
to have a child and signed his letters, when he was writing, "I am as
ever, your lonesomeness [probably he meant to write *lonesomest*]
Buster." He chastised his mother for failing to remember even his
eighteenth birthday. In a letter he wrote, "even Ma thinks [you
should have called on my birthday]." [86] Although Elizabeth loved
Fred deeply, politics, not family, were primary.

Another reason to return home was that Flynn's mother was
quite ill. In fact she died shortly after Elizabeth returned home.
Finally Elizabeth had a chance to mother her mother. In the past
she had been quite dependent on Mama, who took care of the
house, sewed Elizabeth's clothes by hand, and listened to her joys
and sorrows. This poem, written in 1938 after Elizabeth returned
home from a long speaking tour, illustrates this love and reliance:

> Before me home—towards which I
> used to turn my eager feet,
> Anxious to tell her all I did and saw.
> *She is not there; she will never be there.*
> Her sweet blue eyes closed now in endless sleep.
> On her pale lips a faint sad smile of peace.
> [blank line, she writes, x_____x]
> At least we had her with us all those years,
> When she was young, beautiful and sad,
> When she was old, happy and tolerant,
> Serene, proud of us, but always slightly amused. [87]

Returning to political life after ten years was harder than coming home to her family, but Flynn believed she now had the sense
of purpose to begin over again. During her illness and rest cure in
Portland, she had gained almost seventy pounds, and she was now
forty-six years old. This mattered, as her youthful glamour had
been a political asset. Now she was no longer a slender, young firebrand, but an overweight, matronly, middle-aged woman. This
was one of several factors that made her fearful about returning to
public speaking; others included speaking on the radio, which she
had never previously done, and becoming acclimated, in general,

to a political situation that had changed greatly in ten years. She disclosed those fears in a previously unpublished poem:

Thoughts on Autumn

How to accept the Autumn of one's life?
When Spring all wild and wayward rushed so
heedless by in ecstatic dreams?
Spring that was yesterday, had no yesterdays and no tomorrows,
And still sings in my blood.
Came splendor of Summer, high noon of work beyond measure,
The thunder and lightning of great struggles,—ending in blinding crash.
Bruised and spent like a frightened child, I lay inert, then slowly rose
 again,
The call of those great battles quenchless in my blood,
Lighting the present, fortifying the future,
I came alive again.
How does this Autumn creep upon us unawares!
Suddenly the yesterdays stretch out on a long road back,
The tomorrows are the shorter road ahead.
A chance wind chills us with a blast of Winter on a Summer day.
How can the yet unconscious young know the gay lightness of our
 fighting hearts.[88]

EARLY YEARS IN THE COMMUNIST PARTY

Flynn's return east from Oregon was soon followed by her application for membership in the Communist party. She described her transition from IWW syndicalism to Marxism:

I came to the conclusion that Socialism could be achieved not by one splurge of violence, but by persistent political activities of the workers and the people. And so in order to participate in political activities, in the effort to achieve Socialism, I joined the Communist Party. . . . I had become convinced that the Communist Party was the logical inheritor of all the best traditions, history and struggles of the older Socialist movement and the IWW.[89]

The legendary Rebel Girl seemed a perfect candidate to join the Party. She had done defense work for Communists arrested at

Bridgeman, Michigan, in 1922, during the great strike at Passaic, 1926, and on many other occasions. She had applied for membership once before, in the fall of 1926; but as she was to put it later, "it didn't take the first time." She had been recruited by Charles Ruthenburg, then secretary of the Communist party. She

> had reservations but I felt maybe they would disappear in struggle, work and discussion. My reservations were not on basic principles, but rather related to tactics and some personalities. But I decided favorably and filled out the application card he [Ruthenburg] gave me. He was accompanied by Jay Lovestone, then his assistant and later an informer and stoolpigeon against the Communist Party (maybe he was then—who knows?). But the odd thing was I never heard of my application until ten years later. . . . I thought maybe they dropped me because I became sick and decided to wait for my return East to find out what happened.[90]

William Z. Foster and Mother Bloor (Ella Reeve Bloor) presented Flynn's application in the winter of 1937, when she became a member—and, simultaneously, a salaried functionary of the Communist party.[91] Even though she seemed a natural candidate and a great find for the Party, her sisters and socialist, feminist, and bohemian friends were dismayed and saddened when she joined. She remained formally in touch with anarchist and former Wobbly friends, but the close friendships with women such as Marie Equi and Mary Heaton Vorse were put aside.

Perhaps her decision to join the Communist party at this time was motivated by her feelings of rootlessness. She had been removed from politics and the East for ten years. Joining a group would ease her reentry. She would be a member of a party, a ready-made community, and have set tasks and a clear role. Besides, she was a totally political animal; her career was agitation— traveling, speaking, and organizing. These were still depression years. In 1937 fulfilling jobs were hard to find, especially for an overweight, forty-seven-year-old high school dropout. Joining the Party gave her an opportunity to revive her political career, a new sense of purpose, and a continuity with her Wobbly past.

It is significant that Flynn and the Communist Party of the United States of America joined forces in 1937, during Roosevelt's New Deal and the Communist party's Popular Front, a period marked by broad coalitions and mass struggle. Her niece and several friends stated that she considered joining the Democratic party, even discussing it with Eleanor Roosevelt, who was a friend of Dr. Marie Equi's.[92] Would Flynn have joined the Communist party in the earlier "Third Period," 1928–1935, which is remembered as one of the most sectarian in Party history?[93] As she put it in a 1930 letter to Mary Heaton Vorse, "the movement is a mess—torn by factionalism and scandal and led by self seekers with one or two exceptions."[94] The Communists attacked Socialists and other leftists as "social fascists," purged those Communists whose line differed slightly, launched dual revolutionary unions to compete with those of the American Federation of Labor (AFL), and were committed to fight for the right of Negro people in the Black Belt (the South) to self-determination, including their right to establish an independent state, following the lead of the autonomous nations in the USSR. In Germany, during this sectarian phase, the Communists' main enemy was the Social Democrats, not the fascists. During this Third Period, the Communist party believed the Great Depression was the final crisis of capitalism, which would lead inevitably to proletarian revolution. Instead, the depression and New Deal ushered in a new stage of capitalist development, "welfare capitalism."

The Popular Front period, initiated in 1935 (after the Seventh World Congress of the Comintern), represented a tactical reorientation and implied changes in Communist strategy. The central slogan represented the fight against fascism and the defense of the Soviet Union, "a united front under capitalism and a single party under socialism." A united front against fascism, including the middle classes, civil servants, technicians, intellectuals, and peasants, was necessary to defeat Hitler's Germany. The workers in the vanguard were warned to avoid putting forward aims that might alarm the less advanced workers; and the working class to refrain from proclaiming its purpose, proletarian revolution, which might upset the middle classes, who were potential allies of the Soviet Union in its fight against fascists and Japanese expansionists.[95]

This Popular Front did not include all progressive groups; Trotskyites, anarchists, and avant-gardists were excluded. In the Soviet Union this was the period of the mass purges and the wholesale execution of the former Bolshevik ranks. The Popular Front period came to a quick halt in 1939 when the Soviet Union signed a nonaggression treaty with Nazi Germany and invaded Finland. Overnight, Party policy flip-flopped. There was no longer a need to form alliances with moderates and liberals to meet the fascist threat. Franklin Roosevelt, formerly a hero, became a villain trying to drag the United States into a capitalist war on the side of British imperialism. The pacifism line prevailed, and many literal antifascists broke with the Communist party in disgust. However, in 1941 Hitler invaded the Soviet Union and the Popular Front line returned. The Communist party now began agitating for aid to Russia and U.S. entry into the war.

Elizabeth Gurley Flynn recalled that in Portland,

> Anita Whitney brought me a *Daily Worker* in the fall of 1935 with the speech of George Dimitroff called "The United Front Against War and Fascism. . . . This speech [delivered at the Congress of the Comintern, 1935] made a great impression. It addressed communists especially and other progressive people elsewhere to put aside all immediate partisan and sectarian interests or differences or ultimate political aims to stop fascism. . . . I resolved when I read this powerful appeal "Here is where I belong. As soon as I am well I will again apply to the Communist Party."[96]

Since Flynn's days in the Workers Defense Union, she had favored mass-based popular movements rather than sectarian politics, so this was an appropriate moment to join the growing Communist party.

An aura of excitement and drama surrounded this pre–World War II period. With total economic collapse still a possibility and Hitler waiting in the wings, every activity seemed crucial and charged with meaning. In 1935 John L. Lewis led his mine workers and eight other unions with a combined membership of 900,000 out of the tepid AFL and formed the CIO. The Communist party played an influential role in this massive labor organization that was aided by Franklin Roosevelt's legislation and moral support and John L. Lewis's daring maneuvers. Organizing the CIO, an industrial-based union, was a herculean task, and John L. Lewis needed all the help he could get. The Communists were the toughest, most hardworking, and experienced union folks around. For years they had been working relentlessly without much success or recognition, trying to build their own industrywide unions. Within a bare six months the CIO had 2 million members.[97]

During this Popular Front period, Earl Browder, general secretary of the Party in 1930–1945, coined the phrase "Communism is Twentieth-Century Americanism," and sought every means to link communism with the democratic populist tradition and to counteract the idea of communism as an alien, authoritarian system inimical to native traditions and aspirations. The Party tried to align itself with an American revolutionary past. Jefferson, Lincoln, and Paine joined the pantheon of heroes alongside Marx, Engels, and Lenin. The American flag began to appear at meetings. "The Star-Spangled Banner" replaced the "Internationale." Flynn had come from a salt-of-the-earth American-based organization, the IWW, and this new Yankee emphasis suited the New Hampshire–born rebel girl well.

This period did not, however, bring about changes in internal Party democracy or in work on behalf of the Soviet Union. The Party still functioned as an outpost of Russian propaganda and diplomacy, often with considerable fumbling in order to keep pace with changes in Moscow's diplomatic positions.[98] For Flynn, who came out of a crusading anarcho-syndicalist organization in which the individual members had almost total latitude in taking organizational initiatives, entering the Communist party meant a major wrench from her past patterns of organizing.

Tapping new sources of American working-class and middle-class participation, just as the Popular Front goal envisioned, the communist organization still made members' discipline paramount and subordinated individual initiative to the Party line.[99] Flynn saw the problems of reorientation as personal difficulties and chastised herself for not readily adapting to the discipline fundamental to party tenets. Flynn found that she resorted to the "evasive method" of keeping silent about policies of which she disapproved, and she endeavored to get assignments outside New York City, where she could feel more at ease and at home. She later said she was "revolted by the repetition, of acquiescence with everything comrade Browder had said."[100]

In spite of her abhorrence of obsequious admiration, Flynn contributed more than her share to the Browder cult. She wrote at least twenty-five articles and a pamphlet, entitled *Earl Browder: The Man From Kansas*, praising Browder, comparing him to Eugene Debs and John Brown, and even proposing that "he stirreth the people like Jesus." She wrote, "It's hard to find a better American, he's fearless, effective, and modest."[101] In 1940 she campaigned coast to coast for Browder and was the executive secretary of the Free Earl Browder campaign. (Browder had been indicted and jailed on passport fraud.) Browder ran for president in 1940, and some of her hyperboles can be brushed off as campaign rhetoric, but this does not obscure the fact that Flynn followed the Party line and never articulated an alternative. She told her friends that she was no theoretician, merely an agitator and popularizer. The IWW had scorned theory as highfalutin dribble, and Flynn had a touch of this Wobbly antiintellectualism. However, instead of developing theoretical sophistication in the Party, Flynn became typecast as the popular medium for the ideological messages from above. Communist colleagues describe her as a "simple unsophisticated" earthy woman with no patience for abstract thought.[102]

ACLU OUSTER

Flynn had barely settled into Communist party New York City life when she met with persecution from the American Civil Liberties Union (ACLU), many of whose members became disgusted with the Communist party in 1939 when the Soviet Union signed a non-aggression pact with Nazi Germany. Liberals, who formerly considered the Communists as allies in the fight against fascism, now saw them as pawns of Soviet foreign policy and friends of Hitler. In 1940 the ACLU asked all those who were Communists or fascists to resign from official posts. Of course, no fascist had ever held an ACLU position, so Communists alone were under fire. Flynn was a founding member of the ACLU, and at that point a member of the National Board of Directors. While other Party members holding ACLU posts simply resigned, she would not. She said,

> I refuse to resign. I will not be party to saving the face of this anti–civil liberties majority, nor to white washing their red baiting. . . . If this trial occurred elsewhere, it would be a case for the ACLU to defend. I am fighting for civil liberties in the ACLU. Is there any member of this board,

she asked in response,

whose records of militant fighter for these rights can outweigh the records of William Z. Foster and myself, since the first free speech in Spokane, Washington in 1910?[103]

Flynn not only refused to resign but defended her position in forceful articles in the *New Masses* and *Daily Worker*. Board members then filed additional charges against her for insulting the board in print.

Refused a hearing before the entire membership, Flynn was expelled at a hasty meeting of the ACLU's board of directors lasting until two in the morning, in which her accusers acted as her jury and judge. The verdict of guilty was in before the trial began— hardly the norm of justice the ACLU sought for those it was founded to defend.

The charges of Communist party membership (which Flynn had publicly avowed in many speeches as well as in direct notification to the ACLU at the time she took out Party membership) were brought by Dorothy Dunbar Bromley, a Scripps-Howard syndicated woman's page columnist. Apparently the ACLU board believed the purgation scene might be less unsightly if the accuser were also female. Many of those who voted against Flynn had personal as well as anti-Communist motives: Roger Baldwin, the noted civil libertarian, had been her lover and felt vindictive. Margaret de Silver, a wealthy contributor to the ACLU, was now the wife of Carlo Tresca and was threatened by Flynn and Tresca's much publicized passionate affair.[104] Throughout the six-hour debate, no member of the board could cite a single instance where Flynn had written, spoken, or acted in violation of the Bill of Rights or the acknowledged principles of the ACLU. Her crime was guilt by association, an unconstitutional principle the ACLU had fought in the past.

Flynn defended herself by arguing that, ultimately, to purge a Communist was to defeat the explicit aim of the ACLU and that, as for herself, she had not changed one iota since taking out Party membership. The Communist party, she said,

> does not want to control the government . . . the Communist Party is trying to bring about the control by the people of the government, and the setting up of socialism in this country and there is the possibility implied in

all the literature of the Communist Party that socialism is possible under democracy and democratic forms in the USA.[105]

She also quoted from the Constitution of the USSR to prove that in some respects bolshevized Russia was a more democratic nation than the United States.[106]

> As far as women are concerned the USSR is a trail blazer for equal rights and opportunities. Women are elected to the Supreme Soviet in far larger proportions than women have been elected to Congress here in the USA after twenty years of women's suffrage. The attitude of Fascism and Nazism towards women is exactly contrary, driving them out of public life and forcing them into an inferior and subject position.[107]

Not until years after Flynn's death did the ACLU reverse its ouster of her. On June 22, 1976, stating that "the expulsion was not consonant with the basic principles on which the ACLU was founded," the ACLU admitted that

> there was no evidence that she had ever violated the principles and they wanted to remove a serious stain remaining on the ACLU and to clear the memory of Elizabeth Gurley Flynn, who contributed more to and for civil liberties of the United States for working people than all the members who were her colleagues.[108]

FRED FLYNN

Flynn fought bravely for her rights, even though she was personally devastated at the time of the ACLU trial. Her only child, Fred Flynn, age twenty-nine, had recently died during an operation for lung cancer. She had begged the ACLU for a postponement, but the time for a satisfactory personal life always seemed to elude her. She regretted her inability to spend more time with her son, but not her choice to put politics before family. She had strong feelings for Fred Flynn—Buster—and worried whenever she was separated from him. In a 1929 letter to Mary Heaton Vorse, written while ill in Oregon, Flynn said:

> I have also been a great deal disturbed about Buster. He is a good enough boy from all conventional standards—doesn't drink, smoke, run around with girls, etc. I guess he's a reaction from my own wild youth. But my fam-

ily, as usual, decides what he is to do. My father and mother are too old to quarrel with—but the others should know better. However, they sent him off to the University of Michigan, though where they expect him to get the necessary funds to see him through is beyond me. And they do not seem to realize the importance of him getting a job and helping pay his own way though. . . . Buster will never be a radical I fear. He heard too much of it when he was a child and it has no novelty or interest for him. What he heard was mostly criticism, unfortunately, which is destructive of enthusiasm.[109]

Despite his mother's fears, Fred Flynn did become a political radical. He studied engineering at the University of Michigan, but quit after two years because he did not like the unreal, middle-class, small town atmosphere and did not have the funds to continue.[110] After leaving Ann Arbor, Fred worked as a statistician in Washington, D.C., for the Federal Surplus Corporation and the Committee on Economic Security. He was an excellent mathematician, taught by his grandpa, and a good worker, but New Deal jobs were short-lived. After eight months the work ended and he was forced to return to his mother. They made peace, but life was still hard for Fred. In the depression, jobs were difficult to come by. His mother found him some poorly paid but morally gratifying work with the International Workers Order (IWO), a militant left-wing benefit society associated with the Communist party. Unlike most benefit societies, the IWO not only provided unemployment and sickness payments and low-cost doctors, but also campaigned for health and unemployment insurance.[111] Fred and his mother grew emotionally and politically closer, and she hoped eventually that he would join the party. With his mother's encouragement he finally became active in the American Labor party in the Bronx and began associating more with Party people.[112] He was still shy and had few friends of his own, but had a good subtle sense of humor like most of the Flynn clan.

Gurley Flynn never fully recovered from the death of her only child. His absence remained a part of her. She developed affectionate relationships with younger men in the Party (for which she was criticized), substitutes for Fred, like John Gates, the *Daily Worker* editor, Steve Nelson, the commander of the Lincoln Brigade in the Spanish Civil War, and Eugene Dennis, who became head of the Communist party. She wrote affectionate poems to Steve Nelson and Gene Dennis, and while in jail she kept a picture of the handsome Dennis in her room and requested that her ashes be placed beside his in Waldheim Cemetery.[113] During World War II she could sympathize in an immediate way with women whose sons were killed in battle. An undated maudlin poem expresses her identification with mothers:

> I know how you feel, stricken mother, today
> In Scranton or Omaha or Dallas,
> When the message came that your boy was dead.
> I know what it means to hold a golden curl of childhood
> Or the darker curls of later years—
> To realize that is all there is left of him.[114]

Every year she commemorated the anniversary of his death, March 29, 1940, in an ad in the *Daily Worker;* later in 1955 she dedicated her autobiography

> to the ever living memory of my dearly beloved only son Fred Flynn. He was my friend and comrade—loving, encouraging, humorous, active in progressive labor politics—to whom I promised this book would be written, and to whom I consciously dedicated my life's work, before and after his death.[115]

It is said that she only began to appreciate her son after he died. Guilt at not having been a full-time mother remained with her. She tried to sublimate this guilt by becoming the great savior of humanity and mothering the men on the Communist party's national board. She was always the one to visit the ill, remember birthdays, and keep in touch by mail. She kept in touch with her nieces and nephew and was quite close to Kathie's daughter, Frances, with whom she lived.

Elizabeth assisted her family mainly through her many political connections. She got the Communist party to hire her sister Kathie as her secretary, after Kathie was fired from her fourth grade teaching job, during the McCarthy period, because her sister Elizabeth was a Communist. When her nephew Peter could not get into the Longshoremen's Union, she pulled some strings so he could ship out. When her niece Roberta Bobba, called Reb, wanted to tour the Soviet Union in the 1960s with her female lover in a Volkswagen camper, Elizabeth had the Soviet Turkish border opened for them and cleared the whole trip with top Russian officials. Before her long illness, her family provided her with care and monetary aid. After she joined the Party, she mainly provided for them. A system of support and mutual aid operated in the Flynn family, no questions asked. Elizabeth did not try to convert her family to socialism and never even held it against her nephew, Peter, that he joined the Shachtmanites, a Trotskyite group most Communist party members despised.[116] Her family remained important to her, but nothing could replace the loss of her son.

TRESCA'S DEATH

Three years after Fred died—January 11, 1943—Flynn's personal life was shaken again. Carlo Tresca was assassinated. The evidence indicates that Carmine Galante, a Mafia leader, shot Tresca on behalf of his friend Mussolini,[117] though various vicious rumors circulated that Tresca was the victim of a Communist thug, a jealous husband, or even Elizabeth Gurley Flynn's brother or father—both of whom were already dead, although that fact did not seem to matter. The district attorney showed no interest in investigating the murder and released Galante for lack of evidence, even though his abandoned car was found two blocks from the scene. The judge preferred to intimate that the guilt lay with bloodthirsty Communist executioners. Tresca had in fact made many enemies and used the pages of *Il Martello* (*The Hammer*) to bitterly attack almost everyone with whom he differed: the Catholic church, Mayor LaGuardia, John L. Lewis, the IWW, the Communists, and even Arturo Giovannitti and Pietro Allegra, who had been close comrades of his for thirty years. However, "the one consistent fight to which he devoted himself after Mussolini came to power was fighting Fascism."[118]

Flynn and Tresca had not been lovers for some time. However, Flynn was pained and distressed by his death and expressed it in this poem she jotted down in a notebook:

How strange it seems that you are dead
Who were so long the other half of me.
How long it's been that you were dead to me
And now you're dead—you are alive again.
Days, months, have passed without a thought of you
So well I steeled and disciplined my heart,

Pulled out the bleeding roots of love and went far off
Till time had healed and seared the aching wounds.
So when I saw you, you were not yourself to me
Only an old weary disillusioned shadow of the man I knew,
With but a far off glimpse of a glorious past,
Like fading somber echoes of a sun long set.
But deep within the memories long suppressed
Are stored the riches of our young rebellious love,
I saw a melancholy light within your eyes—
As you stood in the doorway the last time we met
And smiling waved goodbye—shortly before you died.
Last night I stood upon the pavement where you died
The merciful rain, like tears soft shed
Had washed away your blood—shed by a fascist assassin
In the dimmed out night of war.[119]

Carlo Tresca remained Flynn's great passion. All her other love affairs, most short-lived, paled in comparison. Her life-style—traveling, long irregular work hours—did not lend itself easily to long-term commitments. Being a Communist celebrity and a fun-loving, sensuous woman meant men were curious about her, but they would not want to adjust their lives to her rigorous work schedule. Her family and political life met some of her emotional needs, but she still longed for an enduring love and passion. However, she settled for loneliness, short secret affairs, and romantic memories of Carlo Tresca.

WOMEN'S ACTIVITIES IN THE COMMUNIST PARTY

Although these tragedies were deeply felt, the Rebel Girl's stamina reasserted itself. In spite of the fact that she had trouble adjusting to Communist party discipline as well as the loss of her son and Tresca, she threw herself into her work. She missed the euphoria of the IWW crusades, but she told herself times had changed and she did not want to be a has been, the last of the buffalos, wallowing in romantic nostalgia. She had to keep up with the times and adhere to Communist party discipline, abstract theory, and more staid strategy.

In her Wobbly period, Flynn had made speeches at rallies, where she educated and organized masses of striking workers for social revolution. Now much of her work was to raise money for

Spanish Republicans and to address fund-raising luncheons, dinners, and other meetings of liberal-minded rich people. Many of these audiences were middle class, and Flynn spoke to them about the importance of cooperating with the New Deal administration in the fight against hunger and fascism. Flynn felt more in her element with working-class folks, although middle- and upper-class people were also moved by her speeches.

In 1937 Flynn started a regular column in the *Daily* and *Sunday Worker,* called "The Feminine Ferment" and devoted, as she stated in the first installment, to discussing labor organization, politics, and economic and social problems from a woman's angle. She wrote this column, almost uninterrupted, until her death, often giving the column different names: "The Life of the Party," "Let's Talk It Over," "Sister Kathie Says," "A Better World." Sometimes she wrote as many as four columns a week, but usually it was three. These columns were very popular. She wrote them in a direct, homey style, sometimes sounding corny and overly folksy and simple like Ma Kettle. The most frequent themes were women, blacks, the Irish, miners, current defense campaigns, and the American labor strikes of the past. She wrote them in union halls, on buses, and in hotel rooms, squeezing them into a busy life, often "wishing I was one of those strong people who can say 'No.'" Her typical schedule was to make four or five trips a year throughout the United States. In seven weeks she would cover ten states, give thirty-five speeches and four radio talks. Even the FBI agents who trailed her noted her rigorous schedule in their lengthy reports. This hectic pace continued all her life. At sixty-eight, she recounted in a column that between April and June she had spoken to twenty-six hundred people in fourteen public gatherings and twelve smaller house parties. In later years she rarely wrote out her speeches, speaking from a few notes, and she was an amazing recruiter for the Party, sometimes enrolling as many as a hundred members a week. Flynn also taught labor history courses at the Party's Jefferson School in New York City, and at a national training school. Even with housework she was a whirlwind, getting the tasks done quickly and well, a virtual superwoman, but impatient about the less significant details.[120]

The political climate greatly affected Flynn's daily life, as politics was the core of her existence. The depression and World War II were a high point for American Communists. At no other time in American history were Communists so numerous and respected. They were involved in reform politics in alliance with Roosevelt's New Deal policy. They were also in the forefront of the fight against fascism and outorganized their left-wing rivals, enjoying the rare prestige that comes from leading a truly popular cause.

During the war fifteen thousand Communist party members, one-fifth of all male members, joyfully enlisted in the armed services, leaving gaps in leadership that women were only too happy to fill.

> By mid-1943 more than half of all the Young Communist League (YCL) members were women and by 1944 nearly half of all party members were women [compared to less than ten percent in 1930 and just over twenty-five percent in 1936]. Women still remained a distinct minority [only Flynn] among the party's top leaders, most of whom were well past military age.[121]

For Flynn the World War II period was a good time as well. Always the Communist party's most popular speaker and recruiter, she was very much in demand and eager audiences awaited her words of wisdom. In 1945 she addressed twenty-five women's conferences and wrote articles and pamphlets encouraging women to participate in industrial war work. In her writing and speeches she educated women about the history of class and sex struggle both in America and in Russia. She also demanded that the government and unions furnish day care, better transportation, laundry, and food services, staggered and part-time work, and equal pay for equal labor. Since unions were often more negligent than either government or private industry, Flynn urged women to join unions to force them to acknowledge women's needs.[122]

During the war female Communists pushed the Party to take a strong stand against the chauvinism of male union leaders, including some of those quite close to the Communist party. In a private memo, Flynn complained to Earl Browder, then head of the Communist party, about the weak organizing effort made by male unionists to recruit women workers and the failure to hire female organizers by some Left-led unions. "They claim they can't find any trained women to do the work [and] assert that women will only be in industry for the duration 'then we'll be rid of them, so why bother.'"[123] Flynn also protested this union intransigence in her writing and speeches.

Flynn, like other militant Communists, saw the war as threatening the very existence of the Soviet Union. Clearly, discipline and self-sacrifice were called for. During the war the Party relaxed recruiting requirements and less devoted types were admitted. The new recruits were more bourgeois and unused to working in a disciplined, unpopular group. Little effort was made to educate these new members in Communist party history or theory. Flynn was drawn into debate when one woman wrote to her complaining that she and other Communists were being pressured by the Party to take on additional organizational responsibilities or to seek work in defense plants, rather than move where their husbands were stationed in the army, which they preferred to do. Flynn's reply was most unsympathetic. She told the woman "not to embarrass our party . . . this is no time to nurse our own private personal feeling. . . . Communists must set an example for others in bravery, understanding and devotion to duty."[124] This controversy on the Woman's Page of the *Daily Worker* about commitment to the war rather than to one's private emotions and family began in the fall of 1942 and continued until July 1943. Flynn also supported conscription for women, which was unpopular with most females.

Flynn asked American women to subordinate personal happiness to win the war and called on them to emulate the Soviet heroines of Sevastopol, who sacrificed their lives and took up guns to defend their city. During the war her articles and letters presented an iron-willed, devoted, revolutionary Flynn who willingly forfeited companionship for the cause. Flynn believed in Lenin's concept of the professional revolutionary and tried to live her life accordingly, but she rarely called on others to do likewise. However, in this wartime situation she extended her own sense of revolutionary discipline to other women, calling upon them to place politics before personal life.

Following the line of the Soviet Union, Flynn's patriotism during the war was limitless: demanding progressive women as well as workers to make sacrifices, urging workers not to strike, and supporting unlimited overtime. When John L. Lewis of the United Mine Workers, a man for whom Flynn claimed a secret admiration, led miners to strike despite the no-strike pledge, he became a

Party villain overnight. Flynn made a trip to Pittsburgh to talk to miners and wrote a pamphlet calling on them to repudiate "John L. Lewis and his swarm of boot licking satellites" who were hampering the nation's victory.[125]

When the war ended, Flynn parted company with the government and Communist party and urged women not to let themselves be driven from their rightful place in the labor market and forfeit their wartime gains. Instead she called for increased militance and agitation so that women could keep their jobs and day care. She, who was usually reserved about openly criticizing the Communist party, now chastised the Party for its failure to include women. She claimed that the National Association of Manufacturers took women more seriously than the Communist party. She noted an increase of male chauvinism in the Party over the years.[126] Perhaps she felt freer to criticize the Communist party for two reasons: the war had given masses of women more power and experience in the workplace, and as a female, Flynn was considered an expert on women's issues.

During this wartime period Flynn's special knowledge of women was given official sanction. From 1945 to 1953 she was chairman of the Women's Commission of the Communist party,[127] whose mission was to carry on the struggle for equal rights for women in shops, unions, and all organizations, including the Party itself. The commission was supposed to inspire female Party members with greater self-confidence to participate in public affairs. Female Communists were to be politically active not only on election day, but the year round, in hearings, delegations, petitions, and statements to all legislative and public bodies on issues of child care, better schools, and housing.[128]

Much of the effort of the commission was directed toward black women. The Party, unlike other leftist groups, fought against the virtual disenfranchisement of southern blacks through violence and the poll tax, as well as racial discrimination in northern factories, especially during World War II. Flynn wrote over thirty articles calling attention to the special plight of black women, pointing out the historic legacy of slavery and the militance of black freedom fighters. Between 1948 and 1953 she wrote and campaigned to free Rose Ingram, a black widow with twelve children who faced death in Georgia for killing a white farmer in self-defense.[129]

Flynn had other honorific positions in Party work with women. She was chairman of the Women's International Democratic Federation (WIDF), an organization that counted 81 million members in thirty-nine nations, and vice president of the Congress of American Women (CAW), its American affiliate. In November 1945 she made her first trip outside the United States to attend the founding of WIDF, which was a coalition of officials brought together by Soviet policy rather than mobilized by the American masses. The program of CAW, its American arm, was an end to fascism; world peace; full economic, political, and legal rights for all women; and the protection of children. CAW showed the potential of an American women's movement that could combine internationalism, anti-imperialism, and women's rights, as a Women's Strike for Peace did twenty years later. CAW's activities included a national meat boycott to combat high prices, a campaign to save the wartime day-care centers, a day-care conference and many meetings in support of the Progressive party, and a campaign for presidential candidate Henry Wallace and against the cold war. CAW ceased functioning in 1948 after the House Un-American Activities Committee (HUAC) vituperatively attacked and red-baited it.[130]

Flynn was the most well-liked leader in the Communist party and therefore was given these prestigious female-focused Party positions. Her power derived from her popularity with the masses, rather than from her standing with the National Executive Committee, the leadership of the Communist party, most of whom did not take her seriously as a leader. Her talent and interest were not in directing or running organizations, but in organizing, agitating, and infusing others with militance. These positions, head of the Women's Commission and vice president of CAW, were honors she could not refuse, even though they never gave her the real respect and power she wanted. Could she have used these posts to mount campaigns against male supremacy, train other women as leaders, and raise issues such as day care, abortion, birth control, and equal pay within the Party? No, women's issues were not her priority, and she correctly sensed that there was little authority attached to women's work; she wanted to be in the center of the decision making, not ghettoized with the second sex.

Whether the Communist party would have committed resources to a full-scale women's liberation program without directives from Moscow is not clear. The Party's support for day care and women's

work during the war was motivated primarily by expediency—the
need to win the war—rather than by the need to liberate women.
After the war women were expected to return happily home.
While Flynn criticized the Party's rescinding of women's wartime
victories, she was unwilling to actively defy the Party and mobilize
women to fight the loss of services and jobs. After the war, left-
wing women, many former Party members, fought successfully in
New York City to keep day-care centers open, in Washington, D.C.,
to lower meat prices, and in Detroit, without success, to keep their
wartime jobs.[131] Flynn did not participate directly in any of these
postwar actions.

Although aware of women's oppression, Flynn did not often act
on her feminist consciousness because the Party had no formal
position on the "woman question," and she was unwilling to initi-
ate a women's rights program. The Communist party perceived
women as an interest group to reconcile; sexism—male chauvinism—was considered a personal problem to be solved individually
within the Party or family. Racism—white chauvinism—on the
other hand was understood as a deep structural, economic, and
political obstacle inherent to United States society. Blacks were
therefore a vanguard; they were second-class citizens deserving
freedom, justice, and equality. The Communist party pioneered in
the fight for black freedom. Programs for black equality were included in every Party platform and huge legal defense campaigns
were mounted, whereas women's equality was not considered a
major issue and indifference and opportunism guided Party policy
on women. The Communist party was nevertheless more enlightened about sexism and women's equality than were the Democratic
and Republican parties, or the other small left-wing groups of the
thirties, forties, and fifties. At least the Communist party talked
about male chauvinism and women's struggles.

PARTY OFFICIAL

Generally, Flynn towed the party line and brought the Communist
party's message to the masses. Elected to the Communist Party
National Committee in 1938, in 1942 she ran for New York State
representative-at-large on the Communist ticket. The war and
postwar were periods of increased commitment to electoral poli-

tics; the Party aided the working class through influence in the liberal state rather than through collective defiance of strikes and massive protest. In 1938 Flynn was appointed to the Party's national board. As she said,

> I was the only person elected in the open convention of the party, and not only by referendum of the district delegations, because I wasn't actually eligible to be a member of the National Committee. I hadn't been a sufficiently longtime member of the Party [seven years], and an exception had to be made, and it had to be done on open convention of the Party.[132]

She had mixed feelings about her rapid ascent to ruling Party circles, and she reflected:

> I came into the Communist Party from the top, and there is great honor to that, but at the same time the great disadvantage of not having the background and experience and solid foundation of having worked through the organization and having the experience that comes from that to make it easier to formulate an opinion.[133]

She was to say she considered herself but a visiting member of the national committee, not a policymaker but a "pitcher full of information" to be sent into the field.[134] These statements were not overly modest; she considered herself a mere vessel, emptying out Party policy. At least she admitted her theoretical weakness. Others were weak but pretended to be knowledgeable. Her fault was in believing other Communist party executives more theoretically sophisticated, and not wishing to master Marxist ideology herself.

Flynn wrote and spoke as a stalwart Party advocate, following each twist and turn of Party line. One column she wrote in July 1940 is called "Stalin, the Moses of the Jews." Sometimes she had nothing but praise for Eleanor Roosevelt ("It's Eleanor and Not Whistler's Mother for Me,"), but during the Hitler-Stalin Pact, Eleanor was nothing but a "Wall Street Whore."[135]

Many people believed that Flynn was but a figurehead, used by Communist party policymakers to push unpopular positions in a populist voice and with the rebellious ring of the former Rebel Girl.[136] The FBI reported that she was "very disheartened by the way she was being ignored by the Party." "It's her feeling," reports another FBI informant, "that the Communist Party is using her and only invites her to affairs where she is needed." "Flynn would like to be released from Communist Party duties so that she could just speak and write and not be involved in 'poolroom politics.'"[137]

Do these remarks, reportedly overheard by FBI agents, prove that the Communist party was exploiting her as a working-class feminine frosting and excluding her from real power? She was used to override dissident Communist party groups and to deliver distasteful messages in rousing familiar phrases.[138] For a Leninist, the Party, and in the final analysis the Soviet state, is the seat of wisdom and the final arbiter of political questions. Therefore it would have been inconsistent with her political commitments if she had contradicted the primary Party line.[139] Flynn perhaps felt even more shaky, as a female and a former Wobbly, about asserting her political differences.

Flynn's apparent sense of powerlessness regarding Party policy changed temporarily in 1945 when William Z. Foster, her old IWW friend, assumed leadership of the Communist party. (Flynn was in favor of the Popular Front but not of dropping revolutionary ideals in order to gain power with the Democratic party and union officials.) With Foster at the helm, she was usually optimistic that the Party would return to class struggle and a program that would articulate socialist goals rather than push the struggle for socialism so far to the background that one needed a phraseology decoder to confirm that the socialist goals remained. As Browder stated, Flynn was "happy for the first time since she entered the Communist organization," and "felt free and equal" to "get her old Wob baggage out of storage and keep her Fenian ancestors."[140]

In the end, Flynn was disappointed with Foster's stale, Soviet-oriented return to cold, conspiratorial, sectarian politics. Foster was no longer the innovating organizer he had been in his youth. He was physically ill and closed to discourse except with Moscow. In 1951 an FBI agent reported that Flynn visited Foster and concluded he was living in the past. Another agent stated that, in a 1960 talk with Andrei Gromyko, Flynn mentioned the pending trip of William Z. Foster, then chairman emeritus of the Communist party, to the Soviet Union, and said, "We will be better off without him because he is a fussy old man." However, to the public, Flynn remained the Party apparatchik.[141] She loyally wrote at least twenty articles, as well as a pamphlet and several book reviews, lauding Foster, his politics, his life, and his work.[142] The 1950s were a troublesome time for the Party and to foment dissent within would have added insult to injury. Flynn remained the compliant rather than rebel girl.

SCOUNDREL TIMES

Times changed. In 1945 the sectarian Foster was at the Communist party helm, the war with Germany was won, and Franklin D. Roosevelt was dead. The Communist party, which had been accepted as an ally during the New Deal in order to popularize liberal legislation and organize the CIO, and which had been needed during the war to fan patriotism and restrain the unions, was now portrayed as a threat to national security and a monster to be curtailed. The government severed the Communist party's New Deal union connection, rearmed Europe to prevent Soviet expansion, and surrounded the USSR with U.S. military installations. The new president, Harry S Truman, moved to involve the United States in a grim and protracted cold war. Communists and their associates became the enemy within, and the Soviet Union, the United States' former ally, the enemy without.

Reaction set in, and the Communist party was unprepared for this sudden shift. A decade of hard work and sacrifice had earned the Party a measure of influence in the American labor movement. In 1945 the Communist party dominated at least a quarter of the CIO's total membership and controlled a third of the votes on the executive board.[143] By 1948 the Communist party had lost its influence in the labor movement and government and had become a hunted and hated sect, scapegoated for all of America's internal and external blunders. Communist leaders were jailed, the Party outlawed, and anyone suspected of associating with Communists was considered an outcast and feared job loss. Communists and those accused of communist sympathy were followed by agents, fired from jobs, and treated like plague carriers. Their children were taunted and even their automobile insurance was canceled. From 1945 to 1953 the *Daily Worker*'s readership dropped 50 percent. So did Party membership,[144] as people avoided contact with Communist party members and literature.

With hindsight it seems the Communist party overreacted to

this precipitous repression with fear and paranoia. They purged
members who were thought to be disloyal and acted like a secret
sect. Flynn disagreed with Foster's policy of purifying the Party as a
first step toward fending off repression and FBI infiltration. Even
though several other National Executive Committee members
agreed with her, they were in the minority and democratic centralism prevailed, which meant going along with majority rule.
Flynn believed in mounting a militant defense which required
the activity of many people, even those outside Communist party
circles. However, the new Foster policy was against the formation
of a broad coalition to actively combat the loss of civil liberties and
democratic rights. In fact Foster closed ranks. In 1947 he eliminated 86 percent of the members of a Communist club at a major
steel plant because he suspected them of disloyalty. People were
also purged for white and male chauvinism, and there were not
even enough loyal Party members left to fight against the forces of
repression.[145]

Several Communist members went underground and took on
new lives, a policy Flynn was totally against.[146] She believed it
would be harmful because it added to the image of the communist
as a bandit on the run, and was unnecessary. She had more faith in
American justice and democracy and recalled the tragic effect that
Haywood's skipping bail and going to the Soviet Union had had on
the IWW. Nevertheless, by the early 1950s much of the Communist party leadership was underground, which cut them off from
daily life, their families, ordinary American workers, and the Party
and created a confusing, double-tiered leadership.

The government and media, especially with the growth of television, bombarded the public with propaganda about Reds, and
even pinkos, who threatened to take over the world and had to be
forcibly contained. No one was immune. The army was suspect,
and even Harry Truman had to prove he was not soft on Reds. So
on the eve of the 1948 election Truman ordered the arrest of
twelve top Communist party leaders. The twelve, all members of
the national board, were charged under the Smith Act (passed in
1940 with the support of the Communist party in order to prosecute Trotskyites) with conspiracy to teach and advocate the overthrow of the U.S. government by force and violence.

Their crime was not the overt act itself, but dangerous thoughts
and inflammatory speeches, articles and books that furthered the

advocacy of force and violence. There had been no peacetime sedition statutes since the Alien and Sedition Act of 1798. The evidence against the Communist party leaders was made up of half sentences and paragraphs torn out of context, with no regard for the time and conditions under which they were written, as illustration that the defendants said or wrote "smash," "abolish," or "overthrow." As Flynn said in her summation speech to the jury in her subsequent trial, a "similar process would achieve the same distortion and perversion of meaning if it was done to the Bible, to Shakespeare or to Gray's *Anatomy*." The works of Marx, Engels, Lenin, and Stalin were labeled instruments of crime and placed in the same category as burglar's tools.[147]

Flynn and Foster (whose case was severed due to illness) were the only national board members not to stand trial in 1948. Her response: "As the only woman member of the Board I felt quite embarrassed and at a loss to explain why I was not arrested with my co-workers. I felt discriminated against by Uncle Sam." But she also feared this was only the beginning and her turn would come unless a broad people's defense campaign was mounted.[148]

Flynn became chairman of a defense committee for the eleven Smith Act victims, characterizing the trial as one to protect the now endangered freedom of speech and assembly and to defend American progressives from further onslaughts. She toured the nation, speaking, raising funds, winning support outside the courtroom, and creating mass protest. Special committees were set up around particular defendants (e.g., a trade union committee, a Harlem committee); briefs and statements were publicized. A families committee was created for mutual aid and protection, to pay for families' visits, to provide the defendants with Christmas and birthday gifts, and to send their kids to camp, even though many of the male defendants resented their wives' activist roles and felt the publicity would harm their children. Some jealousy was involved, as the "Women's Commission said they [the wives and mothers] were better speakers than their husbands." There was also resistance to wives leaving their homes when requests for family speakers flooded in from all over the country.[149] However, Peggy Dennis, wife of Gene Dennis, a Party leader and defendant, argued as Flynn did that the families should work "not in pain and sorrow but in pride and anger."[150]

Anti-Communist hysteria mounted with the Korean War, the

Hiss and Rosenberg spy trials, loyalty oaths, book burnings, deportations, congressional investigations, and legislation to force Communists and sympathizers out of government jobs and labor unions. These were dreary times (1947–1953) for civil liberties, and Flynn found but a few supporters at meetings she addressed, frequently running into cancellations and hostility. This anti-Red weather was a direct result of the cold war climate. Sometimes disruptions were orchestrated by the FBI.[151] Of the Smith Act defendants, seven surrendered to serve their five-year jail terms; the remaining four (Gus Hall, Gil Green, Henry Winston, and Robert Thompson), believing that fascism was on the way, skipped bail and went underground. Elizabeth Gurley Flynn and Martha Stone were the only Communist party board members to vote against this underground policy.[152] Flynn never believed fascism was imminent and saw skipping jail as contributing to a negative image of Communist party members as evaders of law. As women Flynn and Stone also understood the hardship long separations would have for family life.

All in all, under the Smith Act 141 people were indicted and 29 served prison terms; thousands more went underground. Lives were torn apart, and the Communist party lost all semblance and coherence of a social movement. The 1950s Red Scare was different from that of the 1920s, when people acknowledged the repression as brutal and undemocratic but necessary to prevent a Red takeover as had happened in Russia. The repression of the 1950s portrayed itself as the custodian of the Constitution, patriotism, and democracy. Intimidation was all pervasive, yet mental, harder to locate, coming from television sets rather than from police raids and guns. McCarthyism made people afraid to think, speak, and be political. Many Communists refused to fight openly as they figured the only defense was to take cover and adapt protective coloring. Defense then became more difficult because Communists could not spread their ideas. Marxist theory was partially lost for a generation. Certainly, then, the atmosphere did not encourage an open, fair trial.

A second group of Smith Act victims, referred to as the "second-string Communist leadership," was arrested on June 20, 1951. The *New York Times* declared that the most "notorious" as well as important of the sixteen was Elizabeth Gurley Flynn. Acting as her own attorney, even though she was arthritic and overweight at 250 pounds, Flynn bore the brunt of the courtroom offensive, testifying between October 3 and November 7, then submitting to cross-examination until December 2. During her trial she was also forced to serve a thirty-day sentence in the Women's House of Detention when she was ruled in contempt of court for refusing to name names.

Flynn's trial lasted ten months and cost the Party and government millions of dollars. Highly paid agents, John Lautner and Louis Budenz, former Communist party members, said in testimony for the state that when Communists said "peace," they meant "war," and that they meant "repression" when they said "democracy." It was a grotesque trial—Alice in Wonderland without the humor. As Flynn said in her summation speech to the jury on January 6, 1953,

> the government attempts to dispose of all of our day-to-day activities, which cannot be disproved or construed as having any criminal intent, and with one word—insincere. This reply to our exposition of what we really do and say, in refutation of what the government alleges we think and mean, borders on the psychoanalytical—I might also say psychopathic. Who can judge the innermost sincerity of another human being? Even in intimate and personal relations, it is not easy. How can we best judge the sincerity of people in public life? . . . The everyday judgment of sincerity is based not only upon words but upon performance, upon what people do—"By their fruit ye shall know them." . . . What more convincing can anyone say than "This is my life?" "This is what I have believed, said and done year in and year out." I have laid it all here before you to show that I and my comrades are not conspirators nor do we advocate force and violence, but we advocate legal and lawful proposals to change and improve our ways of life. I do not ask you to agree with my ideals. We do not expect you to admit that we are right. We do expect you to admit our right to hold our ideas and advocate them, as you do your own.

Flynn speculated that the Communist party leaders were on trial because

> we passionately oppose the greatest force and violence the world could ever see—an atomic war . . . and because we dare to stand up against the bipartisan policy that is leading our country to national disaster and the slaughter that we are under indictment.[153]

As a fellow defendant remembers, "Elizabeth did a noble job on the stand. Her long, picturesque history in the revolutionary movement, her motherly appearance, her Irish wit hardly conveyed the picture of a violent conspiracy aimed at uprooting American institutions." She rose to the occasion with all of the passion, nerve, and spunk of her early flamboyant years. Some Party leaders, especially Foster, felt that Flynn was turning the Party into a defense organization; others declared that the system was against them and the fight was not worth the energy and effort.[154] But Flynn was a fighter, a believer in people and in America. She wrote, "I am not a fatalist, nor do I have legalistic illusions. But I am convinced it's not all cut and dried and that the American people can influence events even here. I believe we have a fighting chance to win if we take full advantage of our chance now to fight and win."[155] Unfortunately her eloquent defense was not covered by the capitalist press, which stifled the humane trenchant words Communist party officials spoke.

On January 20, 1953, the jury found all the defendants guilty. Flynn made such a moving statement prior to sentencing that Judge Edward S. Dimock was prompted to make an unprecedented offer: "If something like spending the rest of your life in Russia could be worked out as a substitute for prison, would it interest you at all?"

The sixty-two-year-old Flynn answered in the spirit of her entire career as a revolutionary:

> I am an American; I want to live and work in the United States of America. I am not interested in going any place else and would reject any such proposition. . . . The point is we do not want to leave our country. It is like the proposition made to Christians who believe in Heaven: Well, do you want to go there right away? Certainly no one of them would want to answer yes to that question, although their belief in Heaven would be great. The Emperor Nero, without asking that question, took them at their word as history records.[156]

For Flynn this was the second Red Scare. She had experienced the first one during World War I, so she was an old hand and had learned from prior mistakes. This time she did not wheel and deal her way out, calling on special privilege. She felt she should pay her dues like everyone else. In fact, she and Judge Dimock developed quite an affectionate relationship based on mutual respect. They corresponded after the trial and generally kept in touch. Even nearing sixty and exhausted, she was still a charmer and appealed to a wide range of individuals. During these scoundrel, trying times, she kept her spirits up and courageously fought for her party, while the government took a sledge hammer to squash an ailing gnat.

Flynn did not enter prison for another two years because the case lingered on appeal up to the U.S. Supreme Court. During this waiting time Flynn ran for Congress and wrote *I Speak My Own Piece*, the autobiography of her career prior to joining the Communist party. This book is political and factual rather than analytical or personal. Flynn avoids controversial issues and minimizes her central role in the IWW, not because she is modest but to magnify her Communist party years. Unfortunately, she had to go to jail without giving the text a final editing, and it was published with numerous errors, including the title, which she changed in later editions to *Rebel Girl*. Nevertheless, the autobiography is powerful, informative, and often exciting.

TO PRISON

Flynn's twenty-eight-month term in the Federal Reformatory for Women at Alderson, West Virginia, began on January 11, 1955, which she subsequently described in *The Alderson Story: My Life as a Political Prisoner* (1963). Unlike her earlier, briefer incarcerations, Flynn used this time of enforced respite to think and further educate herself, rather than to agitate among fellow prisoners, most of whom were young. At age sixty-five, Flynn felt distant from them. She spent her time in the prison library as she prepared to write a second volume of her autobiography (which was never to be completed): "I've read over 200 books, classics, poetry, plays, philosophy, religion, science, fiction, together with sociology and psychology," she wrote to one of her few approved correspondents.[157] She read many standard texts for the first time, since a busy life had never permitted her this luxury. In writing to Clemens France, a lawyer, teacher, social worker, and leader in prison reform who participated in writing the Constitution of the Irish Free State and ran for governor on the Progressive party ticket in Rhode Island, and with whom Flynn carried on what developed into a romantic correspondence, she rethought and reevaluated her life.[158]

> I feel that one of the most serious mistakes I made in my last years was to move largely in circles of people who agreed with me and I lost contact

with literally hundreds of fine people, many very good friends. It is a mistake common to our people. My father used to say of the old Socialist Labor Party, "they are always absolutely right and dead as a door nail." Its history can well be a warning to all men who are too doctrinaire and sectarian.[159]

Several other Communist party members who were jailed during this period, John Gates and George Charney, commented on how living among criminals, most of whom were poor, proved a sharp break from Party insular life and helped change their consciousness.[160] The disparity between Communist party rhetoric and workers' consciousness was great. With time to contemplate, they reexamined Communist party policy. In jail the younger Communist party members especially, who entered the Party in the high times of the depression and World War II, began to have second thoughts about the Communist party and Marxism. This younger generation acted on these doubts in 1956, when their skepticism, rekindled by the Khrushchev's revelations, led to a mass Party exodus.[161]

In prison Flynn had some misgivings about the current direction of the Communist party, but once she returned to Party life she seemed more committed than ever, despite being occasionally discouraged and tired. Flynn's published jail memoir, *Alderson Story,* does not reveal her hesitations about Party practice, which her letters from Alderson to her sister and certified correspondents uncover.[162] Either she changed her mind when she left prison and consulted with Party people and read Party journals (these were unavailable in prison), or she felt writing candidly might undermine the Party when it was vulnerable.

These prison letters, although read by prison authorities, are spunky, honest, and well written. Many consist of past memories. She requested that her correspondents save them so they would aid her in writing the rest of her autobiography. They indicate Flynn's individual interests in housework, in feminist friends whose obituaries she saw, in childbearing as a vital social vocation, in the absence of female dais-sitters at such events as a Lawyer's Guild dinner, in her disgust for slacks on women, in her admiration of Mae West, in her hatred of Howard Fast's novels filled with "arrogant male egotism—not a single true-to-life, well-drawn woman character."[163] She remarked that only a single member of the Soviet

Communist party's Central Committee on its visit to England—
Ekatarina Furtseva—was a female.

The Alderson letters express more concern with women's issues
than her columns evidence, but this might be because her correspondents, Muriel Symington (a wealthy suffragist and socialist
who did publicity work for General Foods and secretarial work for
Elizabeth Gurley Flynn and W. E. B. DuBois) and her sister Kathie
were feminists. Lawyer and lesbian Rene Hanover revealed that
Flynn complained that the Communist party had forced her to
change her chapter "Lesbianism in Alderson."[164] Originally, Flynn
is said to have told Rene Hanover that she came out as gay in this
chapter, but as the chapter now stands, not only did Flynn remain
silent about herself, but she described lesbian behavior in rather
unsympathetic and stereotypical terms. She sees the

> masculine-type lesbians as flat-chested, narrow-hipped, no curves, some-
> times extremely thin. They actually looked better in masculine-like attire
> and probably wore men's sports clothes outside. . . . Jealousy was ram-
> pant and brutal fights resulted. They called each other "husband" and
> "wife," and exchanged rings. . . . The masculine partner dominated the
> relationship, demanding and getting service.[165]

A chapter on lesbians shows Flynn's interest in the subject, which
was unusual at that time, especially for a Communist party official.

In Alderson, her only companion was Claudia Jones, a black
Smith Act victim. Given the tradition of segregation—the prisons
had just been integrated—their companionship made an important
political statement to the Alderson population as well as providing
Flynn with a close friend. When Jones's sentence expired eighteen
months prior to Flynn's, the latter was left without anyone who
shared her past or who cared about what she read or heard from
the outside.[166] This little poem marked her despondency: "The
longer you are gone, my dearest friend/The harder are the lonely
days to bear." Claudia Jones, "tall, slender, beautiful," was born in
Trinidad and emigrated to the United States with her parents
while she was quite young.[167] She joined the Communist party
through her work on the Scottsboro Defense Committee and in
the Party assumed major responsibility for the Women's Commission. Soon after her release from Alderson she was deported
to England, where, until her untimely death, she edited a lively

monthly journal, the *West Indian Gazette,* which called attention to the plight of the "coloureds" in England.

Summarizing the Alderson days in a letter, Flynn said,

> Boredom is a mild word. One begrudges a piece out of my own life, especially at my age when days are getting shorter. Frustration, futility, loneliness, monotony, undesirable company, force one to live alone and within oneself, until nearing the end one feels the surge of spring again. It would be an illusion to say that one is ever happy but it is a weakness to indulge in self pity. Books are my great escape—associating with the best minds of humanity. The study of people palls, there is no great diversity of types and little pathos but no available cures, it must be terribly disheartening to conscientious workers who do their best.[168]

At age sixty-seven Flynn found prison life hard to endure. However, several people remarked that when she came out of jail she talked a great deal about her prison mates and seemed like a graduated college student, lonesome for her room-cell mates but pleased to move out in the world and on. She summarized her stay for the press, saying: "I had no reason to reform, repent or recant so I simply reduced." She had lost seventy-five pounds.[169]

THINGS FALL APART

While Flynn was behind bars, much happened again to alter the political situation. In the USSR the Party first secretary Nikita Khrushchev delivered a top-level "secret" speech incriminating Stalin for his terrorist leadership of the Russian Communist party and world Communism. The Soviet Union invaded Hungary, and this move and the Khrushchev speech, which necessitated a new look at Party policy, created widespread dissension in Communist ranks everywhere. (In the United States this dissension took the form of a split between the Gates "revisionists" and the "hard-line" Foster adherents.) In U.S. ruling circles, Sen. Joe McCarthy, arch-symbol of the Red witch-hunts, died of alcoholic poisoning and, although the cold war had wrought havoc among liberal and progressive forces, Martin Luther King, Jr., launched a bus boycott in Montgomery, Alabama. The bleak season of cold war was thawing.

Because Gurley Flynn was a prominent American Communist and the debates over the events and revelations were so heated, people would ask her sister Kathie which side Elizabeth was on. "Oh, don't you know?" Kathie would say, "she's on the inside."[170] While this was a cute and evasive answer, Flynn really did not have the information in jail to judge the great splits in world Communism, including the beginnings of the Sino-Soviet rift, that were causing a mass exodus from the Communist party in 1956. (By the summer of 1957 the Communist party had 3,000 members, down from 15,000.)[171] Thus, Flynn temporarily avoided having to take sides in these great debates, which no doubt pleased her because she generally sought to avoid philosophical confrontation; this meant she was not identified with a faction. It also meant she missed much vital educational and political process.[172]

However, Flynn's letters from jail indicated criticism of the Foster faction and support for the Gates group. On November 22, 1956, she wrote to Clemens France: "What happened in Hungary seemed to be regrettable! I had wished the Soviet Union to withdraw her troops." On December 2, 1956, she wrote Clemens France again about Hungary: "I feel a great error in judgment was made in Hungary which reflects diplomatically but more important injures the status of Socialist countries with the *people* of the world and reflects on their relationships especially with friendly countries."[173] A letter from Alderson to her liberal friend Muriel Symington indicates intolerance of a narrow Party line and agreement with John Gates, the editor of the *Daily Worker,* whom she admired, whose forces, numerically a majority, stood for inner-party democratization, open criticism of the Russian leadership, opposition to Soviet troops in Hungary, and advocacy of a peaceful road to socialism like the one taken by the Communist party in Italy. The Gates group, a loose collection of individuals with no coherent point of view and little adeptness at administrative wheeling and dealing, eventually withdrew from the Party. On September 4, 1956, Flynn wrote to Muriel Symington: "Dr. France quoted a Chinese paper that said that the Soviet Union's actions in Hungary were 'entirely just.' I told him I do not agree. He is a devotee not an analyst of political events."[174] In another letter Flynn identified with a dissident and stated:

Yes, it looks as if Tito made a major blunder in arresting Djilas, who was sentenced I see, to three years—the same sentence as mine and apparently

the same "offense," political difference. *But* the people who criticize him
see no analogy with themselves. I like Gates' statement as you report it in
your letter.[175]

At some point during these great debates Flynn jotted down a
list of twelve mistakes the Communist party had made. She apparently kept this list secret, as none of her many colleagues knew of it
and seemed surprised it had been written.[176] The almost tele-
graphic, penciled list criticizes:

1. Too great idolatry of Soviet Union, Foster's Soviet America.
   [One of Foster's slogans was Toward a Soviet America.]
2. Too close identity with Comintern. [The Comintern was the
   Soviet-dominated international policy-making body.]
3. Theory of self-determination in the Black Belt as applied
   to Negro people—What Browder said, "Here a right but
   should not exercise it." [Flynn meant the Communist party
   wanted the idea but not the reality. As the USSR established
   the Ukraine and Armenia as "autonomous" nations, so the
   Communist party in the United States wanted the South to become an independent black nation. Browder said blacks had
   the right to establish this independent nation but they should
   not use the right. Browder stopped organizing in the South
   and, to please Roosevelt, stopped pressing for black rights in
   the North as well.]
4. Browder—change to Communist Political Association. [Brow-
   der's dissolution of the Party and establishment of an
   association.]
5. Browder dropping of foreign born. [Browder dropped the
   foreign-born from Party membership to eliminate that pre-
   text for their prosecution and dropped organizing by ethnic
   group.]
6. Teheran—Imperialism at an end—Peaceful co-existence applied to ideology without theoretical struggle. [Browder felt
   that because Roosevelt and Stalin had been allies during World
   War II and had made peace at Teheran, this amity would continue. With peaceful relations between the United States and
   the USSR, there would be no need for a Communist party.]
7. Smith Act trials policy exposition of news rather than right to

admit and correction of misrepresentation. What Wellman said on M and L trial. [Flynn might be referring to Marxist-Leninist theory, rather than to the Communist party's accomplishments. Wellman was a Party leader in Michigan.]

8. Wrong estimation of period—1948—as fascism coming to USA. [Many Party leaders went underground, expecting fascism in the United States. A whole underground network was created. This policy was based on the real need for an underground in the Fascist European countries—Germany, Spain, Italy and France.]

9. Underground—"No shows" etc. result. [Party leaders Gil Green, Robert Thompson, Gus Hall, and Henry Winston went underground rather than show up for their Smith Act trial.]

10. Voluntary departures *wrong* except where fascist countries were destination. [The involuntary departures of Party leaders John Williamson and Irving Potash who were not citizens were not wrong.]

11. Wrong Labor Policy—try to cut to Party patterns, Local 64-Maritime-Transport-Fur etc. alienated friends in leadership. Effects still felt. [The Communist party tried to direct friendly unions in a dogmatic fashion.]

12. Failure to frankly admit and discuss these and other mistakes—no self-criticism.[177]

Flynn's list was critical of both the overly revisionist Browder and the narrowly Soviet-identified Foster. In the end she identified herself with Eugene Dennis's cautious compromise position, calling for a "united mass party of socialism."[178] Many of her younger colleagues left the Party in 1956–1957, but she stayed. As Al Richmond wrote,

She was a woman of sixty-seven whose organic attachment to the party was a primary source of her intellectual and spiritual sustenance. She wanted very much to be freed of organizational chores and responsibilities, so that she could devote her time and energy to writing the second half of her autobiography. But this desire to get out of the structural harness did not reflect any weakening of her fundamental commitment to the organization.[179]

Most of Flynn's generation stayed in the Party. In
was too late for them to remake their lives, and
loyalty was to the Party not to whatever it may have
stood for.[180]

Her plan, after prison, was to settle down on the West
write the second part of her autobiography, *My Life as a*
in the United States. But the Party needed her now more th
So less than a month after her release from Alderson she
full swing, running as a candidate from the Lower East S
the New York City Council, speaking, although the listeners
still few, writing her weekly columns for the *Daily Worker*,
teaching public speaking and American labor history at the Sc
of Marxist Studies in New York City.

In 1960 she went to Copenhagen as a delegate to a conferen
on the fiftieth anniversary of International Women's Day. Instea
of returning, she accepted some of her many invitations to spea
in Europe and, not least, at a May Day celebration in Moscow. This
was her first visit to the socialist world. For eight months she traveled in the Soviet Union and five other socialist nations, where she
was lionized and from whence she sent back joyful accounts for
her *Daily Worker* readers.[181] Even the readers of her columns protested that she was "too ecstatic" and "saw nothing to criticize" and
suggested that she did not "meet the people sufficiently" as she was
too protected by officials. Her reply was: "Nothing is perfect anywhere and they do such a thorough job of self criticism there that I
leave criticism here to the capitalist press."[182]

In Russia Flynn looked into the role of women and was unduly
impressed with what she found. Women constituted 30 percent of
Party leadership; women workers were afforded special facilities
such as day care, kindergartens, nursing homes, and health resorts; and women occupied many vocations they were largely denied in the United States. The sanctimonious attitude the Soviets
displayed toward their own heritage did upset her somewhat:
"Every second building in Leningrad is a holy ground," she jotted
in a notebook, but she never made any public criticism.[183]

Flynn's trip to the Soviet Union provided her with the rest and
pleasures she was deprived of under capitalism. She was treated
like royalty and for the first time she lived in the best hotels, ate
choice Soviet cuisine, and attended ballet, circuses, and theater. In

the United States she had never had the time or the money for ordinary entertainment unconnected with Party activities. In the USSR, dinners and celebrations with dignitaries were held in her honor. She lapped up the luxury and dreaded returning to her exhaustive routine. In her old age she needed the esteem, comfort, and recognition that should come from a long life of toil and devotion. No wonder she looked at Soviet life with rose-colored glasses. At last her half century of committed class struggle and political activism was rewarded and the socialist state, from Khrushchev on down, paid her respect. She came back from the Soviet Union more orthodox than ever, convinced the Soviets were correct in invading Hungary and that the Russians were creating a new democratic technological state.[184] Finally she had found a country in which the values she had spent her life creating were actualized and in which the Communist party was in power rather than being a small outcast, outlaw sect.

Just a month after her return, Eugene Dennis, chairman of the Communist party, died of cancer. Elizabeth Gurley Flynn was chosen as his successor. The capitalist press responded to her new distinction in typical male chauvinist fashion—describing her garments and face. From the way she wore a black dress, wrote the *New York Times* (Mar. 15, 1961), she looked like "a retired grammar school teacher." Her face, said Murray Kempton, "would be irresistible on the label of an apple pie mix; she is the aunt Dorothy longed to get back to from Oz" (*New York Post,* Mar. 15, 1961). The *Baltimore Sun* (Mar. 25, 1961) refused to tarry over the visible traits and wrote instead—refusing to accept women in decision-making roles—of a "reluctantly obedient puppet whose strings are worked by unseen hands." The characterization of her as "Mother Flynn" or a "sweet old lady" most aggravated her, she told the *San Francisco Chronicle* (Apr. 5, 1961), because they sounded like epitaphs. Actually the communist party's choice of Flynn was a pragmatic compromise that few could oppose. The leading contender was Ben Davis, a black former New York City congressman attached to the hard-line Foster group. A woman and the most personally liked of the whole leadership group, and one who, like Gus Hall, executive secretary, had not been around during the 1956–1957 crisis fights, seemed an ideal choice.[185]

As chairman of the Communist party, Flynn made countless appearances at colleges, on radio, and sometimes television. Newspaper, radio, and TV reporters, editors, and photographers (*New York Times, Los Angeles Examiner and Mirror, San Francisco Chronicle*) sent detailed reports to the FBI alerting the bureau to Flynn's statements.[186] Her remarkable voice and charismatic presence stayed with her to the end of her days. Her niece, Jane Bobba, remembers visiting her aunt in the early 1960s and being awakened to a voice from the next room, "Arise ye prisoners of Starvation," then again, then again, louder. After forty minutes warming up, her niece recalls, her voice was downright scary—rich, full, and magnificent.[187]

Flynn spoke loudly and clearly against the McCarran Act, which required Communists to register with a Subversive Activities Control Board as agents of a foreign power. Members of the Communist party refused to register because it involved supplying names of Party officers and members, identifying and detailing all expenditures, and stamping all outgoing mail and publications as disseminated by a Communist organization. Flynn felt that to register was to admit one was a traitor, a saboteur, a seditionist, and a conspirator.

Labor agitation and labor defense had almost always shared her attention, but if Flynn found the defense of the Party's right to exist to be paramount in the early 1960s, she still combined this task with positive agitational steps to build the socialist movement. Certain Party hard-liners believed no effort should be undertaken at that time to persuade nonmembers or former members to join, but Flynn sensed a reawakened militance in blacks, students, and women and cheered and encouraged the new spirit of resistance, the end of the silent generation. Fresh winds were blowing, and she could recognize them as the Freedom Riders used old familiar IWW techniques of militant confrontation. Most of her Communist party cohorts denigrated these "infantile disorders," rather than recognizing as Flynn did that the "sixties were to be a landmark in progressive history—to surpass the eighties of the last century and the thirties of this." In the early sixties the Communist party made alliances with the more cautious, established NAACP (National Association for the Advancement of Colored People), and Martin Luther King, Jr.'s, SCLC (Southern Christian Leadership Conference), rather than with the militant SNCC (Student Nonviolent Coordinating Committee) or Malcolm X.[188]

Flynn continued to agitate against the McCarran Act, which did not seek her out personally, as it did Gus Hall and Benjamin Davis, the other top Party leaders. The FBI reported that although Flynn was chairman of the Communist party, she was not indicted because "she would make too good a defendant."[189] But Flynn was denied a passport to travel abroad. With Herbert Aptheker, she successfully fought the case to the Supreme Court, upsetting this section of the act. With her right to travel reinstated, Flynn went to the Soviet Union for a rest. And it was for her, at this point in a ceaselessly eventful life, a "quiet, peaceful land," where she hoped to complete her autobiography.[190]

Instead she lived the final chapter of her life. Elizabeth Gurley Flynn died after a month in the Soviet Union. The autopsy found inflammation of the stomach and intestinal lining, aggravated by a blood clot in the lungs of the workers' Joan of Arc, as Dreiser had dubbed the great-voiced girl of sixty years earlier. At seventy-four, the flesh was no longer willing, although the spirit was still strong.[191] Flynn received a full-scale state funeral in Red Square. More than twenty-five thousand people gathered for the tribute, as Moscow came to a standstill. Such Red veterans as Dolores Ibarruri—the Spanish Civil War's Pasionaria—rose to eulogize the fallen comrade. Nina Khrushchev joined the pall bearers carrying the flower-decked bier with Elizabeth Gurley Flynn's black-edged portrait. Nikita Khrushchev stood solemnly in the honor guard just before the body was cremated, and the band played the "Internationale." Her obituary appeared on the front page of the *New York Times* and *Izvestia*. Throughout the United States she was eulogized as "the grand old lady of American Communism," one of the "brightest personalities of the twentieth century," or vilified as "a matronly looking character with the personality of a cobra," "a fire eater turned Communist politician and party hack." Some of her ashes were placed on a dais before Lenin's tomb and then buried beneath the Kremlin Wall. The rest, in Waldheim Cemetery in Chicago, lie with those of America's legendary radicals—Big Bill Haywood, Eugene Debs, Emma Goldman, and the Haymarket Martyrs of 1886.[192]

To die in a foreign country, although a Communist one, which treated her better than her own country, seemed an unfitting end. She was an American rebel. It was in America that she stirred millions, fought bravely, and tried, even if she often fell short, to live a revolutionary life.[193]

Child Prodigy

Elizabeth Gurley Flynn (front row, right) with her class at Public School #9, 1904. She is wearing the gold medal given her by the New York Times *for a prize essay.*

Early Essay on Women (1905)

THIS essay, one of Flynn's earliest, written in 1905 when Elizabeth Gurley Flynn was a mere fifteen, was based on her prizewinning high school debate topic, "Why Women Should Vote?" Her debate style was described by newspapers of the time: "there is not a dull line in her speeches. She draws the crowd with her beauty and holds it with her logic." [1]

Elizabeth Gurley Flynn hypnotized the crowd before she had got far in her discourse. She has an odd manner of making what might be called short hand gestures, pot hooks, curves, dots and dashes written in the air. Soon they [audience] were frowning when she frowned, laughing when she laughed, growing terribly earnest when she grew moderately so. [2]

This speech, which is not preserved in its entirety, was influenced by her reading at the time: suffrage literature and feminist theory, Mary Wollstonecraft's Vindication of the Rights of Women, *John and Harriet Mill's* The Subjection of Women, *Edward Carpenter's* Love's Coming of Age, *and Olive Schreiner's* Women and Labor, *all liberal, socialist, feminist, nineteenth-century non-Marxist classics.* [3] *According to these texts, women's advancement depended on their position in the church, school, and legal system and not on their position in capitalist production, as a scientific socialist would have emphasized. Flynn's essay reflects this bourgeois and utopian thought; men, not a specific class, the ruling class, as Marx indicated, make laws. Flynn might have defined herself as a Marxist at this time, but her writing and speeches show that she was still an anarchist or utopian socialist.*

[1] From a clipping in Flynn Papers, Tamiment, marked Philadelphia 1907.

[2] From a clipping in *Morning Public Ledger*, Kensington, N.Y., Aug. 28, 1906, Flynn Papers, Tamiment. By age seventeen she was referred to as "The Platform Wonder of NY." Clipping in Chicago paper, Sept. 17, 1907, Flynn Papers, Tamiment.

[3] Penciled reading list, 1905–1906, from Flynn Papers, Tamiment. Later in an article for the *Sunday Worker*, Jan. 26, 1941, "How I Made My First Public Speech," she said that at this time she was reading two Marxist texts as well, August Bebel's *Women under Socialism* and Engels's *Origin of the Family*.

WHEN we think of the woman of today, we see in our minds the athletic, the business, the college, the society, the home-managing women, "new women" they are derisively called; then we compare them with the women of yesterday, meek, domestic, and religious household drudges for men, submitting themselves in a way that would delight Old Saint Paul and usually we say, "How they have improved! How sensible, intelligent, strong they are, these maids of the twentieth century! We are glad those backboneless women have gone."

But they have not gone. The new women are in the minority still, the backboneless women are in the large majority and they are *seldom* sensible, educated and strong.

The feminine sex have not advanced as men have advanced. Their progress has been retarded, first by the church, second by lack of education, third by laws and customs, and fourth by their own submission.

The girls of today are being retarded as their mothers were retarded, but we may hope that a few more generations will remedy this evil, and give us *free* girls and free women.

The church has always retarded Woman, has wronged her for centuries and for this reason if for no other, the church should and will fall! It has taught that woman is inferior to man, that she is his subject and was created for him and his desires. The man has willingly acquiesced to this false doctrine and the woman has slavishly bowed her head and submitted to this decree of tyranny. St. Paul has done more harm to Christian womankind than any other human being, but his reign will soon be completed and he will be consigned to his well deserved grave, where he should have been nearly nineteen hundred years ago.

The second factor that brought about the wrong condition of women was their lack of education. Men and women alike have declared, "Home is woman's place, she does not need education." But our weary ears have heard it long enough and although at present few women know anything of science, astronomy, medicine, geography, politics, even of that important subject physiology (this lack of knowledge causing them to twist and squeeze their bodies into horrible shapes in a mistaken idea of beauty), yet why should not women be educated as well as men? Why should not women know something of the earth, of themselves, just as much as men?

The third factor was the senseless customs and tyrannical laws in regard to women. Laws giving a man his wife's property, as if she were his slave, allowing a man to own her, body and soul, and forbidding her the right to govern herself, to help make the laws of her country. Men make the laws, men enforce the laws, men try women accused of breaking the laws, and men sentence and punish them if found guilty. Is this justice? Does the star-eyed Goddess of Liberty look down on this scene, this injustice to her sex? Is this country a Republic or a monarchial government? It matters little as far as women are concerned.

Do you wonder that women break laws, laws made by others conflicting with their interests? Until women get the right to vote and rule themselves we cannot blame all women if they become Anarchists. Any woman who will tamely admit to seeing men the rulers and women the subjects, who has no interest in how she is governed, is either a lover of slavishness or has lost the last vestige of intelligence and spirit and self-respect.

Further the absurd, yet cruel unwritten laws of conventionalities, laws that say even as mother of the world, woman should be ashamed, should feel degraded. The act of creation, the power of increasing the race, the process of life giving which lies with woman is treated as shameful, as something to be spoken of in whispers. And why? Why this custom? Has it brought great honor to woman? Indeed not. For today, instead of deep and holy reverence for Motherhood, in the minds of the race, it is treated as a disgrace to woman, to be ignored by cultured people. How terrible to think the most necessary function of human life is the most dishonored, and that woman, the Eternal Mother, is forced to be ashamed of it! What false customs! What false conventionalities! What false unworthy civilization! May we become civilized before many ages.

Speaking of civilization reminds me of one objection a worthy masculine friend brings up against giving woman her rights. It is, "Well when women are so independent they won't be treated as chivalrously as now!" Chivalry! A sort of sneering charity! Men cant of chivalry, they carry a little bundle or umbrella for a woman, but seldom carry a baby, they give up a seat to a fast, gaudily-dressed butterfly woman, but let a poor working girl stand, they take the pretty girls home from a party or a club while the less attractive ones must trot off alone, they tell their wives of their simpering silly adoration for them, but clasp their pocketbooks with the iron hand, they are willing to do all the foolish little nothings that a sensible woman does not want, but refuse to give us our *rights,* and they talk of Chivalry. Chivalry never existed, never will till women are given their own place as equals of men. I do not argue that woman is higher than man, but I do argue she is his equal. She is to the man and the man is to her as the two parts of a pair of shears are to each other. Together they are useful, separated they are worthless, but they are equals and men and women are equals, and always will be equals. Woman's submission is the last cord that binds her. Is it because she doesn't want her rights, or does not know enough to become educated, or does not appreciate her importance to Humanity?

Woman has become, I believe, slightly degenerated after ages of submission and now it is only a few women, "daughters of their fathers," who appreciate their condition and try to remedy it. But if the cause were removed according to the theory of cause and effect, the effect would very soon disappear also. If the conditions were changed, if her political, religious, and sex freedom were given to her, then the degenerate effect would be removed and woman would be again the true mother of men and women, the true companion of men.

Women have mastered the great studies, others can and will do it, many women want self-government, the others will soon want it and learn how to use it, and soon women will understand, let us hope, that they need *never* be ashamed of their function in life as mother.

And then, Ah! then, when women get out of the rut, think less of clothes, fashion, style, sentimental nonsense, consider the vital questions, the great issues of knowledge, of government, of Liberty, of Humanity, when they become *WOMEN*, not sensless brainless idiots, as so many are today, when the church drops its doctrine of inferiority, when the government gives women their rights, when the unwritten law written in the hearts of men and women decrees woman's duty is not debasing but honorable and glorious, she will be herself, the True Woman, The Sister, The Daughter, The Wife, The Mother of the race.

We will then take one great step towards the millenium, for depraved servile mothers have depraved servile children and free mothers will have free children.

When we have glorious intelligent women we will soon have a race of men reared by free Mothers. As the poet Whitman says, "A man is a great thing thru eternity; but every jot of greatness of the man is unfolded out of the woman."

Man will never be free till woman is free. When woman is free man is free, then and then only.

SOURCE: Flynn Papers, Tamiment.

Education and the School System (1906)

ELIZABETH *Gurley Flynn first submitted this essay to a contest at Morris High School, where it caused great consternation among the teachers. The master-piece was rejected, and so, undaunted, she delivered it in front of the school building while the more ingratiating winner accepted within. "Huh. What do you know about education?" demanded a heckler. "What don't I know about education," flashed Flynn, "I'm getting educated."* [1]

Flynn later delivered this speech as a sermon to the Unity Congregation, a socialist church that met every Sunday morning at the Apollo Hall, near the New York City Library. Again the speech caused a stir, touching off a series of letters to the editor in the New York Times. *A New Jersey man was shocked by her socialist tirade against the public school system, while others defended her.* [2] *Flynn in fact delivered this speech many times.*

This essay was Flynn's swan song to formal education. She quit school at age seventeen and only returned as a teacher at the Jefferson, later called the Marxist School.

EDUCATION is exemplified by the school system. To come to any right conclusion on this question we must understand exactly what the school system is—its merits and faults. Thus far, its loudest-voiced exponents have equally been old and gray, and since "things were different when I was a boy," quoting themselves they don't know anything about their subject. This is our question—it belongs to us—the young folks in the school; it is about time we grasped the problem, consid-

---

[1] Clippings from the *Journal American*, Apr. 11, 1906, Flynn Papers, Tamiment.
[2] Clippings from the *New York Times*, May 29, 1906, Flynn Papers, Tamiment.

ered it well and took part in the discussion ourselves. They have arranged it, they have forced us into it, they have demanded of us, it is now time we demand of them "why have you done thus?"

Since there can be but few better qualified to speak than one in the midst of a school course, I will proceed to define what our present day school system is—from a scholar's point of view.

. . . The aim of the school system is to produce a well-trained, well-knowledged human being. Why does it fail? . . .

Firstly, because you cannot crowd the *education of a life time* into a few years, or the subjects suitable for a man's understanding into a child's brain. Secondly, all human beings are not alike and just as long as the parents and teachers continue feeding us, very different tho we be, on exactly the same intellectual diet, there will be many cases of mental indigestion.

Thirdly, the whole course is a memory course and not a thinking course, it is not an incentive to knowledge-seeking but kills it and as such is bound to fall in defeat.

Fourthly, we are taught no useful work that will make us a benefit to society, help us produce more than we consume, and cultivate the spirit of independence.

Fifthly, we go into the world from the groping hands of educators, utterly ignorant of the world and ourselves, the relation of the two, what we must do for the world and it for us.

Lastly and most important they force, force, force education at us and until we know the reason or right of it the system must be a failure, because we cannot cooperate with them on any mutual basis.

. . . When we are young and growing, we are active. We can't help it, you may preach at us to cultivate repose but we can't do it. We must laugh and sing and frolic for are we not young with all the world before us? But when we are old we get stiff and lame and lose this activity. We become sedate and like to sit by the fire and read or dream and think. Then it is when we forget our youth and say "children should be seen and not heard" and preach about the utility of having children understand the laws of physics. Why? Because they, the active young, like it? No, because we, the tired old folks, understand it and *because we like* it, and that brings me to the point. Why not follow nature's plan, get back to Mother Earth as the exponents of the simple life advise us, by studying agriculture, by learning manual training where there is plenty of field for our activity when we are young? I hardly recall one young person I ever knew, who did not enjoy this sort of work. Where is the girl or boy who would not delight in a little garden all their own, who couldn't "putter" around the fields and woods day after day, learning more about nature than you wise teachers and your biology books can ever hope to teach them? What child doesn't like to make something with his own hands? I remember a look of pleasure I once saw on a boy's face when he brought home a little breadboard he had cut out, a look that no arithmetic paper however fine could bring to his face. I, myself, have always wanted to know how to work in wood, yet I never could do it because I was under a school system that wanted to pommel geography into my head which was no sooner learned than it slipped away again.

Then since the grown-up folks like the intellectual, brain work, leave that for them. Let us know how to read and write so that the key to knowledge lies with us, then if we want knowledge we can take it and if we don't want it all your school system can't succeed in making us take it. These studies which are disliked at twenty are very interesting at forty. The philosophical subjects "the passion-less pursuit of passion-less knowledge" are for the deep thinkers, the fully matured, not children.

Education is never ending, why should we be forced to act the glutton over it?

. . . I stated that all people are not alike and the intellectual food given to us is not suited to our individual needs. I can see no sense in a system that tries to teach a boy, who has a mathematical turn of mind and would make a first class civil engineer, how to tell the parts of a flower and what key is denoted in music by one sharp; why should a good cook be spoiled to make a poor stenographer; or a good carpenter be lost in educating a poor teacher? One occupation is just as honorable as the other; the point is to do your work well in whatever line your talents lead you.

This present day method of education tends to produce the unsatisfactory race of men and women we are today. We are all poured into the same educational mold, we all come out the same, mediocre, uninteresting, conventional, lacking in individual thought or action. . . . Did Good Mother Nature give us each our own little peculiarities and talents to have them knocked out of us by wise educators? Individuality is discouraged and not fostered, but just as long as we are patterns of each other, I am trying to be you and you are trying to be me, there is little hope for progress and the world. You and I must rule someday.

Then further, I said, the course is one to cultivate memory and not thought and rather than give an incentive to knowledge seeking, kills any desire for it.

. . . There are in New York five school sessions a week of five hours each. (I speak principally of New York because I know it best.) Now five hours a day sounds like an easy, short, school day. If that were all I might not object so vigorously. The work of education however is done at home, usually by poor gaslight, for after you once enter the grammar department, you have from three to five hours homework. Five hours is not a fabrication, I have it myself every Tuesday night.

That makes from 8 to 10 hours mental work for children. Talk about the 8 hour labor law, better conditions shorter hours! We'll have to form a labor union and go on strike ourselves! . . .

And then the studies are so dead, there is so little chance for outside reading and thinking that the incentive is gradually destroyed. To use a personal illustration, if I gave as much time as is required to each of my lessons, which I don't do, I could never have done any outside reading. . . .

. . . Without my gleanings from Marx, George and Proudhon, Thomas Paine and Ingersoll, Walt Whitman and Emerson and Thoreau, Shelley, Byron, even Ibsen and Bernard Shaw and many more such literary teachers, what sort of crude ideas would I have? Does the school training open the door of Knowledge? I would emphatically say no. Instead of giving you the key to the realms of booklore and *then letting you alone* to explore for yourself, they must pick and choose for you and finally give you such overpowering doses of heavy, dry, lessons *which you don't want to know,* that finally in the end they drive you away and you never find out *what you did want to know.* . . .

It's no use telling me it's a Utopian dream, it's justice and common-sense and must in the end triumph over all difficulties. One of the greatest troubles in the labor world today is that there are so many idlers, the capitalists who shirk and live on the profit of the laborer's toil, the unemployed who have been forced out by the competitive, profit making system and even We, the school children too, must be counted in this idle class. The result is that the work for all these people must be done by the workers, who are thus overtaxed and the work is neither well nor completely done. My objection, which may be easier to understand after this explanation, means this—our school system is radically wrong, because it makes us a burden on the backs of the workers; because it does not help us produce as much as we consume, a duty of every able-bodied person. Lastly, if we pass over these reasons we could condemn it because it makes no attempt to prepare us and make us as competent to do our share to the last iota of the world's work, when we do leave its rule and enter the realms of the grown-ups. Reason why it does not? After this decision that we must do our share of the work, we can consider the topic from a physiological point of view. I have always heard stated that you should not exercise one part of the body to the detriment of the other, or, in fact, that you should never overexercise one muscle or set of muscles. I may not quote exactly right; it sounds like very sensible advice however. It would not be considered a sane act if a man exercised his child's arms day after day, yet never allowed him to walk. But is it any more sane to exercise a child's brain day after day yet make no attempt to exercise his muscles, teach him no useful work for his hands?

The brain is worked to the detriment of the rest of the body. It is not in accordance with the laws of health or science. Exercise strengthens, overexercise hardens. Can it be this that explains the hard heads of so many grown-ups who won't think if they can possibly help it?

. . . Now what is taught me as a girl of womankind? Do they come out truthful and sincere and tell me just how society treats women today and where her place is in its plan so that I may judge for myself whether it is right or wrong and whether I am satisfied with it or not. No, they read about woman's creation from the rib of a man, they murmur about woman's sphere and some indefinite woman's calling, and then their attitude says "Hush! We are on forbidden subjects." No more is said and here is one of the great root-evils of the perverted notions of conventionality and morality, the ignorance of woman and the wrong attitude of the majority of people towards clean, pure subjects. They leave us ignorant of vital subjects, how can we be expected to handle them with honest frankness?

The inconsistencies stand out clearly when they attempt to explain even how man came to exist. Altho no one really knows, still if they must instruct about the question it is well to have consistent teachings to give or keep silent on the subject.

In the morning we heard from the Bible how man was created in the full vigor of his manhood from the dust, by a Divine Being, but in the afternoon we were told that he slowly evolved thru long ages from the lowest forms of life. Now altho whatever proof there is goes to the side of the evolution theory, still they shouldn't expect us to believe both and did they suppose we were all fools and did not see the glaring inconsistency? . . .

Lastly, I claimed the system fails because they force, force, force, education at us and until we know the reason or right of it, their system will be a failure because we cannot cooperate with them on any mutual basis.

. . . This is my credo, I believe in education that never ends, that goes on thru life, an education that never hurries, crowds or forces, that helps people learn what they like and want to know when they want to know but never forces them to learn what they don't want to know, that educates the hands and heart as well as the head. I believe the fields and gardens are as much the schools as any buildings, that play is as useful for children as work, that teachers should be the parents or the friends, should be comrades and companions who take joy in their work. I believe in the gospel of friendship in helping each other meanwhile.

SOURCE: Flynn Papers, Tamiment Library.

The Wobbly Years, 1908–1917

Elizabeth Gurley Flynn (circled, center right) addressing a crowd in City Hall Park, Seattle, during the Free Speech Battle, May 25, 1915

Story of My Arrest and Imprisonment (1909)

ELIZABETH *Gurley Flynn's free speech activity began with direct action in defense of the freedom to speak, assemble, and organize. The IWW was the first labor organization to dramatize the constitutionally guaranteed right of free speech. Whenever a Wobbly chapter would become involved in a free speech battle, it would notify the general office, which would send all footloose men; occasionally women came along. Twenty-six free speech battles occurred between 1909 and 1916.[1] In response to these calls, Wobblies converged on the town that had violated their free speech, usually by forbidding the IWW to hold street meetings. One after another the itinerant Wobblies would test their rights by mounting a makeshift soap box in the town center and beginning to read the Bill of Rights. Just as quickly, the police would haul them off to jail.*

Jail then became another weapon in the IWW drama to defend Wobblies' rights. Wobs crowded into the jails, sang and carried on, demanded separate trials, cluttered the courts, and burdened the local taxpayers with the expenses. Incarceration became another stage for effective propaganda. In prison the Wobblies spread the IWW gospel and won new recruits to the organization.[2] Eventually the town's citizens, worn down by the noise, notoriety, and expense of feeding the prisoners and paying for their trials, demanded that free speech prevail. At this point the victorious Wobbly activists moved to another town, for another battle and drama.

In Seattle the free speech battles lasted more than a year, and over twelve hundred were arrested.[3] Seattle was the largest center of migratory workers, and the IWW had its largest western chapter there. The immediate reason for

---

[1] *New York Times*, May 9, 1912; and Paul Brissenden, *The IWW: A Study of American Syndicalism* (New York: IWW, 1919), 387.

[2] Melvyn Dubofsky, *We Shall Be All: A History of the Industrial Workers of the World* (Chicago: Quandrangle Books, 1969), 196–197.

[3] Elizabeth Gurley Flynn, "The Free Speech Fight at Spokane," "The Shame of Spokane," and "Latest News from Spokane," *International Socialist Review*, Dec. 1909, 483–489; Jan. 1910, 610–619; Mar. 1910, 828–834; and William Z. Foster, "47 Days in the Spokane City Jail," *Workingman's Paper*, Seattle, Jan. 22, 1910.

the battle was that fraudulent employment agencies, the Wobblies called them "sharks," were cheating job applicants, in alliance with unscrupulous lumber and agricultural employers. The sharks sent men to jobs that did not exist and insisted on collecting a fee beforehand. The job applicant not only lost the fee but the railroad fee to and from the nonexistent job. A single firm employing a hundred men at a time was alleged to have hired and fired five thousand during the season.[4]

In the fall of 1908 the Wobblies began attacking the employment agencies and demanding that employers hire through the union. The Don't Buy Jobs campaign of the IWW so frightened these sharks that they got the Seattle City Council to pass an ordinance against public street meetings, effective January 1, 1909. Religious organizations like the Salvation Army were exempt from this ordinance. The IWW protested. Even the AFL and the Socialist party petitioned the city council to remove the ordinance.

The free speech arrests caused severe overcrowding of the jails in Seattle; twenty-eight men were forced into a cell seven-by-eight feet in size.[5] Gurley, who was pregnant at the time, tried to avoid arrest by not mounting a soap box; instead she spoke inside and raised funds. Eventually though, because she was a leader and dubbed a dangerous firebrand, she was jailed anyway. Gurley's arrest, however, backfired on the Seattle authorities and only accelerated IWW activity. The IWW then threatened the city and individual officials with damage suits of $150,000 and vowed to carry the suits to the Supreme Court.

On March 5, 1910, the city officials finally made peace with the Wobblies. The ordinance against public speech was repealed, and employment agencies agreed to pay the losses suffered by defrauded workers. The licenses of nineteen employment agencies were revoked and female matrons introduced in the female jails, altogether an overwhelming victory. One unhappy result of the dramatic struggle was that Gurley had a miscarriage, undoubtedly triggered by her jail stay.

O N Tuesday, November 30th at about eight o'clock I was walking towards the IWW hall. As I reached the corner of Stevens and Front I was accosted by officer Bill Shannon with the demand, "Are you Miss Flynn?" I replied yes—when he grunted "well we want you." I asked, "Have you a warrant?" "Naw, we haven't," he rejoined, when the other plainclothes man stepped up and remarked, "There is one in the station." I accompanied them to the police station where I was booked and the warrant read for "Criminal conspiracy." I was then taken to the Chief's office, where the Prosecuting Attorney Pugh put me thru the "third degree."

[4]*Proceedings of the First Convention of the Industrial Workers of the World* (New York: IWW, 1905), 82.
[5]Ibid., 575.

. . . They were all extremely courteous, probably due to information conveyed to them over the phone that my physical condition was such that it would be dangerous to be otherwise.[6] But the ordeal of a rapid firing of questioning is not as easy as it looks from the outside. Every trick known to a shyster lawyer is resorted to—every possible appeal made to honesty, sincerity and truthfulness of the average citizen, that the questioners have no respect for themselves.

Frankly the only mistake I made was to talk at all, but what I forgot, "refused to answer," "didn't remember," and "couldn't recall" would fill a book. A man they would put in a sweat-box and break his physique and spirit and eventually get him so faint and sick that he wouldn't know what he was saying.

The idea of the "third degree" is evident, to trap you into proving yourself innocent, into forgetting that it's up to them to prove you guilty. Some of the cross questions were highly humorous. For instance Mr. Pugh remarked, "You know its useless denying what you know is an apparent fact, easily proven by scores of witnesses"—to which I retorted, "Well, why do you ask me so many questions about *an apparent fact?*"

The Chief of police was anxious to know if Katherine Flynn who signed the Irish Socialist communication happened to be any relation of mine. Irish on both sides of this fight annoys the Chief, in face of his assertion that we are all foreigners. With an assumption of innocence Pugh asked, "Who are the Executive Committee?" and "Who handles the finances?" The first I didn't know, the second I refused to answer. He asked, "Do you know?" and I answered, "Of course I know." And he asked "you refuse to answer?" I said "I certainly do." He asked Did you say so and so in your speeches? to which I replied "I talk so much I don't know what I say." They all gave him the laugh— and he asked if that statement wouldn't probably, if published, injure my reputation as a speaker. Anxious he was for me to maintain my standing as an agitator, indeed! Finally he said with a very smooth preliminary about not caring to prosecute a woman, etc., that I might go if I would state that I had no connection with the free speech fight, was not in sympathy with the tactics of the IWW and had not induced men to go to jail etc. I refused to either deny or affirm, declined and that settled me. I was allowed to see Mr. Moore[7] and Mr. Rogers in the Chief's office after which I was taken to the county jail in the patrol wagon.

. . . I was placed in a cell with two other women, poor miserable specimens of the victims of society. One woman is being held on the charge that her husband put her in a disorderly house—the other is

[6] Flynn was pregnant.
[7] Her lawyer, Fred Moore?

serving ninety days for robbing a man in a disreputable resort in
Spokane. Never before had I come in contact with women of that
type, and they were interesting. Also I was glad to be with them, *for in
a jail one is always safer with others than alone.* One of the worst features
of being locked up is a terrible feeling of insecurity, of being at the
mercy of men you do not trust a moment day or night, unable to defend yourself or call for help. These miserable outcasts of society did
everything in their power to make me comfortable. One gave me the
spread and pillow cover from her own bed, when she saw my disgust
at the dirty gray blankets. I could not eat the heavy soggy food, stews,
etc. nor drink the terrible stuff called coffee, but the girls gave me
fruit that had been sent into them. They moderate their language,
apologize, and pathetically try to conform to some of the standards of
decency when they see you are *"different."* They have been so accustomed to being ill used and brow beaten they rather expect it, yet become indignant when it is done to another. In the morning they gave
me soap and clean towels that I might not have to use the common
soap or dirty jail towels.

The jailers are on terms of disgusting familiarity with these
women—probably because the latter cannot help themselves, or don't
care. Imprisonment doesn't seem to have any horrors for them. Content to sleep and eat, they seem as happy inside of jail as out. They are
unconscious of their degradation and solicit no sympathy. And they
shouldn't be conscious for society is to blame not they. I was put in
with them at about eleven o'clock, yet the lights were burning bright
and they showed no signs of retiring. Three little iron beds were the
furnishings for sleeping facilities—so I threw my cloak over me and
tried to sleep. The younger girl remained up, though she turned the
light down that I might rest, several times as she went to and fro asking if she disturbed me. Finally the jailer came and opened the cell-
door and took her out. She remained a long time and I gathered from
the whispered conversation with the older woman the following—that
he had taken her down to see a man on the floor below—"a sweetheart" she called him to me afterwards. She went again and remained
a long time and whispering told the other woman on her return that
Bert (I judged to be the jailer) would have brought "Jack" up, but for
this woman indicating me. "They don't trust her," she said. Perhaps I
am carrying out their suspicion in writing this—but the whole performance bore the earmarks to me of a *putrid state of morals inside the
county jail of Spokane.*

Taking a woman prisoner out of her cell at the dead hours of night
several times to visit a sweetheart looks to me as if she was *practicing
her profession inside of jail* as well as out. And what particular interest
did this man Bert, so intimately designated by his first name, have in

the matter? It would bear investigation. Readers may well imagine the horrible night of restlessness I put in. Early in the morning a man by the name of Bigelow, a jailer I presume, came into the cell with "breakfast," instead of leaving it in the anteroom of the cell where we were all still in bed. He laid his cold hand on my cheek and I awoke with a start—my anger blazed up and I said "Take your hand off me—I didn't come here to be insulted." He murmured some inarticulate excuse "of course not" or something to that effect and got out.

It certainly is a shame and disgrace to this city that a woman can be arrested because of union difficulties, bonds placed so high that immediate release is impossible, thrown into a county jail where sights and sounds horrible, immoral and absolutely different from her ordinary *decent* mode of life can be forced upon her, her privacy invaded while trying to steal some sleep by a brute of a man in a jail that hasn't attained the ordinary of civilization that requires a matron for the care of women prisoners. This all in for law and order! "Oh, Liberty, *what crimes* are committed in thy name."

SOURCE: *Workingman's Paper of Seattle,* formerly the *Socialist,* Dec. 11, 1909, Flynn Papers, Tamiment. The piece is dated 1910 and handwritten.

Women in Industry Should Organize (1911)

GURLEY *wrote this newspaper article one year after her son Fred was born. When she wrote that women were in industry to stay, she was talking not only to the IWW reader, but to her husband Jack Jones, whom she had just left because he wanted her to stop working, stay home, and become a full-time mother. In this piece Gurley commented on the conservative qualities of mothers, but unlike most socialists and trade unionists, she did not blame women for wanting to protect their families. Instead she understood women's fears; she blamed men for failing to educate women about politics, and she encouraged women to organize on their own behalf.*

Gurley differentiated her position from other political activists of the pe-
riod—suffragists, social workers, Women's Trade Union Leaguers, and So-
cialist party women—who participated in the political process. Her views were
closer to the anarchist Emma Goldman and syndicalist Mother Jones, who be-
lieved that politics corrupted was meaningless and wasted energy. Along with
these revolutionaries, Gurley emphasized economic equality and called for di-
rect action and industrial organization as the path to female freedom.

F ROM the viewpoint of a revolutionary socialist there is certainly
much to criticize in the present labor organizations. They have their
shortcomings of so pronounced a character that many thoughtful but
pessimistic workers despair of practical benefit from assisting or considering them further. Yet unionism remains a vital and burning question to the toilers, both men and women.

. . . A labor trust of all workers, in all industries, regardless of skill,
nationality or sex; to obliterate all craft lines; to cast aside all binding
and traitorous contracts; to throw barriers down for the admission of
all workers; such a union inspires the workers through its unity of the
practical every day needs with the ultimate revolutionary ideal of
emancipation. Through it we are able to live our ideals, to carry our
revolutionary principles into the shops, every day of the year: not to
the ballot box one day alone.

Now as to women's relationships to the old and new unionisms. In
the final analysis, women's sufferings and inequalities, at least in the
working class, which is our only concern, are the results of either wage
slavery directly or personal dependence upon a wage worker.

. . . Women to the number of seven million have been driven forth
from the home, by dire necessity, into the industrial arena, to be even
more fiercely exploited than their brother workers; they are constantly
seeking relief and release from the labor market on the marriage mart,
which marks woman the wage worker as a transitory being; and the
social or co-operative spirit engendered in the factory is usually neu-
tralized by the struggle for husbands [living] outside. Multitudes of
wives and mothers are virtually sex slaves through their direct and debasing dependence upon individual men for their existence, and
motherhood is all too often unwelcome and enforced, while the
struggle for existence even in the homes where love and affectionate
understanding cast their illuminating rays is usually so fierce that life
degenerates to a mere animal existence, a struggle for creature comforts—no more and it is impossible for love to transcend the physical.
The mental horizon of the average housekeeper is exceedingly limited because of the primitive form of labor in the household, the cooking, cleaning, sewing, scrubbing, etc., for an individual family. How

can one have depth or mental scope when one's life is spent exclusively within the four walls of one's individual composite home, and workshop, performing personal service continually for the same small group, laboring alone and on the primitive plan, doing work that could be better done by socialization and machinery, were not women cheaper than machines today?

We are driven to the conclusion, after the admission of all these facts, that much more than the abstract right of the ballot is needed to free women; nothing short of a social revolution can shelter her cramping and stultifying spheres of today. Yet, I have a firm and abiding conviction that much can be done to alleviate the lot of the working class women today. I have never been one of those possessed of the audacity and hard-hearted courage to face a crowd of hungry strikers and console them with the hope that the next November they could vote the Socialist ticket and thereby strike a blow at freedom. Thoreau has said, "Even voting for the right, is doing nothing for it. It is only expressing to men feebly your desire that it should prevail." Likewise, I feel the futility, and know many other Socialist women must, through our appreciation of these sad conditions and our deep sympathy for our sister women of extending to them nothing more than the hope of an ultimate social revolution. I am impatient for it. I realize the beauty of our hopes, the truth of its effectiveness, the inevitability of its realization, but I want to see that hope finds a point of contact with the daily lives of the working women, and I believe it can through the union movement.

The only appeal that craft unions make to the wives of their membership is on the matter of the label.[1] But the small number of women shoppers who trouble to inquire about the label or the union affiliations of the clerks testify to the ineffectiveness of this appeal. Men unionists are not themselves stirred to great enthusiasm over the label on shoes, hats, overalls, cigars, etc. The reason is not far to seek—namely, that men steeped of craft interests and craft selfishness cannot be suddenly lifted to the plane of class interests and solidarity. How much less can we expect the women in the homes, many of whom know nothing of the significance of the label, to demand it on the countless purchases they make. No special efforts have ever been made seriously to interest the wives in what the men consider "man's affairs." Many a wife hasn't the remotest idea of what the union that John goes [to] every Friday night consists of, or at least her knowledge

---

[1] A consumer movement that asked shoppers to buy only garments with union labels was a large movement among the middle class. Nonunion garments were often made in individual tenements and contained typhoid and tuberculosis germs, so buying union meant the products were free of disease as well.

is grumbling expressed about John having to pay 50 cents a week to "that union." Stubborn insistence on the two hundred odd labels that mark union-made goods is difficult, sometimes as sacrificed from the point of view of personal comfort as an actual strike. Usually it means boycotting all the tradespeople for miles around, and it stands to reason that women who are not vitally and intelligently interested are not going to trudge miles searching for the union label.

But if one is willing to make a sacrifice for the sake of the union movement, one's ardor is dampened by a realization that demanding the union label usually means simply increasing the demand for some manufacturer's product to the exclusion of another. All too often the union label does not represent improved conditions, as witness the wage scale and price lists in the Wickert and Gardiner shoe factory in Brooklyn before the strike, lower than in the non-union shops which struck. And even where higher wages are paid for the production of union-made products, they are simply to one craft, not to all who handle the goods in the course of production, and the union dues of this craft are utilized to advertise the goods of the company. In short, the union label is open to suspicion and is a very weak weapon at best. Certainly not clean enough to appeal to women with as yet.

But more important than the label is the relation of the women to strikes. Many of the strikes of the Western Federation of Miners have been famous for the exceptional courage and fortune displayed by their women folk. Strikes of foreigners in the mining and steel districts of Pennsylvania have been the scenes of wonderful bravery among the women. Yet all strikes are not thus fortunately aided. Many a smooth-tongued agent of the employers has discovered on approaching the wives of strikers that he can induce them to influence their husbands. Many a striker has been taunted by his wife, who has been an eager listener to the emissary, that he is lazy, doesn't care about his family and that "Mr. Smith always treated you all right, will take you back to work," and so forth, ad infinitum. The meeting of the union may be enthusiastic, the speakers eloquent, convincing, and capable of stirring all that is stanch and courageous in man, but if when he trudges home he finds a desolate, poverty-stricken household, sees hardships visited on his family, and worst of all, finds that his wife is alienated through her lack of understanding—there comes a terrible reaction. No influence is more piercing, more subtle through the voices of his dear ones; the speakers, the union, the enthusiasm that was as wine in his blood fades before it. Yet the woman cannot be blamed, even if she helps to drive the husband to cowardice and treason to his fellows. All the instincts of maternity are aroused to protect her little ones, and she is in the grasp of a foe that "calls for

something more than brawn or muscle to o'ercome"—namely—ignorance. Woman's influence is one of the strongest in the world, though
we may scorn the idea of influence. But it must be made an educated
influence and used to help on the battle that is for her and hers, if she
but realized it. Every gain made by a union man means more of the
necessities and some of the luxuries, for the family depending on
him. There is the best of reasons from the view of enlightened selfishness why women should endorse and support the unions in their
strikes.

Little need be said of the seven million wage-earning women. That
unionism is their one great weapon hardly admits of an argument.
Even more than their brother toilers do these underpaid and overworked women need co-operative effort on their own behalf. Yet
many of their experiences with the old unions have been neither
pleasant nor encouraging. Strike after strike of cloak makers, shirt
waist makers, dressmakers, etc. on the East Side of New York has been
exploited by the rich faddists for woman's suffrage, etc., until the
points at issue were lost sight of in the blare of automobile horns at-
tendant on their coming and going. A band of earnest, struggling
workers made the tail of a suffrage kite in the hands of women of the
very class driving the girls to lives of misery or shame, women who
could have financed the strike to a truly successful conclusion were
they seriously disposed, is indeed a deplorable sight. But the final
settlement of the many widely advertised strikers left much to be de-
sired. A spontaneous revolt, a light with glowing enthusiasm and ardor that kept thousands of underfed and thinly clad girls on the
picket line, should be productive of more than "a contract." Contracts
binding dressmakers in one union, cloak makers in another, shirt
waist makers in another, and so on through the list of clothing workers—contracts arranging separate wage scales, hours, dates of expira-
tion, etc., mean no more spontaneous rebellions on the East Side of
New York. Now union leaders arbitrate so that you may go back to
your old job "without discrimination," the new concept of "victory,"
and if you dare to strike under the contract you will be fired from
both shop and union for violation of it. . . .

Women are in industry to stay. They cannot be driven back to the
home. Their work left the home and they followed. They are part of
the army of labor and must be organized and disciplined as such . . .
organized they are tenacious and true fighters. And the union factory
girl of today is the helpful and encouraging wife of the union man of
tomorrow. Mutual aid replaces suspicion, and distrust in the home
and the benefit of mutual effort between women and men workers
and husbands and wives should not be underestimated.

Then through intelligent criticisms and systematic efforts to re-mold the old—a new fighting union will come forth eventually to flower into the co-operative commonwealth.

Men and women workers unite.

SOURCE: *Industrial Worker*, June 1, 1911, microfilm, Tamiment. The *Industrial Worker* was a weekly newspaper published by the General Executive Board of the IWW, from Spokane, Wash. It was advertised as a "red hot fearless newspaper, representing the spirit of the west."

One Boss Less: The Minersville Strike (1911)

IN *the early 1900s some garment manufacturers moved to Schuykill County, Pennsylvania, where Minersville is located, from New England and New York to take advantage of a nonunion labor force of the wives and daughters of the anthracite miners and steelworkers. These male workers were often unemployed due to injury, illness, or strikes. To fuel the family economy, younger women worked in the factories while older ones took in boarders, did piecework, and tended their gardens.*

But if the garment manufacturers moved to escape the union, they were quickly surprised to find the union following them. The Amalgamated Clothing Workers Union found a fertile field to organize. The female garment workers were immigrants—Polish, Lithuanian, Croatian, Dutch, Scotch, and Irish—from families with strong union traditions. In childhood their lullabies were the sounds of their daddies "drumming the scabs home" in the great anthracite strike of 1902, and they cut their teeth on a union button. Long and often violent organizing drives went on until the 1920s and 1930s, when the Amalgamated Clothing Workers finally organized the region.[1] *However, by the 1940s and 1950s these shirt factories moved to the South to exploit another nonunion, racially divided, labor force.*

As a result of the strike Gurley wrote about in "One Boss Less," the Coombs

[1] Mary Heaton Vorse, *A Footnote to Folly* (New York: Farrar and Rinehart, 1935), 313–325.

Garment Company factory closed, after operating for twelve years, and some two hundred girls were forced to seek work elsewhere.

THE particular employer engaged in this conflict is typical. Over twelve years ago he came to Minersville and opened a factory. Since that time a chain of factories have been installed throughout the anthracite regions and the farming belt that lies South of Pottsville, absorbing all the unused labor of women and girls, who previously engaged in domestic tasks at home, until, through marriage, they established homes of their own.

Dependent for a living upon brothers, fathers and husbands, the factory gate seemed the door of opportunity to them. Life had been a stepping from their father's threshold to their husband's, a sheltered, healthy, but often monotonous and uneventful existence. Many of the younger generation were educated in the public schools and felt the lure of the big cities; others were not satisfied with the domestic life, and so the factory spelled a varied experience, a wider life and independence. They welcomed it eagerly and were engulfed in its hungry maw.

When Coombs came to Minersville he was poor and unknown. He was financed by a man named Phillips, a Jewish occulist and rabbi, who likewise commenced his career poor. But running expenses of shirt and underwear factories are less in Pennsylvania towns than in New York or Philadelphia, and girls are cheaper. In the large cities girls are supposed to secure at least a living wage, as most of them are dependent solely upon their earnings. Often they do not, and lives of shame and horror are the result. But the majority attempt to secure it, and a pretence is made by the employers to pay it. Not so here. Wages are simply fit for *spending money* and do not nearly equal living expenses. The girls still live at home. They have lost the illusion of being self-supporting, and make no pretence of being. They are as dependent on their families as they ever were, and the outrageous condition prevails of miners and farmers raising and caring for daughters to turn them over to the factory owners as instruments of production, practically free of charge.

They lend their children to Coombs and Phillips, and receive them back physical wrecks, hollow-eyed, flat-chested, nervous from overwork. Young girls are taken from schools at a tender age and crushed in the industrial prisons that disfigure the hills and valleys. The vitality of future generations is sapped through the grinding toil these future mothers must endure. From every point of view—financially, physically and morally—these factories have been a blight and a curse to every region they invade.

At first, Coombs employed the girl operators at twelve cents per dozen pieces, but they made too much at this rate, and were reduced to ten cents, and finally to eight. Working day and night on piece work, one girl was able to earn twenty-four dollars in two weeks at the ten-cent rate, and Mr. Coombs quotes this astounding amount as an instance of the good wages the girls earned, but he conveniently forgot the little girls of fifteen and sixteen years, who earned as low as $1.50 and $2.00 per week, and all the others graded between this and $9.00 earned by the forewoman. Ignorant of unionism and completely unorganized, the girl operators courageously refused to work for the eight cents, and deserted the factory. They formulated their demands for the ten-cent scale, and included a recognition of their personal rights, which had been ruthlessly trampled upon. More is involved in this strike than a question of wages.

I have been informed by one of the forewomen that Coombs was accustomed to use the vilest of profanity to drive the girls to greater efforts, and would grab their scarfs, even tearing them to shreds. In one case he shook a girl so severely that she went into hysterics.

For twelve weeks, these operators have been out. Soon they realized that as long as the cutters, binders, pressers and teamsters remained at work, Coombs could the more easily replace them, and as a result of a great open-air mass meeting, addressed by Con F. Foley, of Pottsville, and myself, in which the entire population enthusiastically participated, a general tie-up was effected. The factory is closed from cellar to roof.

Coombs became desparate. He threatened to move his factory to Brooklyn, where he claims a site has already been purchased, but the girls realize that he is bound to this region by economic ties which cannot be easily severed. He rents houses and owns a splendid residence in Minersville, and controls factories for Phillips in Tremont, Valley View, Mahoney City, Trackville and other places. Here he is a pillar of society, hobnobs with judges, and has his own automobile. Whereas, his importance would sink into insignificance in a great industrial center.

We are making efforts not only to tie up all of his other plants, but every factory and mill in this region, where wages are inadequate and women are shamelessly exploited. Our attempts in Tremont illustrate our difficulties and Mr. Coombs' methods. While we were addressing the girls from one factory, Mr. Coombs rushed past in his machine and into his factory, where he detained the girls for about five minutes. His intimation that if they listened to the agitators they need not report to work further had effect, for when he dismissed them, they marched convict-like, arm in arm, past the meeting, and could not be induced to listen.

These girls had their wages raised to nine cents to head off a strike. Thus, they are profiting by the struggle of the girls in Minersville, while virtually scabbing on them. Far from being discouraged, however, we feel that Coombs has shown his fear, and we intend to arouse these girls to a realization of the situation.

This strike, the first of its kind in the anthracite region, has been invaluable, as it has served to set ablaze the smouldering rebellion of other women workers. It was followed by a strike in the silk mill of Pottsville.

We are hopeful that it is the beginning of a real union movement among the women. Craft unionism had ignorantly segregated the workers until the women, neglected and unorganized, were left to the mercy of the capitalist wolves. Miners worry only for miners, brewery workers for themselves, and so on through the list. . . .

Committees of business men played their usual role of urging the girls to compromise for nine cents, but the girls, on the advice of the local comrades, refused the offer. As for the craft unionists, the girls could have been sold out and defeated, and no aid or advice extended to them, had not the Socialists taken up their cause. Coombs approached Foley "to fix up things," but was confronted by a committee of his own girls, with whom he refused to deal.

. . . We have talked industrial unionism to the girls throughout the progress of the strike, and have advanced the IWW as the union in which they belong. The girls are embracing the ideas of Socialism and the strike cannot be a failure. Successful, they will organize for better things. Defeated, the spirit that can never die will have been infused into their beings.[2]

SOURCE: *International Socialist Review,* July 1911, which was the monthly theoretical journal of the Socialist Party of America.

[2]The strikers were visited by Eugene Debs as well as by Big Bill Haywood.

Men and Women (1915)

THIS lecture reveals Flynn's syndicalist ideas. Like most Wobblies she viewed labor as the measure of people's power and creativity. Most IWW members were foreigners, migrant workers, and women and therefore ineligible to vote; political franchise was irrelevant to them. Economic democracy, that is, decent wages and working conditions, and the right to organize were the vital demands. Two books provide the underpinnings for this talk: the Marxist Frederick Engels's Origin of the Family, *and the Fabian or evolutionary socialist Charlotte Perkins Gilman's* The Home *and* Women and Economics.

THERE are about 5 million women in the industrial and professional fields, side by side with the men, and although there are more and more being forced into earning their own living every day, nevertheless the great majority are still what we call "home women," mothers and wives, whose livings are being made for them on the industrial arena. Until a comparatively short while ago however all the women were home-workers, and so when the pressure of capitalism came, they were driven out as competitors against the men, exactly as today when the Japanese are entering San Francisco they do so as competitors against the natives and the results were and are the same. The women sold their labor power cheaper, replaced the men, drove them out, or lowered their wages and incurred their enmity. In the case of the Japanese it became what they call "race hatred," based on an economic reason; in the case of women it becomes a "sex-war" based on an economic reason, and the claim of many men that women forfeit their power over men etc. etc. in lowering themselves to laboring, is but an expression of this economic contest between them. But although forced into the struggle for existence by capitalism's ruthless hand, like a starving mouse will rush into the trap for a tiny bite of cheese and then starve there trying to get out, so woman strive to get out of the struggle back into the home life, so that "the advent of women into the industrial field," loudly heralded as "the emancipation of women," is but a transient thing, a step from her father's home to her husband's home and that is about all to the average woman-worker today. The Indian squaw left her father's wigwam, and entered her husband's; the modern woman does hardly any different, except for this short breath of the industrial atmosphere.

Now while they are out in the industrial world, what are their conditions? The same as man's only worse, infinitely worse in every occupation where she has usurped his place. Do we not all know girls in department stores who work for as low a wage as $3 per week; in offices for $7 and $8 per week; girls in needlework factories and cigar factories and clothing "sweatshops" for anywhere from $2 per week to $6 and $7; woman doing housework, and scrubbing work and nursing in the interest of health and cleanliness, waitresses and various other kinds of workers for $7, $8, or $9 per week. I remember once a girls' meeting in Newark N.J.—girls all under 18 years coming together for the purpose of organizing a union—and when I mentioned a salary of $15 a week at least, as what I thought they might well need, they looked at each other in amazement and then laughed, explaining to me they never got over $8 a week and never hoped to, even with a union.

I heard a young man remark on last Friday "that young women were over-anxious to marry and were only too glad to take the first man who offered himself." Any wonder, when the lash of capitalism bears so harsh? The young man need give no thanks to his great powers of attractiveness etc. He need only give the credit to economic and social conditions. Women are not only scratching each other's eyes out over any man, or will they, though they may over the "living" he can give them. So that a vast number of your every-day marriages hark back to the economic problems, the woman's struggling for existence and natural desire to throw the burden on other shoulders wherever possible, become a parasite (in an economic sense) in a parasitic age.

Women have been dependent for many ages, but not always. Frederick Engels in his *Origin of the Family* tells of the primitive communism of tribal society and how women did their share of the work and were equals of men.

. . . Woman stands in much the same position to man, as man does to his employer. He runs the industrial system and in return gets a bare living for himself and his family; she runs his home and in return gets her bare living. She is in a proletarian-like position, he in a bourgeois-like position, and must submit to man's government in all its extremes, as the proletarian must submit to bourgeois government to the last limit.

Woman's labor in the home has not kept step with modern progress, for the reason I believe, that it has not been organized and secondarily because it is in about its cheapest condition today, which brings me to another point in the comparison of the woman and the worker, the cost of her labor-power and its relation to its value. Value is computed in economic [terms], I suppose I need hardly say, by the amount of labor power necessary to produce it. In the case of a human being and his labor power, the value is the food, clothing and shelter necessary to keep him alive. This is exactly what a woman gets in return for her household labor, food, clothing and shelter to keep her alive, so that while the cost of the regular workingman's labor in the market still has not reached by "the iron-law of wages" the low water mark of value, his wife's seems to have done so. Machine labor, organized and perfected in the home, is costlier than plain woman's labor, since the woman is necessary in any case and so woman's simple, primitive household methods have lived and kept her digging the best part of her life in a dirty kitchen; separated from the life current of the civilization, its politics, its culture, its interests, clinging to the conservatism of by-gone days, bringing up her children along these lines, a retainer and a retarder; sometimes forced out by lack of support to the industrial field but slipping back into parasitism as soon as possible. Women shared, divided, and subdivided their movements into many sections and parts, each with some special object, for political advantage, social, religious, or sexual rights, etc., but according to the Socialist conception, harsh as it may seem, women can have no rights until they have economic freedom, for all their other rights depend on this one.

. . . The only sex problem I know of is how are women to control themselves, how be free, so that love alone shall be the commandment to act, and I can see but one way thru controlling their one problem of how to live, be fed and clothed—their own economic lives.

When you consider these reasons for marriage, these hypocrises, deceits, woman's dependency on a man, especially after she has borne him children, then we are at no loss to understand why marriage in the majority of cases loses all semblance of love and becomes legalized prostitution, why most marriages are unhappy, at no loss whatsoever for no institution could remain pure amid such vile surroundings.

Sexual enslavement then follows economic enslavement, and is but a gentle way of saying prostitution, whether it be for one night or one whole life. The woman who bears her children faithfully every year or so, who "submits herself to her husband" in a truly Christian way, whose life is that of a breeder of children, may be President Roosevelt's ideal, to guard against race-suicide. To me she is a miserable sex slave and my ideal is far different. Is your ideal that sort of woman? The men and women with whom love and passion are dead, who keep up appearances, live as man and wife, raise children, may be Cardinal Gibbons's ideal.

. . . The proposition of Mary Wollstonecraft, that "woman should have equal rights in government with men," a dunce could not deny, but it is with what is, not what ought to be that we must deal, and there is little or no chance of women getting this right and further little or no chance of getting any benefits out of it, if she did get it.

There would be but one reason for giving women the suffrage—to exploit their conservatism and use it against the overwhelming forces of radicalism, otherwise her vote would be useless to "the powers that be" and would not be granted. The cry of women suffragists, "taxation without representation," may be heeded, votes given to women with property and their class interests would line them up with capitalism, but this suffragist slogan has no appeal to class conscious working women, who have no interest in taxes on property until they have the property. Further if she received the vote, it would mean only another form of *political enslavement*, for her economic necessity would make her have no opinion but some man's opinion, no party but his party, no mind but his mind, to guide her to the ultimatum, no vote but his kind of vote. Understanding that "the political power is but the power of one class to keep another in subjection," that it is an expression of class rule and dies with class rule, therefore we Socialists can see only a waste of time in specializing on the woman suffrage movement, when political emancipation is impossible as long as there is *economic slavery*.

. . . We know without going into further detail that we are absolutely going into Socialism, where the means of production will be concentrated in the hands of the workers' industrial organization, where each man and each woman who works will get the value of the product of labor, and classes and parasitism must come to an end, and I can see nothing for women but an opportunity to earn their own living, too, and organizing and centralizing household work must be one of the first results. But for women to take their place in the social labor means so much—so much we can scarcely conceive of the vast results that will come in natural order. It means a revolution in woman's position such as the world has never known, a reaction against all the horror of the ages, and it is possible for us to measure but few of these with our puny, childish standards of today. We can however say this, that since economic dependence is the cause of social and sexual enslavement, then economic independence means a free woman socially and sexually, a woman who thinks as she pleases, does as she pleases, works as she pleases, speaks as she pleases, and belongs to herself alone.

SOURCE: Flynn Papers, Tamiment. The manuscript is handwritten and dated 1915. Many of Flynn's lectures at this time were written in longhand. In fact, she didn't type. She never read her lectures, and people describe Flynn as speaking without notes.

The IWW Call to Women (1915)

GURLEY was the IWW expert on women; her statements became official policy. The IWW was far more advanced than any other union in its open attitude toward organizing both women workers and worker's wives. The union was successful in organizing many female textile workers and some telephone operators, secretaries, teachers, housewives, and prostitutes.

The Wobblies did not have many female organizers, nor did they seem to make special efforts to recruit them. However, two women, Mother Jones and Lucy Parsons, were at the founding convention in 1905 which was more than most unions could boast.

This newspaper article articulates Flynn's belief, a belief that separated her from the suffragists, that working-class women should organize as workers and that solidarity among all women was neither desirable nor possible. Flynn, however, like Charlotte Perkins Gilman and other suffragists of her day, put great hope in the ability of technology to free women from housework. Recent feminist books on housework prove that technology increases, rather than decreases, the hours of women's labor in the home.[1]

I N the tremendous process of merging all groups of labor into a unified whole; of infusing their humblest daily struggle with the urge of a great ideal—industrial freedom—women are as vitally concerned as men. But the IWW, the instrument through which "the world for the workers" is taking concrete form, makes no special appeal to women as such. To us society moves in grooves of class, not sex. Sex

---

[1]Ruth Cowan, *More Work for Mother: The Ironies of Household Technology, from the Open Hearth to the Microwave* (New York: Basic Books, 1983); Susan Strasser, *Never Done: A History of American Housework* (New York: Pantheon, 1982).

distinctions affect us insignificantly and would less, but for economic differences. It is to those women who are wage earners, or wives of workers, that the IWW appeals. We see no basis in fact for feminist mutual interest, no evidence of natural "sex conflict," nor any possibility—nor present desirability—of solidarity among women alone. The success of our program will benefit workers, regardless of sex, and injure all who, without effort, draw profits for a livelihood.

I have seen prosperous, polite, daintily-gowned ladies become indignant over police brutality in the Spokane free speech fight of 1901, and lose all interest—even refuse to put up bail for pregnant women—when they realized that the IWW intended to organize the lumber, mining, and farming industries, whence the golden stream flowed to pay for their comfort and leisure.[2]

Yet more horrible a glimpse into the chasm that divides woman and woman is afforded by the bloodthirsty approval of the Ludlow massacre by the "good women" of Trinidad, Colorado.[3] . . . Mrs. Northcutt, wife of the lawyer, said: "There has been a lot of maudlin sentiment about those women and children. There were only two women and they make such a fuss!" Mrs. Rose, wife of the superintendent of the coal railroad, said: "The miners probably killed the women and children themselves, because they were a drain on the union!" and, "They ought to have shot Tikas to start with!" This of the Greek leader who had over thirty bullets in his body and his head laid open with the butt of a gun. The solution of labor troubles agreed upon by a dozen representative women was, "Shoot them down."

The "queen of the parlor" has no interest in common with the "maid in the kitchen"; the wife of the department store owner shows no sisterly concern for the seventeen-year-old girl who finds prostitution the only door to a $5 a week clerk. The sisterhood of women, like the brotherhood of man, is a hollow sham to labor. Behind all its smug hypocrisy and sickly sentimentality loom the sinister outlines of the class war.

---

[2] See "Story of My Arrest and Imprisonment" in this section. Many of these prosperous ladies' husbands owned lumber, mining, and farm industries.

[3] The Ludlow massacre occurred during the Colorado miners strike against the Rockefeller-dominated Colorado Fuel and Iron Company. The miners were forcibly evicted from their company-owned houses and lived in tents surrounded by the National Guard. The militiamen occasionally shot into the colony, particularly at night. The women were afraid their children would be shot, so they dug a cave inside the biggest tent and thirteen children and a pregnant women were hidden there. On Easter 1914 the company employed gunmen and members of the National Guard to drench the miners' tents with oil and light them. It was nighttime, and the miners and their families fled from the burning tents, where they were gunned down. Many miners and their wives were wounded, but the thirteen children and the pregnant woman were killed, some shot and some suffocated.

Fifty years ago earnest advocates of woman's rights were demanding "economic independence." Today Olive Schreiner, in her book, "Woman and Labor," expresses woman's need "for our share of honored and socially useful human toil—labor and the training that fits us for labor."[4] This may be applicable to an insignificant group of white-handed idlers, whose life consists of pleasure-seeking to counteract ennui; but it is meaningless to eight million women wage earners and the innumerable housekeepers. Women have been engaged in useful human toil since the dawn of time. True enough, much that was once "woman's work"—spinning, weaving, churning, etc.—has been absorbed by the factory system. The old division—men doing the outdoor and women the indoor tasks—ended with the advent of power-operated machinery. But woman was not left idle-handed. Rather it was now possible and inevitable that she should follow her work and take her place with man, at the factory gate; 21 per cent of the total employees in the U.S. are women, 45 per cent of the total in England.

The private ownership of industry and the propertyless status of labor become a common problem. But entering the industrial arena later than her brother, she is under the disadvantage in common with the immigrant, of being compelled to work cheaper to secure the job. Hunger, want, scarcity of work, drives all workers to accept an ever lower standard, and the women the lowest.

. . . Ancient illusions die hard, and one of the most hoary is "the sanctity of the home." But a visit to Lawrence, Mass., would bring rapid disillusionment. The golden dream of youth, that marriage brings release from irksome toil, is rudely shattered by the capitalist system. Whole families toil for a living wage. The heaviest burden is on the tired frame of the woman. Child-bearing and housework remain. Pregnant women stand at the looms until the labor pains commence. A few weeks after, the puny babe is left at a day nursery with amateur "nurses"—with the result that 300 babies out of every thousand born die in the first month. The gutter is the baby's playground, and amid the deafening clatter of the looms the mother's heart is torn with anxiety about her children. Miscarriage from overstrain is common, and unscrupulous doctors secure exorbitant sums to perform abortions, that the women may keep at work. But to tell these women toilers how to control birth is a state prison offense in the United States; and so they die, 25,000 yearly from operations. The burden of family, added to the day's mill work, means that while father smokes his pipe and takes his ease, mother has the innumerable household tasks still to do.

[4]Olive Schreiner, 1855–1920, was a South African novelist, social theorist, and socialist-feminist.

As soon as her children's tiny hands can handle machinery, and their tender forms pass for legal age, they too, are fed to the insatiable looms. Tragic indeed is the lot of the woman toiler! Her youth, her love, her home, her babies are "ground into dollars for parasites' pleasure."

Hardly more attractive is the lot of the young girl toiler, who sells beautiful articles she is denied, who weaves delicate fabrics she never wears, who makes fine garments and shivers home in winter's snows with barely enough to cover her nakedness. Full of life and spirit, craving enjoyment, good clothes and youthful pleasures—is it any wonder that when resistance is weakened by hunger, many in despair sell their sex to secure what honest effort denies them; 350,000 prostitutes in the U.S.; 20,000 added every year, five per cent of the total working group (although all do not come from that source)—is a staggering condemnation of our present society.

"Starvation or prostitution?"—how many girls last winter, with three million unemployed in the land, were compelled to face that question?

The IWW relies upon the organized power of labor to sweep away such nauseous conditions. White slaves, investigation, rescue houses, etc., help a hundred, but the juggernaut of industry crushes a thousand. The department store owner is the largest procurer today, and the fresh, youthful faces of our daughters and sisters should spur us on to break his power. POVERTY, the root of all crime and vice, must be destroyed and labor be free to enjoy the plentitude it creates. Carefree childhood, flowering youth, happy homes, are denied to countless girls who work in the textile towns of the East, and the boys driven into the migratory life of the West, and will be until industry is owned by labor and adjusted to the happiness of the toiler.

The IWW appeals to women to organize side by side with their men folks, in the union that shall increasingly determine its own rules of work and wages—until its solidarity and power shall the world command. It points out to the young girl that marriage is no escape from the labor problem, and to the mother, that the interest of herself and her children are woven in with the interests of the class, and to both that this industrial ENFRANCHISEMENT is possible for all, women and children, citizens and immigrants, every nation and color.

Where a secluded home environment has produced a psychological attitude of "me and mine"—how is the IWW to overcome conservatism and selfishness? By driving women into an active participation in union affairs, especially strikes, where the mass meetings, mass picketing, women's meetings, and children's gatherings are a tremendous emotional stimulant. The old unions never have considered the women as part of the strike. They were expected to stay home and worry about the empty larder, the hungry kiddies, and the growling landlord, easy prey to the agents of the company. But the strike was "a man's business." The men had the joy of the fight, the women not even an intelligent explanation of it.

Never does a bricklayers' or street carmens' union have a woman's meeting. So the women worry and wait, and weaken the spirit of the men by tears and complaining.

Women can be the most militant or most conservative element in a strike, in proportion to their comprehension of its purpose. The IWW has been accused of putting the women in the front. The truth is, the IWW does not keep them in the back, and they go to the front. Mothers nursing their babes stood in the snow at the Lawrence common meetings. Young girls, Josephine Liss, Hannah Silverman, were flaming spirits in Lawrence and Paterson. Hundreds went to jail, with a religious devotion to the cause.

. . . A familiar query is, "What effect would the democratization of industry have on the family?" The IWW is at war with the ruthless invasion of family life by capitalism, with the unnatural and shameful condition of a half million able-bodied unemployed men in New York City alone, last winter, yet there are 27,000 children under 16 years of age in cotton mills in the South. We are determined that industry shall be so organized that all adults, men and women, may work and receive in return a sufficiency to make child labor a relic of barbarism. This does not imply that mothers must work, or that women must stay at home, if they prefer otherwise. Either extreme is equally absurd. House work will probably be reduced to a minimum through the application of machinery, now more costly than the labor of women— but the care of children will remain an absorbing interest with the vast majority of women. The free choice of work is the IWW ideal—which does not mean to put women forcibly back into the home, but certainly does mean to end capitalism's forcibly taking her out of the home.

Exact details of the readjustment of human relations after an economic revolution cannot be mapped out. The historical destiny of our times is to establish industrial freedom. What mighty superstructure our progeny will rear upon our work, we can only vaguely prophesy.

SOURCE: *Solidarity*, July 31, 1915. This newspaper was an IWW weekly published in New Castle, Pa. It is on microfilm at the University of Wisconsin.

The Truth about the Paterson Strike (1914)

PATERSON *was a grimy industrial city in New Jersey; one-third of the popula-*
tion, 73,000, worked ten hours a day in the mills. The factories were cold in
winter and suffocating in summer. Humidifiers were used to make the silk damp,
and the workers choked on the steam and dye fumes. Early deaths from tuber-
culosis and other respiratory diseases were frequent. Beginning in 1913 Pater-
son experienced an economic depression that did not end until World War I.

    The Paterson strikers demanded an eight-hour day and an end to the four-
loom system, the docking system for female apprentices, kickbacks in wages to
the foreman, and different wage scales for the same work. The strike was a
failure in that the demands were not met. The IWW had expected a glorious
victory, as in Lawrence, and poured enormous organizational resources into
Paterson. When the contrary happened they were badly bruised.

    Gurley was the central figure in this strike and was tormented by responsibil-
ity for the strike failure. She developed chronic bronchitis from speaking so
much and began to slowly gain weight. IWW leader Big Bill Haywood shuttled
back and forth between Paterson and Akron, Ohio, where he was leading a
strike of five thousand rubber workers. He developed an ulcerated stomach and
lost eighty pounds during the strike. Haywood never fully recovered his health.
Gurley was there throughout and was jailed for inciting to riot and preaching
anarchy.

    Fifty-six percent of the silk workers were women and children, and they were
among the most devoted and enthusiastic strikers. They worked most of the un-
skilled jobs. Special meetings were scheduled for women and children. When
teachers spoke against the strike in school, the children picketed; at one chil-
dren's meeting they demanded less homework. The IWW male leadership
learned some lessons from these meetings. At one of the women's meetings,
Carlo Tresca remarked that with an eight-hour day, couples would have more
time to spend making more babies. The audience of tired workingwomen and
wives looked glum. Haywood, who was at this meeting, intervened, "No Carlo,

we want fewer babies well cared for, we believe in birth control." Then the women laughed and applauded.[1]

A special, much-touted feature of the strike was the pageant. Flynn, always leary of the bohemian set, was against the pageant from the beginning. However, when she was outvoted, she participated and lent her full support. New York City was a mere two-hour commute from Paterson, and New York radicals usually ventured out on Sunday to imbibe the working-class culture and militance. One New York radical, John Reed, a great, daring reporter fresh out of Harvard, came. He was arrested, thrown into a four-by-seven-foot cell with eight picketers, and was without food and water for twenty-four hours. New York City newspapers picked up the story and featured a Harvard boy jailed with a bunch of immigrants for four days. Reed became enthralled with the strike and wanted to help. He conceived of the idea of a pageant to save the strike financially and break the deadlock with the employers. So, with Haywood's blessings and the help of the Greenwich Village art world, Reed trained over a thousand textile workers to reenact the strike and sing labor songs for a performance at Madison Square Garden.

Reed managed to raise only enough money to rent Madison Square Garden for a day. IWW members and strikers were let in free, and only twelve hundred people paid. As a result the pageant failed financially, even though it was a theatrical and media success and everyone who saw it and participated in it was deeply moved. The IWW letters blazed in red lights outside the Garden. Inside each ethnic group sang their songs and joined in to harmonize in such classics as the "Marseillaise" and the "Internationale." Led by a twenty-six-piece band, strikers paraded up the aisles through the audience. Gurley on stage told the audience how their hungry children would be fed and cared for by families in New York City for the remainder of the strike. She told the audience how she hoped the children would get "the rose put back in their cheeks and class solidarity in their hearts."[2]

Only Gurley blamed the pageant for the decline in worker morale and the defeat of the strike. She believed the middle-class intellectuals were concerned only about the media; the pageant was a spectacle to promote attention rather than to promote working-class solidarity. (Many historians today adopt Flynn's interpretation, including Philip Foner, William Conlin, Robert Rosenstone, Granville Hicks, and Peter Carlson.) The speech "The Truth about the Paterson Strike," given to an audience of liberals, shows Flynn's analytical acumen and her ability to publicly dissent from IWW policy, qualities she would not demonstrate later in the Communist party.

[1] Elizabeth Gurley Flynn, *Rebel Girl: An Autobiography, My First Life, 1906–1926* (New York: International Publishers, 1973), 166.

[2] Steve Golin, "The Paterson Pageant," *Socialist Review* 13 (May–June 1983): 49. Steve Golin, while writing a book on the Paterson strike, shared his insights and material with me. Much of my interpretation of this strike comes from him.

The Paterson strike was a dramatic, complicated event with many historical ramifications. After the strike, and again with Flynn dissenting, the IWW became a more centralized and hierarchical organization under Haywood's primary leadership, but it was never able to regain the initiative in organizing factory workers. The lost battle became a lost war and proved fatal for the IWW in the East. Male historians devote more attention and space to Lawrence, perhaps because the strikers won and the Socialist party backed that strike. Is it possible Paterson is neglected in historical accounts because it was a strike lead by a female, and one who later joined the Communist party?

After the strike was lost Flynn continued going to Paterson to speak and to fight the remaining free speech battle. She believed it had been a serious error to leave Lawrence after the strike and wanted to learn from that experience. (After the Lawrence strike was won, the employers fired many IWW strikers and then moved the mill to the South.) Flynn attracted an impressive group of feminists, social workers, liberals, and wealthy women to support her work in Paterson. Lillian Wald, Fola La Follette, Walter Lippmann, Lincoln Steffens, Mrs. O. H. Belmont, and Mrs. J. Sargeant Cram assisted her in waging an eventually successful free speech battle—an example of her willingness to accept assistance, on her terms, from the professional and upper class.

Comrades and Friends:

The reason why I undertake to give this talk at this moment, one year after the Paterson strike was called, is that the flood of criticism about the strike is unabated, becoming more vicious all the time, drifting continually from the actual facts, and involving as a matter of course the policies and strike tactics of the IWW. To insure future success in the city of Paterson it is necessary for the past failure to be understood, and not to be clouded over by a mass of outside criticism. It is rather difficult for me to separate myself from my feelings about the Paterson strike, to speak dispassionately. I feel that many of our critics are people who stayed at home in bed while we were doing the hard work of the strike. Many of our critics are people who never went to Paterson, or who went on a holiday; who did not study the strike as a day-by-day process. Therefore it's rather hard for me to overcome my impatience with them and speak purely theoretically.

What is a labor victory? I maintain that it is a twofold thing. Workers must gain economic advantage, but they must also gain revolutionary spirit, in order to achieve a complete victory. For workers to gain a few cents more a day, a few minutes less a day, and go back to work with the same psychology, the same attitude toward society, is to have achieved a temporary gain and not a lasting victory. For workers to go back with a class-conscious spirit, with an organized and a determined attitude toward society, means that even if they have made no economic gain they have the possibility of gaining in the future. In other words, a labor victory must be economic and it must be revolutionizing. Otherwise it is not complete.

. . . So a labor victory must be twofold, but if it can only be one, it is better to gain in spirit than to gain economic advantage. The IWW attitude in conducting a strike, one might say, is pragmatic. We have certain general principles; their application differs as the people, the industry, the time and the place indicate. It is impossible to conduct a strike among English-speaking people in the same way that you conduct a strike among foreigners; it is impossible to conduct a strike in the steel industry in the same manner you conduct a strike among the textile workers, where women and children are involved in large numbers. So we have no ironclad rules. We realize that we are dealing with human beings and not with chemicals. And we realize that our fundamental principles of solidarity and class revolt must be applied in as flexible a manner as the science of pedagogy. The teacher may have as her ultimate ideal to make the child a proficient master of English, but he begins with the alphabet. So in an IWW strike many times we have to begin with the alphabet, where our own ideal would be the mastery of the whole.

The Paterson strike divides itself into two periods. From the 25th of February, when the strike started, to the 7th of June, the date of the pageant in New York City, marks the first period. The second period is from the pageant to the 29th of July, when every man and woman was back at work. But the preparation for the strike had its roots in the past, the development of a four-loom system in a union mill organized by the American Federation of Labor. This four-loom [system] irritated the workers and precipitated many small outbreaks. At any rate they sent to Mr. John Golden, the president of the United Textile Workers of America,[3] for relief, and his reply was substantially, "The four-loom system is in progress. You have no right to rebel against it." They sought some other channel of expressing their revolt, and a year before the historic strike the Lawrence strike occurred.[4] It stimulated their spirit and it focused their attention on the IWW.

. . . We had three elements to deal with in the Paterson strike: the broad silk weavers and the dyers, who were unorganized and who were, as you might say, almost virgin material, easily brought forth and easily stimulated to aggressive activity. But on the other hand we had the ribbon weavers, the English-speaking conservative people, who had behind them craft antecedents, individual craft unions that

[3] United Textile Workers of America was a skilled craft union, which was part of the AFL.

[4] The Lawrence strike occurred in 1912.

they had worked through for thirty years. These people responded only after three weeks, and then they formed the complicating element in the strike, continually pulling back on the mass through their influence as the English-speaking and their attitude as conservatives. The police action precipitated the strike of many workers. They came out because of the brutal persecution of the strike leaders and not because they themselves were so full of the strike feeling that they could not stay in any longer. This was the calling of the strike.

The administering of the strike was in the hands of a strike committee formed of two delegates from each shop. If the strike committee had been full-force there would have been 600 members. The majority of them were not IWW; were non-union strikers. The IWW arranged the meetings, conducted the agitation work. But the policies of the strike were determined by that strike committee of the strikers themselves. And so [with] this strike committee dictating all the policies of the strike, placing the speakers in a purely advisory capacity, there was a continual danger of a break between the conservative element who were in the strike committee and the mass who were being stimulated by the speakers. The socialist element in the strike committee largely represented the ribbon weavers, this conservative element making another complication in the strike. I want if possible to make that clear before leaving it, that the preparation and declaration as well as the stimulation of the strike was all done by the IWW, by the militant minority among the silk workers; the administering of the strike was done democratically by the silk workers themselves. We were in the position of generals on a battlefield who had to organize their forces, who had to organize their commissary department while they were in battle, but who were being financed and directed by people in the capitol. Our plan of battle was very often nullified by the democratic administration of the strike committee.

The industrial outlook in Paterson presented its difficulties and its advantages. No one realized them quicker than we did. There was the difficulty of 300 mills, no trustification, no company that had the balance of power upon whom we could concentrate our attack. In Lawrence we had the American Woolen Company. Once having forced the American Woolen Company to settle, it was an easy matter to gather in the threads of the other mills. No such situation existed in Paterson. Three hundred manufacturers, but many of them having annexes in Pennsylvania, meant that they had a means whereby they could fill a large percentage of their orders unless we were able to strike Pennsylvania simultaneously. And those mills employed women and children, wives and children of union weavers, who didn't need actually to work for a living wage, but worked simply to add to the family income. We had the difficulty that silk is not an actual necessity.

In the strike among coal miners you reached the point eventually where you had the public by the throat, and through the public you were able to bring pressure on the employers. Not so in the silk industry. Silk is a luxury. We had the condition in Paterson, however, that this was the first silk year in about thirty years. In 1913 fortunately silk was stylish. Every woman wanted a silk gown, and the more flimsy it was the more she wanted it. Silk being stylish meant that the employers were mighty anxious to take advantage of this exceptional opportunity. And the fact that there were over 300 of them gave us on the other hand the advantage that some of them were very small, they had great liabilities and not very much reserve capital. Therefore we were sort of playing a game between how much they could get done in Pennsylvania balanced off with how great the demand for silk was and how close they were to bankruptcy. We had no means of telling that, except by guesswork. *They* could always tell when our side was weakening.

The first period of the strike meant for us persecution and propaganda, those two things. Our work was to educate and stimulate. Education is not a conversion, it is a process. One speech to a body of workers does not overcome their prejudices of a lifetime. We had prejudices on the national issues, prejudices between crafts, prejudices between competing men and women—all these to overcome. We had the influence of the minister on the one side, and the respect that they had for government on the other side. We had to stimulate them. Stimulation, in a strike, means to make that strike, and through it the class struggle, their religion; to make them forget all about the fact that it's for a few cents or a few hours, but to make them feel it is a "religious duty" for them to win that strike. Those two things constituted our work, to create in them a feeling of solidarity and a feeling of class consciousness—a rather old term, very threadbare among certain elements in the city of New York, but meaning a great deal in a strike. It means, to illustrate, this: the first day of the strike a photographer came on the stage to take a picture, and all over the hall there was a quiver of excitement: "No, no, no. Don't let him take a picture." "Why not?" "Why, our faces might show in the picture. The boss might see it." "Well," I said, "doesn't he know you are here? If he doesn't know now, he will know tomorrow."

From that day, when the strikers were afraid to have their pictures taken for fear they might be spotted, to the day when a thousand of them came to New York to take part in a pageant, with a friendly rivalry among themselves as to which one would get their picture in the paper, was a long process of stimulation, a long process of creating in them class spirit, class respect, class consciousness. That was the work of the agitator. Around this propaganda our critics center their volleys: the kind of propaganda we gave the strikers, the kind of stimulation and education we gave them. Many of our critics presume that the strikers were perfect and the leaders only were human; that we didn't have to deal with their imperfections as well as with our own. And the first big criticism that has been made (of course they all criticize: for the socialists we were too radical, for the anarchists we were too conservative, for everybody else we were impossible) is that we didn't advocate violence. Strange as it may seem, this is the criticism that has come from more sources than any other.

I contend that there was no use for violence in the Paterson strike; that only where violence is necessary should violence be used. This is not a moral or legal objection but a utilitarian one. I don't say that violence should *not* be used, but where there is no call for it, there is no reason why we should resort to it. In the Paterson strike, for the first four months there wasn't a single scab in the mills. The mills were shut down as tight as a vacuum. They were like empty junk boats along the banks of the river. Now, where any violence could be used against non-existent scabs passes my understanding. Mass action is far more up-to-date than personal or physical violence. Mass action means that the workers withdraw their labor power, and paralyze the wealth production of the city, cut off the means of life, the breath of life of the employers. Violence may mean just weakness on the part of those workers. Violence occurs in almost every American Federation of Labor strike because the workers are desperate, because they are losing their strike. In the street car strikes, for instance, every one of them is marked with violence because the men in the power house are at work, the power is going through the rails, and the scabs are able to run the cars. The men and women in desperation, seeing that the work is being done, turn the cars off the track, cut the wires, throw stones, and so on. But the IWW believes that it is far more up to date to call the men in the power house out on strike. Then there won't be any cars running, any scabs to throw stones at, or any wires that are worth cutting. Physical violence is dramatic. It's especially dramatic when you talk about it and don't resort to it. But actual violence is an old-fashioned method of conducting a strike. And mass action, paralyzing all industry, is a new-fashioned and a much more feared method of conducting a strike. That does not mean that violence shouldn't be used in self-defense. Everybody believes in violence for self-defense. Strikers don't need to be told that. But the actual fact is that in spite of our theory that the way to win a strike is to put your hands in your pocket and refuse to work, it was only in the Paterson strike, of all the strikes in 1913, that a strike leader said what Haywood said: "If the police do not let up in the use of violence against the strikers the strikers are going to arm themselves and fight back." That has, however, not been advertised as extensively as was the "hands in your pockets" theory. Nor has it been advertised by either our enemies or our friends that in the Paterson strike police persecution did drop off considerably after the open declaration of self-defense was made by the strikers. In that contingency violence is of course a necessity and one would be stupid to say that in either Michigan or West Virginia or Colorado the miners have not a right to take their guns and defend their wives and their babies and themselves.

The statement has been made by Mrs. Sanger in the *Revolutionary Almanac* that we should have stimulated the strikers to do something that would bring the militia in, and the presence of the militia would have forced a settlement of the strike.[5] That is not necessarily true. It was not the presence of the militia that forced a settlement of the Lawrence strike. And today there is militia in Colorado; they have been there for months. There is the militia in Michigan; they have been there for a long period. There was the militia in West Virginia, but *that* did not bring a successful termination of the strike because coal was being produced, and copper was being produced, in other parts of the world, and the market was not completely cut off from its product. The presence of the militia may play a part in stimulating the strikers or in discouraging the strikers, but it does not affect the industrial outcome of the strike, and I believe to say so is to give entirely too much significance to political or military power. I don't believe that the presence of the militia is going to affect an industrial struggle to any appreciable extent, providing the workers are economically in an advantageous position.

Before I finish with this question of violence I want to ask you men and women here if you realize that there is a certain responsibility about advocating violence. It's very easy to say, "We will give up our own lives in behalf of the workers," but it's another question to ask them to give up their lives; and men and women who go out as strike agitators should only advocate violence when they are absolutely certain that it is going to do some good other than to spill the blood of the innocent workers on the streets of the cities. I know of one man in particular who wrote an article in the *Social War* about how "the blood of the workers should dye the streets in the city of Paterson in protest," but he didn't come to Paterson to let his blood dye the streets, as the baptism of violence. In fact we never saw him in the city of Paterson from the first day of the strike to the last. This responsibility rests heavily upon every man and woman who lives with and works with and loves the people for whom the strike is being conducted.

[5] Margaret Sanger, in the anarchist paper *Revolutionary Almanac*, criticized the IWW for not urging the strikers to fight back.

. . . The free speech fight that we have in Paterson is something far more intricate than just having a policeman put his hand over your mouth and tell you you can't speak.

. . . In Paterson we had this peculiar technicality, that while you had the right to speak, they said, "We hold you responsible for what you say, we arrest you for what you say, what you meant, what you didn't say, what we thought you ought to have said, and all the rest of it." Our original reason for going to Haledon, however, was not on account of the Sunday law only, but goes deep into the psychology of a strike.[6] Because Sunday is the day before Monday! Monday is the day that a break comes in every strike, if it is to come at all during the week. If you can bring the people safely over Monday they usually go along for the rest of the week. If on Sunday, however, you let those people stay at home, sit around the stove without any fire in it, sit down at the table where there isn't very much food, see the feet of the children with shoes getting thin, and the bodies of the children where the clothes are getting ragged, they begin to think in terms of "myself" and lose that spirit of the mass and the realization that all are suffering as they are suffering. You have got to keep them busy every day in the week, and particularly on Sunday, in order to keep that spirit from going down to zero. I believe that's one reason why ministers have sermons on Sunday, so that people don't get a chance to think how bad their conditions are the rest of the week. Anyhow, it's a very necessary thing in a strike. And so our original reason for going to Haledon—I remember we discussed it very thoroughly—was to give them novelty, to give them variety, to take them en masse out of the city of Paterson some place else, to a sort of picnic over Sunday that would stimulate them for the rest of the week. In fact that is a necessary process in every strike, to keep the people busy all the time, to keep them active, working, fighting soldiers in the ranks. And this is the agitator's work—to plan and suggest activity, diverse, but concentrated on the strike. That's the reason why the IWW has these great mass meetings, women's meetings, children's meetings; why we have mass picketing and mass funerals. And out of all this continuous mass activity we are able to create that feeling on the part of the workers, "One for all and all for one." We are able to make them realize that an injury to one is an injury to all; we are able to bring them to the point where they will have relief and not strike benefits, to the point where they will go to jail and refuse fines, and go hundreds of them together.

. . . People learn to do by doing. We haven't a military body in a strike, a body to which you can say "Do this" and "Do that" and "Do

[6] Haledon was an adjacent city with a socialist mayor, William Brueckmann, which did not follow the New Jersey blue laws prohibiting Sunday meetings.

the other thing" and they obey unfailingly. Democracy means mistakes, lots of them, mistake after mistake. But it also means experience and that there will be no repetition of those mistakes.

. . . Sabotage was objected to by the Socialists. In fact they pursued a rather intolerant attitude. It was the Socialist organizer and the Socialist secretary who called the attention of the public to the fact that Frederic Sumner Boyd made a sabotage speech. Why "intolerant"? Because nobody ever objected to anything that the Socialists said. We tried to produce among those strikers this feeling: "Listen to anything, listen to everybody. Ministers come, priests come, lawyers, doctors, politicians, Socialists, anarchists, AFL, IWW—listen to them all and then take what you think is good for yourselves and reject what is bad. If you are not able to do that then no censorship over your meetings is going to do you any good." And so the strikers had a far more tolerant attitude than had the Socialists. The strikers had the attitude: "Listen to everything." The Socialists had the attitude: "You must listen to us but you must not listen to the things we don't agree with; you must not listen to sabotage because we don't agree with sabotage." We had a discussion in the executive committee about it, and one after the other of the members of the executive committee admitted that they used sabotage, why shouldn't they talk about it? It existed in the mills, they said. Therefore there was no reason why it should not be recognized on the platform. It was not the advocacy of sabotage that hurt some of our comrades but denial of their right to dictate the policy of the Paterson strike.

What the workers had to contend with in the first period of this strike was this police persecution that arrested hundreds of strikers, fined hundreds, sentenced men to three years in state's prison for talking; persecutions that meant beating and clubbing and continual opposition every minute they were on the picket line, speakers arrested, Quinlan arrested, Scott convicted and sentenced to fifteen years and $1,500 fine.[7] On the other side, what? No money. If all these critics all over the United States had only put their interest in the form of finances, the Paterson strike might have been another story. We were out on strike five months. We had $60,000 and 25,000 strikers. That meant $60,000 for five months, $12,000 a month for 25,000 strikers; it meant

[7] A hundred pickets a day were arrested through May and June; most received ten-day sentences. By the end of the strike three thousand had been arrested.

Patrick Quinlan was from Limerick, Ireland, and had worked as a coal miner, steelworker, longshoreman, sailor, and union organizer. Originally he was a Socialist party organizer and then joined the IWW in 1912. He was jailed during 1913–1915. After jail he rejoined the Socialist party. Alex Scott was a local Socialist editor whose case was reversed by the New Jersey Supreme Court.

an average of less than 50 cents a month. And yet they stayed out on strike for six months.

. . . I saw men go out in Paterson without shoes, in the middle of winter and with bags on their feet. I went into a family to have a picture taken of a mother with eight children who didn't have a crust of bread, didn't have a bowl of milk for the baby in the house, but the father was out on the picket line. Others were just as bad off. Thousands of them that we never heard of at all. This was the difficulty that the workers had to contend with in Paterson: hunger; hunger gnawing at their vitals; hunger tearing them down; and still they had the courage to fight it out for six months.

Then came the pageant. What I say about the pageant tonight may strike you as rather strange, but I consider that the pageant marked the climax in the Paterson strike and started the decline in the Paterson strike, just for the reason that the pageant promised money for the Paterson strikers and it didn't give them a cent. Yes, it was a beautiful example of realistic art, I admit that. It was splendid propaganda for the workers in New York. I don't minimize its value but am dealing with it here solely as a factor in the strike, with what happened in Paterson before, during and after the pageant. In preparation for the pageant the workers were distracted for weeks, turning to the stage of the hall, away from the field of life. They were playing pickets on the stage. They were neglecting the picketing around the mill. And the first scabs got into the Paterson mills while the workers were training for the pageant, because the best ones, the most active, the most energetic, the best, the strongest ones of them went into the pageant and they were the ones that were the best pickets around the mills. Distraction from their real work was the first danger in Paterson. And how many times we had to counteract that and work against it!

And then came jealousy. There were only a thousand that came to New York. I wonder if you ever realized that you left 24,000 disappointed people behind? The women cried and said, "Why did *she* go? Why couldn't I go?." The men told about how many times they had been in jail, and asked why couldn't they go as well as somebody else. Between jealousy, unnecessary but very human, and their desire to do something, much discord was created in the ranks.

But whatever credit is due for such a gigantic undertaking comes to the New York silk workers, not the dilettante element who figured so prominently, but who would have abandoned it at the last moment had not the silk workers advanced $600 to pull it through.[8]

---

[8] Gurley was referring to wealthy bohemians such as Mabel Dodge Luhan, who helped plan the pageant.

And then comes the grand finale—no money. Nothing. This thing that had been heralded as the salvation of the strike, this thing that was going to bring thousands of dollars to the strike—$150 came to Paterson, and all kinds of explanations. I don't mean to say that I blame the people who ran the pageant. I know they were amateurs and they gave their time and their energy and their money. They did the best they could and I appreciate their effort. But that doesn't minimize the result that came in Paterson. It did not in any way placate the workers of Paterson to tell them that people in New York had made sacrifices, in view of the long time that *they* had been making sacrifices. And so with the pageant as a climax, with the papers clamoring that tens of thousands of dollars had been made, and with the committee explaining what was very simple, that nothing *could* have been made with one performance on such a gigantic scale, there came trouble, dissatisfaction, in the Paterson strike.[9]

Bread was the need of the hour, and bread was not forthcoming even from the most beautiful and realistic example of art that has been put on the stage in the last half century.

. . . But there came one of the most peculiar phenomena that I have ever seen in a strike; that the bosses weakened simultaneously with the workers. Both elements weakened together. The workers did not have a chance to see the weaknesses of the employers as clearly, possibly, as we who had witnessed it before, did, which gave us our abiding faith in the workers' chances of success, but the employers had every chance to see the workers weaken. The employers have a full view of your army. You have no view of their army and can only guess at their condition. So a tentative proposition came from the employers of a shop-by-shop settlement. This was the trying-out of the bait, the bait that should have been refused by the strikers without qualification. Absolute surrender, all or nothing, was the necessary slogan. By this we did not mean that 100 per cent of the manufacturers must settle, or that 99 per cent of the workers must stay out till 1 per cent won everything. The IWW advice to the strikers was—an overwhelming majority of the strikers must receive the concession before a strike is won. This was clearly understood in Paterson, though misrepresented there and elsewhere. Instead, the committee swallowed the bait and said, "We will take a vote on the shop-by-shop proposition, a vote of the committee." The minute they did that, they admitted their own weakness. And the employers immediately reacted to a position of strength. There was no referendum vote proposed by this committee; they were willing to take their own vote to

[9]The bourgeois press accused the IWW of stealing the profits.

see what they themselves thought of it, and to settle the strike on their own decision alone.

Then it was that the IWW speakers and Executive Committee had to inject themselves in contradistinction to the strike committee. And the odd part of it was that the conservatives on the committee utilized our own position against us. We had always said, "The silk workers must gain their own strike." And so they said, "We are the silk workers. You are simply outside agitators. You can't talk to this strike committee even." I remember one day the door was virtually slammed in my face, until the Italian and Jewish workers made such an uproar, threatening to throw the others out of a three-story building window, that the floor was granted. It was only when we threatened to go to the masses and to get this referendum vote in spite of them that they took the referendum vote. But all this came out in the local press, and it all showed that the committee was conservative and the IWW was radical; more correctly, the IWW and the masses were radical. And so this vote was taken by the strikers. It resulted in a defeat of the entire proposition. Five thousand dyers in one meeting voted it down unanimously. They said, "We never said we would settle shop by shop. We are going to stick it out together until we win together or until we lose together." But the very fact that they had been willing to discuss it made the manufacturers assume an aggressive position. And then they said, "We never said we would settle shop by shop. We never offered you any such proposition. We won't take you back now unless you come under the old conditions."

. . . On the 18th of July the ribbon weavers notified the strike committee, "We have drawn out of your committee. We are going to settle our strike to suit ourselves. We are going to settle it shop by shop. . . . And the ribbon weavers stayed out till the very last. Oh yes. They have all the glory throughout the United States of being the last ones to return to work, but the fact is that they were the first ones that broke the strike, because they broke the solidarity, they precipitated a position that was virtually a stampede. The strike committee decided, "Well, with the ribbon weavers drawing out, what are we going to do? We might as well accept"; and the shop-by-shop proposition was put through by the strike committee without a referendum vote, stampeded by the action of the English-speaking, conservative ribbon weavers.

So that was the tragedy of the Paterson strike, the tragedy of a stampede, the tragedy of an army, a solid phalanx being cut up into 300 pieces, each shop-piece trying to settle as best for themselves. It was absolutely in violation of the IWW principles and the IWW advice to the strikers. No strike should ever be settled without a referendum vote, and no shop settlement should ever have been suggested in the

city of Paterson because that was the very thing that had broken the
strike the year before. So this stampede came, and the weaker ones
went back to work and the stronger ones were left outside, to be made
the target of the enemy, blacklisted for weeks and weeks after the
strike was over, many of them on the blacklist yet. It produced discord
among the officers in the strike. I remember one day at Haledon the
chairman said to Tresca and myself, "If you are going to talk about the
eight-hour day and about a general strike, then you had better not
talk at all." And we had to go out and ask the people, "Are we expected here today and can we say what we think, or have we got to say
what the strike committee has decided?" We were unanimously welcomed. But it was too late. Just as soon as the people saw that there
was a break between the agitators and the strike committee, that the
ribbon weavers wanted this and others wanted that, the stampede had
started and no human being could have held it back.

It was the stampede of hungry people, people who could no longer
think clearly. The bosses made beautiful promises to the ribbon weavers and to everybody else, but practically every promise made before
the settlement of the Paterson strike was violated, and the better conditions have only been won through the organized strikes since the big
strike. Not one promise that was made by the employers previous to
breakup on account of the shop-by-shop settlement was ever lived up
to. Other places were stranded. New York, Hoboken, College Point
were left stranded by this action. And on the 28th of July everybody
was back at work, back to work in spite of the fact that the general
conviction had been that we were on the eve of victory. I believe that if
the strikers had been able to hold out a little longer by any means, by
money if possible, which was refused to us, we could have won the
Paterson strike. We could have won it because the bosses had lost their
spring orders, they had lost their summer orders, they had lost their
fall orders, and they were in danger of losing their winter orders, one
year's work; and the mills in Pennsylvania, while they could give the
bosses endurance for a period, could not fill all the orders and could
not keep up their business for the year round.

I say we were refused money. I wish to tell you that is the absolute
truth. The *New York Call* was approached by fellow worker Haywood,[10]
when we were desperate for money, when the kitchens were closed
and the people were going out on the picket line on bread and water,
and asked to publish a full page advertisement begging for money,
pleading for money. They refused to accept the advertisement. They
said, "We can't take your money." "Well, can you *give* us the space?"
"Oh, no, we can't afford to give you the space. We couldn't take money

---

[10] The *New York Call* was a socialist newspaper.

from strikers, but we couldn't give space either." And so in the end there was no appeal, either paid for or not, but a little bit of a piece that did not amount to a candle of light, lost in the space of the newspaper. However, on the 26th of July, while the ribbon weavers and some of the broad silk weavers were still out, the *Call* had published a criticism by Mr. Jacob Panken of the Paterson strike.[11] Lots of space for criticism, but no space to ask bread for hungry men and women. And this was true not only of the *Call*, but of the other socialist papers. So, between these two forces, we were helpless.

. . . Our position to the strikers was, "If the IWW conception had been followed out you would have won all together, or you would have lost all together, but you would still have had your army a continuing whole." Every general knows it is far better for an army to retreat en masse than it is to scatter and be shot to pieces. And so it is better to lose all together than to have some win at the expense of the rest, because losing all together you have the chance within a few months of recovering and going back to the battle again, your army still centralized, and winning in the second attempt.

What lessons has the Paterson strike given to the IWW and to the strikers? One of the lessons it has given to me is that when the IWW assumes the responsibility of a strike, the IWW should control the strike absolutely through a union strike committee; that there should be no outside interference, no outside non-union domination accepted or permitted. . . . That direct action and solidarity are the only keys to a worker's success or the workers' success. That the spirit throughout this long weary propaganda has remained unbroken, and I will give you just three brief examples.

. . . Every time I go to Paterson some people get around and say, "Say, Miss Flynn, when is there going to be another strike?" They have that certain feeling that the strike has been postponed, but they are going to take it up again and fight it out again. That spirit is the result of the IWW agitation in Paterson.

And so, I feel that we have been vindicated in spite of our defeat. We have won further toleration for the workers. We have given them a class feeling, a trust in themselves and a distrust for everybody else. They are not giving any more faith to the ministers, even though we didn't carry any "No God, no master" banners floating through the streets of Paterson. You know, you may put a thing on a banner and it makes no impression at all; but you let a minister show himself up, let all the ministers show themselves against the workers, and that makes more impression than all the "No God, no master" banners from

[11] Jacob Panken was a socialist lawyer and legal adviser for the unions that attacked the IWW in the *New York Call*.

Maine to California. That is the difference between education and sensationalism.

And they have no more use for the state. To them the statue of liberty is personified by the policeman and his club.

SOURCE: Speech delivered on Jan. 31, 1914, at New York Civic Club Forum.

Sabotage (1915)

FLYNN wrote Sabotage: The Conscious Withdrawal of the Workers' Industrial Efficiency *in 1913, during the Paterson strike, to lend support to the New York socialist Frederic Sumner Boyd, who had been arrested and charged with advocating sabotage and sentenced to five years in prison. Sabotage was a highly controversial topic, and Flynn dared to tackle it. In 1912 the Socialist party expelled Big Bill Haywood for opposing political action and advocating sabotage. Many Wobblies did not approve of it either. On the other hand many anarchists criticized the IWW for not preaching sabotage openly, especially during the Paterson strike. Flynn herself only justified sabotage because the workers considered it necessary, not as a moral principle.*

This piece of writing haunted Flynn throughout her life; as Flynn explained, "It has bobbed up like a bad penny from time to time." It was mentioned in her Smith Act trial in 1951, in her Subversive Activities Control Board hearing in 1952, and in her FBI files.[1] Sabotage was originally published as a pamphlet in 1915, taken by the Cleveland, Ohio, IWW from a speech Flynn had given, supposedly without the national headquarters' permission. The pamphlet was later withdrawn and the Cleveland chapter dissolved.[2] By the time the pamphlet was printed, Frederic Boyd had signed a petition for pardon, denouncing sabotage. Thus on the last page of the pamphlet Flynn

[1] Flynn, *Rebel Girl*, 163. FBI files, Aug. 15, 1949, NY, No. 100-1696, 8-12.
[2] Fred Thompson and Patrick Murfin, *IWW: Its First Seventy Years* (Chicago: IWW, 1976), 86.

noted Boyd's cowardice; it had been too late to change the many complimentary references to Boyd in the text proper. In her autobiography Flynn went further, even suggesting that Boyd may have been a provocateur.[3]

In 1916, in a letter to President Wilson, Flynn herself noted her misgivings about the pamphlet. She said: "the only conceivable basis for my indictment is a pamphlet on sabotage written four years ago in defense of a man arrested during the Paterson strike. I had no intention that it should apply to any other times or conditions than those of which I wrote, and long before my arrest [for espionage, during World War I] had requested that the IWW not publish it further until I could rewrite it."[4] *It is not clear whether Flynn changed her mind about the use of sabotage or whether she was stretching the truth to persuade the president to dismiss her case.*[5]

ITS NECESSITY IN THE CLASS WAR

I am not going to attempt to justify sabotage on any moral ground. If the workers consider that sabotage is necessary, that in itself makes sabotage moral. Its necessity is its excuse for existence. And for us to discuss the morality of sabotage would be as absurd as to discuss the morality of the strike or the morality of the class struggle itself. In order to understand sabotage or to accept it at all it is necessary to accept the concept of the class struggle. If you believe that between the workers on the one side and their employers on the other there is peace, there is harmony such as exists between brothers, and that consequently whatever strikes and lockouts occur are simply family squabbles; if you believe that a point can be reached whereby the employer can get enough and the worker can get enough, a point of amicable adjustment of industrial warfare and economic distribution, then there is no justification and no explanation of sabotage intelligible to you. Sabotage is one weapon in the arsenal of labor to fight its

[3] Flynn, *Rebel Girl*, 162; Joseph Conlin, *Bread and Roses Too: Studies of the Wobblies* (Westport, Conn.: Greenwood Press, 1969), 108. Conlin agreed with Flynn, but I believe this scenario was unlikely.

[4] Haywood Defense File No. 2, Nos. 188032, 120249, National Archives, Washington, D.C.

[5] In July 1916 a section of *Sabotage*, "Limiting the Supply of Slaves," was published in *Melting Pot*, a small, iconoclastic, socialist monthly published in St. Louis during 1913–1920. This article was brought to my attention by Neil Basen. Steve Golin, "Defeat Becomes Disaster: The Paterson Strike of 1913 and the Decline of the IWW," *Labor History* 24 (Spring 1983): 238–240. Golin suggested that Flynn changed her mind about sabotage after the Paterson strike, but this could not be the case unless the article in *Melting Pot*, written three years after the strike, was also printed without her permission, or that she still agreed with this section of *Sabotage*.

side of the class struggle. Labor realizes, as it becomes more intelligent, that it must have power in order to accomplish anything; that neither appeals for sympathy nor abstract rights will make for better conditions. For instance, take an industrial establishment such as a silk mill where men and women and little children work ten hours a day for an average wage of between six and seven dollars a week. Could any one of them, or a committee representing the whole, hope to induce the employer to give better conditions by appealing to his sympathy, by telling him of the misery, the hardship and the poverty of their lives; or could they do it by appealing to his sense of justice? Suppose that an individual working man or woman went to an employer and said, "I make, in my capacity as wage worker in this factory, so many dollars' worth of wealth every day and justice demands that you give me at least half." The employer would probably have him removed to the nearest lunatic asylum. He would consider him too dangerous a criminal to let loose on the community! It is neither sympathy nor justice that makes an appeal to the employer. But it is power.

SHORT PAY, LESS WORK

. . . I have heard of my grandfather telling how an old fellow came to work on the railroad and the boss said, "Well, what can you do?"

"I can do 'most anything," said he—a big husky fellow.

"Well," said the boss, "can you handle a pick and a shovel?"

"Oh, sure. How much do you pay on this job?"

"A dollar a day."

"Is that all? Well,—all right. I need that job pretty bad. I guess I will take it." So he took his pick and went leisurely to work. Soon the boss came along and said:

"Say, can't you work any faster than that?"

"Shure I can."

"Well, why don't you?"

"This is my dollar-a-day clip."

"Well," said the boss, "let's see what the $1.25-a-day clip looks like."

That went a little better. Then the boss said, "Let's see what the $1.50-a-day clip looks like." The man showed him. "That was fine," said the boss, "well, maybe we will call it $1.50 a day." The man volunteered the information that his $2-a-day clip was "a hummer." So, through this instinctive sort of sabotage this poor obscure workingman on a railroad in Maine was able to gain for himself an advance from $1 to $2 a day. We read of the gangs of Italian workingmen, when the boss cuts their pay—you know, usually they have an Irish or American boss and he likes to make a couple of dollars a day on the side for himself, so he cuts the pay of the men once in a while without consulting the contractor and pockets the difference. One boss cut them 25 cents a day. The next day he came on the work, to find that the amount of dirt that was being removed had lessened considerably. He asked a few questions: "What's the matter?"

"Me no understan' English"—none of them wished to talk.

Well, he exhausted the day going around trying to find one person who could speak and tell him what was wrong. Finally he found one man, who said, "Well, you see, boss, you cutta da pay, we cuttada shob'." . . .

INTERFERING WITH QUALITY OF GOODS

The second form of sabotage is to deliberately interfere with the quality of the goods. And in this we learn many lessons from our employers, even as we learn how to limit the quantity. You know that every year in the western part of this United States there are fruits and grains produced that never find a market; bananas and oranges rot on the ground, whole skiffs of fruits are dumped into the ocean. Not because people do not need these foods and couldn't make good use of them in the big cities of the east, but because the employing class prefer to destroy a large percentage of the production in order to keep the price up in cities like New York, Chicago, Baltimore and Boston. If they sent all the bananas that they produce into the eastern part of the United States we would be buying bananas at probably three for a cent. But by destroying a large quantity, they are able to keep the price up to two for 5c. And this applies to potatoes, apples, and very many other staple articles required by the majority of people. Yet if the worker attempts to apply the same principle, the same theory, the same tactic as his employer we are confronted with all sorts of finespun moral objections. . . .

"DYNAMITING" SILK

Let me give you a specific illustration of what I mean. Seventy-five years ago when silk was woven into cloth, the silk skein was taken in the pure, dyed and woven, and when that piece of silk was made it would last for 50 years. Your grandmother could wear it as a wedding dress. Your mother could wear it as a wedding dress. And then you, if you, woman reader, were fortunate enough to have a chance to get married, could wear it as a wedding dress also. But the silk that you buy today is not dyed in the pure and woven into a strong and durable product. One pound of silk goes into the dye house and usually as many as three to fifteen pounds come out. That is to say, along with the dyeing there is an extraneous and an unnecessary process of what is very picturesquely called "dynamiting." They weight the silk. They have solutions of tin, solutions of zinc, solutions of lead. . . .

And so when you buy a nice piece of silk today and have a dress made for festive occasions, you hang it away in the wardrobe and when you take it out it is cracked down the pleats and along the waist and arms. And you believe that you have been terribly cheated by a clerk. What is actually wrong is that you have paid for silk where you have received old tin cans and zinc and lead and things of that sort. You have a dress that is garnished with silk, seasoned with silk, but a dress that is adulterated to the point where, if it was adulterated just the slightest degree more, it would fall to pieces entirely.

Now, what Frederic Sumner Boyd advocated to the silk workers was in effect this: "You do for yourselves what you are already doing for your employers. Put these same things into the silk for yourself and your own purposes as you are putting in for the employer's purposes. . . ."

NON-ADULTERATION AND OVER-ADULTERATION

Now, Boyd's form of sabotage was not the most dangerous form of sabotage at that. If the judges had any imagination they would know that Boyd's form of sabotage was pretty mild compared with this: Suppose that he had said to the dyers in Paterson, to a sufficient number of them that they could do it as a whole, so that it would affect every dye house in Paterson: "Instead of introducing these chemicals for adulteration, don't introduce them at all. Take the lead, the zinc, and the tin and throw it down the sewer and weave the silk, beautiful, pure, durable silk, just as it is. Dye it pound for pound, hundred pound for hundred pound." The employers would have been more hurt by that form of sabotage than by what Boyd advocated. And they would probably have wanted him put in jail for life instead of for seven years. In other words, to advocate non-adulteration is a lot more dangerous to capitalist interests than to advocate adulteration. And non-adulteration is the highest form of sabotage in an establishment like the dye houses of Paterson, bakeries, confectioners, meat packing houses, restaurants, etc.

Interfering with quality, or durability, or the utility of a product, might be illustrated as follows: Suppose a milkman comes to your house every day and delivers a quart of milk, and this quart of milk is half water and they put some chalk in it and some glue to thicken it. Then a milk driver goes on that round who belongs to a union. The union strikes. And they don't win any better conditions. Then they turn on the water faucet and they let it run so that the mixture is four-fifths water and one-fifth milk. You will send the "milk" back and make a complaint. At the same time that you are making that complaint and refusing to use the milk, hundreds and thousands of others will do the same thing, and through striking at the interests of the consumer once they are able to effect better conditions for themselves and also they are able to compel the employers to give the pure product. That form of sabotage is distinctly beneficial to the consumer. Any exposure of adulteration, any over-adulteration that makes the product unconsumable, is a lot more beneficial to the consumer than to have it tinctured and doctored so that you can use it, but so that it is destructive to your physical condition at the same time.

Interfering with quality means can be instanced in the hotel and restaurant kitchens. I remember during the hotel workers strike they used to tell us about the great cauldrons of soup that stood there month in and month out without ever being cleaned, that were covered with verdigris and with various other forms of animal growth, and that very many times into this soup would fall a mouse or a rat and he would be fished out and thrown aside and the soup would be used just the same. Now, can anyone say that if the workers in those restaurants, as a means of striking at their employers, would take half a pound of salt and throw it into that soup cauldron, you as a diner, or consumer, wouldn't be a lot better off? It would be far better to have that soup made unfit for consumption than to have it left in a state where it can be consumed but where it is continually poisonous to a greater or less degree. Destroying the utility of the goods sometimes means a distinct benefit to the person who might otherwise use the goods.

INTERFERING WITH SERVICE—"OPEN MOUTH" SABOTAGE

But that form of sabotage is not the final form of sabotage. Service can be destroyed as well as quality. And this is accomplished in Europe by what is known as "the open mouth sabotage." In the hotel and restaurant industry, for instance—I wonder if this judge who sentenced Boyd to seven years in state's prison would believe in this form of sabotage or not? Suppose he went into a restaurant and ordered a lobster salad and he said to the spick and span waiter standing behind the chair, "Is the lobster salad good?" "Oh, yes, sir," said the waiter, "It is the very best in the city." That would be acting the good wage slave and looking out for the employer's interest. But if the waiter should say, "No, sir, it's rotten lobster salad. It's made from the pieces that have been gathered together here for the last six weeks," that would be the waiter who believed in sabotage, that would be the waiter who had no interest in his boss' profits, the waiter who didn't give a continental whether the boss sold lobster salad or not. And the judge would probably believe in sabotage in that particular instance. The waiters in the city of New York were only about 5,000 strong. Of these, about a thousand were militant, were the kind that could be depended on in a strike. And yet that little strike made more sensation in New York City than 200,000 garment workers who were out at the same time. They didn't win very much for themselves, because of their small numbers, but they did win a good deal in demonstrating their power to the employer to hurt his business. For instance, they drew up affidavits and they told about every hotel and restaurant in New York, the kitchen and the pantry conditions. They told about how the butter on the little butter plates was sent back to the kitchen and somebody with their fingers picked out cigar ashes and the cigarette butts and the matches and threw the butter back into the general supply. They told how the napkins that had been on the table, used possibly by a man who had consumption or syphilis, were used to wipe the dishes in the pantry. They told stories that would make your stomach sick and your hair almost turn white, of conditions in the Waldorf, the Astor, the Belmont, all the great restaurants and hotels in New York. And I found that that was one of the most effective ways of reaching the public, because the "dear public" are never reached through sympathy. I was taken by a lady up to a West Side aristocratic club of women who had nothing else to do, so they organized this club. You know—the white-gloved aristocracy! And I was asked to talk about the hotel workers strike. I knew that wasn't what they wanted at all. They just wanted to look at what kind of person a "labor agitator" was. But I saw a chance for publicity for the strikers. I told them about the long hours in the hot kitchens; about steaming, smoking ranges. I told them about the overwork and the underpay of the waiters and how these waiters had to depend upon the generosity or the drunkenness of some patron to give them a big tip; all that sort of thing. And they were stony-faced. It affected them as much as an arrow would Gibraltar: And then I started to tell them about what the waiters and the cooks had told me of the kitchen conditions and I saw a look of frozen horror on their faces immediately. They were interested when I began to talk about something that affected their own stomachs, where I never could have reached them through any appeal for humanitarian purposes. Immediately they began to draw up resolutions and to cancel engagements at these big hotels and decided that their clubs must not meet there again. They caused quite a commotion around some of the big hotels in New York. When the workers went back to work after learning that this was a way of getting at the boss via the public stomach, they did not hesitate at sabotage in the kitchens. If any of you have ever got soup that was not fit to eat, that was too salty or peppery, maybe there were some boys in the kitchen that wanted shorter hours, and that was one way they notified the boss. In the Hotel McAlpin the head waiter called the men up before him after the strike was over and lost and said, "Boys, you can have what you want, we will give you the hours, we will give you the wages, we will give you everything, but, for God's sake, stop this sabotage business in the kitchen!" In other words, what they had not been able to win through the strike they were able to win by striking at the taste of the public, by making the food non-consumable and therefore compelling the boss to take cognizance of their efficiency and their power in the kitchen.

FOLLOWING THE BOOK OF RULES

Interfering with service may be done in another way. It may be done, strange to say, sometimes by abiding by the rules, living up to the law absolutely. Sometimes the law is almost as inconvenient a thing for the capitalist as for a labor agitator. . . .

That book of rules exists in Europe as well. In one station in France there was an accident and the station master was held responsible. The station masters were organized in the Railwaymen's Union. And they went to the union and asked for some action. The union said, "The best thing for you men to do is to go back on the job and obey that book of rules letter for letter. If that is the only reason why accidents happen we will have no accidents hereafter." So they went back and when a man came up to the ticket office and asked for a ticket to such-and-such a place, the charge being so much, and would hand in more than the amount, he would be told, "Can't give you any change. It says in the book of rules a passenger must have the exact fare." This was the first one. Well, after a lot of fuss they chased around and got the exact change, were given their tickets and got aboard the train. Then when the train was supposedly ready to start the engineer climbed down, the fireman followed and they began to examine every bolt and piece of mechanism on the engine. The brakeman got off and began to examine everything *he* was supposed to examine. The passengers grew very restless. The train stood there about an hour and a half. They proceeded to leave the train. They were met at the door by an employe who said, "No, it's against the rules for you to leave the train once you get into it, until you arrive at your destination." And within three days the railroad system of France was so completely demoralized that they had to exonerate this particular station master, and the absurdity of the book of rules had been so demonstrated to the public that they had to make over their system of operation before the public would trust themselves to the railroads any further. . . .

SABOTAGE AND "MORAL FIBER"

I remember one night we had a meeting of 5,000 kiddies. (We had them there to discuss whether or not there should be a school strike. The teachers were not telling the truth about the strike and we decided that the children were either to hear the truth or it was better for them not to go to school at all.) I said, "Children, is there any of you here who have a silk dress in your family? Anybody's mother got a silk dress?" One little ragged urchin in front piped up. "Shure, me mudder's got a silk dress."

I said, "Where did she get it?"—perhaps a rather indelicate question, but a natural one.

He said, "Me fadder spoiled the cloth and had to bring it home."

The only time they get a silk dress is when they spoil the goods so that nobody else will use it: when the dress is so ruined that nobody else would want it. Then they can have it. The silk worker takes pride in his product! To talk to these people about being proud of their work is just as silly as to talk to the street cleaner about being proud of his work, or to tell the man that scrapes out the sewer to be proud of his work. If they made an article completely or if they made it all together under a democratic association and then they had the disposition of the silk—they could wear some of it, they could make some of the beautiful salmon-colored and the delicate blues into a dress for themselves—there would be pleasure in producing silk. But until you eliminate wage slavery and the exploitation of labor it is ridiculous to talk about destroying the moral fiber of the individual by telling him to destroy "his own product." Destroy his own product! He is destroying somebody else's enjoyment, somebody else's chance to use his product created in slavery. There is another argument to the effect that "if you use this thing called sabotage you are going to develop in yourself a spirit of hostility, a spirit of antagonism to everybody else in society, you are going to become sneaking, you are going to become cowardly. It is an underhanded thing to do." But the individual who uses sabotage is not benefiting himself alone. If he were looking out for himself only, he would never use sabotage. It would be much easier, much safer not to do it. When a man uses sabotage he is usually intending to benefit the whole; doing an individual thing but doing it for the benefit of himself and others together. And it requires courage. It requires individuality. It creates in that workingman some self-respect for and self-reliance upon himself as a producer. I contend that sabotage instead of being sneaking and cowardly is a courageous thing, is an open thing. The boss may not be notified about it through the papers, but he finds out about it very quickly, just the same. And the man or woman who employs it is demonstrating a courage that you may measure in this way: How many of the critics would do it?

How many of you, if you were dependent on a job in a silk town like Paterson, would take your job in your hands and employ sabotage? If you were a machinist in a locomotive shop and had a good job, how many of you would risk it to employ sabotage? Consider that and then you have the right to call the man who uses it a coward—if you can.

LIMITING THE OVER-SUPPLY OF SLAVES

It is my hope that the workers will not only "sabotage" the supply of products, but also the over-supply of producers. In Europe the syndicalists have carried on a propaganda that we are too cowardly to carry on in the United States as yet. It is against the law. Everything is "against the law," once it becomes large enough for the law to take cognizance that it is in the best interests of the working class. If sabotage is to be thrown aside because it is construed as against the law, how do we know that next year free speech may not have to be thrown aside? Or free assembly or free press? That a thing is against the law does not mean necessarily that the thing is not good. Sometimes it means just the contrary: a mighty good thing for the working class to use against the capitalists. In Europe they are carrying on this sort of limitation of product: they are saying, "Not only will we limit the product in the factory, but we are going to limit the supply of producers. We are going to limit the supply of workers on the market." Men and women of the working class in France and Italy and even Germany today are saying, "We are not going to have ten, twelve and fourteen children for the army, the navy, the factory and the mine. We are going to have fewer children, with quality and not quantity accentuated as our ideal who can be better fed, better clothed, better equipped mentally and will become better fighters for the social revolution." Although it is not a strictly scientific definition, I like to include this as indicative of the spirit that produces sabotage. It certainly is one of the most vital forms of class warfare there are, to strike at the roots of the capitalist system by limiting their supply of slaves and creating individuals who will be good soldiers on their own behalf.

SOURCE: *Sabotage: The Conscious Withdrawal of the Workers' Industrial Efficiency* (Cleveland: IWW Publishing Bureau, 1915).

Problems Organizing Women (1916)

UNLIKE *Elizabeth Gurley Flynn, few prominent IWW members fought for women's inclusion in the brotherhood of labor. Gurley was categorized as the lone female expert, even though she pleaded to write on other issues and to organize strikes where women workers were not the majority.*

In 1916 Gurley initiated a special woman's edition of Solidarity, *where "Problems Organizing Women" was published. The article expresses the traditional Marxist position that under socialism, with the end of the profit system, sexual inequality will vanish. Gurley added to the classic socialist view to insist that the IWW enter the kitchen as well as the factory, for she saw sex-segregated socialization as responsible for women's inferior status. Men and women had to change as well as the economy. In many of Gurley's IWW articles and speeches, including this one, she underlined the importance of birth control for female emancipation. Most Wobs stressed the glorious romantic role of motherhood, rather than the prevention of children.*

I N extending an enthusiastic welcome to the Women's Edition of *Solidarity* I am merely reiterating my conviction that we must here study our materials and adapt our propaganda to the special needs of women. Some of our male members are prone to underestimate this vital need and assert that the principles of the IWW are alike for all, which we grant with certain reservations. They must be translated for foreigners, simplified for illiterates, and rendered in technical phrases for various industrial groups. The textile workers discuss "one big union" in terms of warp and woof, the Joplin miners in terms of "cans of ore," and the harvest hand in the job dialect of his seasonal work. The Western locals feel the need of a paper written in the style peculiar to their district and thus the general education progresses from the Atlantic to the Pacific. I have heard revolutionists present a large indictment against women, which if true, constitutes a mine of reasons for a special appeal based upon their peculiar mental attitudes and adapted to their environment and the problems it creates.

Women are over-emotional, prone to take advantage of their sex, eager to marry and then submerged in family life, more interested in personal than social problems, are intensely selfish for "me and mine," lack a sense of solidarity, are slaves to style, and disinclined to serious and continuous study—these are a few counts in the complaint. Nearly every charge could be made against some men and does not apply to all women, yet it unfortunately fits many women for obvious reasons. It is well to remember we are dealing with the sex that has been denied all social rights since early primitive times, segregated to domestic life up to a comparatively recent date, and denied access to institutions of learning up to half a century ago. Religion, home, and childbearing were their prescribed spheres. Marriage was their career and to be an old maid a lifelong disgrace. Their right to life depended on their sex attraction, and the hideous inroads on the moral integrity of women, produced by economic dependence, are deep and subtle. Loveless marriages, household drudgery, acceptance of loathsome familiarities, unwelcome childbearing, were and are far more general than admitted by moralists, and have marred the mind, body, and spirit of women. . . .

After a few generations, custom will accept it as natural and ethical. When Mary Wollstonecraft wrote her "Vindication of the Rights of Woman" in 1702, she was dubbed a "hyena in petticoats," yet her views would be considered mild and conservative today. The early suffragists were mobbed and occupied the same plane in popular opinion allotted to the IWW now, yet slowly the changing economic status of woman has made suffrage respectable, even fashionable. While women were merely instruments of passion or household drudges, so long as "the ideal woman was she of whom neither good nor evil was heard outside her own home" and education stopped with reading the catechism—there was no soil in which the roots of new ideals could cling or be nourished. Today we see calm, clear-eyed women deliberating in conventions, marching in peace or suffrage parades, and enthusiastic militant ones in long and bitter strikes. It thrills us as mighty cosmic upheavals when the static of centuries moves, rises, and is changed. From this larger viewpoint, one must admit that women are forging ahead, and have really accomplished much with their limited opportunities. Given a fraction of the long eras of public, cooperative life men have passed through, the new woman whose outline we already dimly see will surely develop.

But one should not exaggerate the number of real rebel women and become over sanguine about the general outlook. There are many intelligent women who have only arrived at an intense rebellion against the handicaps placed on women, which is pithily expressed in the slogan, "Give a woman a man's chance." The rebel woman realizes that "a man's chance" is not enviable under the present order and that her fight is to secure relief for all workers, irrespective of sex. Ideas do not change automatically with environment and many hold-over ones, a century behind actually, aggravate and humiliate self-respecting women. With the past dominating in education, we found girls and boys equipped differently for wage-earning. . . .

Combat and struggle are considered essentially *manly* endeavors. . . .

Mis-education further teaches girls to be lady-like, a condition of inane and inert placidity. She must not fight or be aggressive, mustn't be "tomboy," mustn't soil her dresses, mustn't run and jump as more sensibly attired boys do. In Scranton recently I heard a boy say to his sister, "You can't play with us, you're only a girl!" I hoped she would beat him into a more generous attitude, but in her acquiescence was the germ of a pitiable inability to think and act alone, characteristic of so many women. In the arrogance of the male child was the beginning of a dominance that culminates in the drunken miner who beats his wife and vents the cowardly spleen he dare not show the boss! Feminist propaganda is helping to destroy the same obstacles the labor movement confronts, when it ridicules the lady-like person, makes women discontented, draws them from sewing circle gossips and frivolous pastimes into serious discussions of current problems and inspires them to stand abuse and imprisonment for an idea. A girl who has arrived at suffrage will listen to an organizer, but a simpering fool who says, "Women ain't got brains enough to vote!" or "Women ought to stay at home" is beyond hope.

A single girl is deluded by expectations of escape through marriage, a state which gives to the man additional incentive to fight for better conditions. The married woman worker has a two-fold burden from which her husband is immune—childbearing and housekeeping. To counteract these tremendous handicaps and draw the women of labor into its warfare is a task pitted to the IWW. Women and foreigners have been step-sisters and brothers in the AFL. The IWW must be capable, large-spirited, all-inclusive to bring a message of hope into the noisiest workshop and dingiest kitchen. . . .

To the wives and mothers the IWW ideal could be presented from many angles. A happier, more wholesome family life, conditional on economic security for the breadwinner, certainly appeals. The abolition of child labor and of the toil of mothers who must neglect their babies to feed them should gladden every mother's heart that feels "the child's sob in the silent curses deeper than the strong man in his wrath." The home of the future will eliminate the odd jobs that reduce it to a cluttered workshop today and electricity free the woman's hand from methods entirely antiquated in an era of machinery. There is no great credit attached to making a pie like mother used to make when a machine tended by five unskilled workers turns out 42,000 perfect pies a day! Cook stoves, washboards, and hand irons are doomed to follow the spinning wheel, candles, and butter churns, into the museums, and few tears will be shed at their demise. Catherine Alsopp, a washerwoman, committed suicide in London eleven years ago and left the following poem written on a sugar bag, a fitting epitaph for woman's labor:

> Here lies a poor woman, who always was tired;
> She lived in a house where help was not hired.
> Her last words on earth were, "Dear friends, I am going
> Where washing ain't done, nor sweeping, nor sewing;
> But everything there is exact to my wishes,
> For where they don't eat there's no washing of dishes.
> I'll be where loud anthems will always be ringing,
> But, having no voice, I'll be clear of the singing.
> Don't mourn for me now; don't mourn for me ever,
> I'm going to do nothing for ever and ever.

Birth control propaganda opens up another avenue of assault on the system, and women readers will agree upon its vital importance. Masculine opposition is theoretical, not practical, since few can understand the hopeless, hapless lot of involuntary maternity, which bequeaths a heritage of submissive despair to the offspring. Recently I met the wife of a miner, mother of six, the oldest eight, the youngest a nursing baby. She was suffering from general debility due to excessive childbearing and when I said, "I hope you'll feel better," she said scornfully, "I hope I die soon!" Certainly there would be more rebellion in our people if this crushing burden were lifted from women. I am besieged by pleas for information on the subject and know the desperate chances women take with their lives under our puritanical laws, yet it is amazing how few members bring their wives when the subject is selected by a local. Our men should realize that the large family system rivets the chains of slavery upon labor more securely. It crushes the parents, starves the children, and provides cheap fodder for machines and cannons.

If women are to be active, however, their ability should not be disparaged. I know a local where members forbid their wives speaking to an IWW woman "because they get queer ideas!" I heard a member forbid his wife, who had worked nine hours in a mill, from coming to the meeting "because she'd do better to clean the house." When I suggested an able woman as secretary of a local, several men said, "Oh, that's a man's job! She couldn't throw a drunk out!" With lots of husky men around to attend to such unpleasantries, a good secretary need hardly be a Jesse Willard.[1] The secretary of the Italian Syndicate of Agricultural Workers (their AWO) is a woman of twenty-five, Maria Rugiery. It has 35,000 members, laborers in the vineyards, olive, fruit and mulberry groves, and in the fields. She was imprisoned in 1912 and led a strike of 12,000 marble cutters in 1914. In recent large struggles women have fought bravely.

SOURCE: *Solidarity*, July 15, 1916, microfilm, Tamiment.

[1] Flynn means Frances Willard, leader of the Women's Christian Temperance Union and a socialist and feminist.

Sons, Lovers, and Mothers

Carlo Tresca, 1934 (left) and Fred Flynn, 1938 (right)

Letter to Mary Heaton Vorse (1926)

THIS *intense letter to Mary Heaton Vorse reveals some of the personal and political tensions in Flynn's life in the late 1920s. It was written after she returned from the Chicago Convention of the International Labor Defense League (ILD), a united front organization formed in 1925 to defend the Left, labor, blacks, and women from the growing right-wing onslaught. In Chicago Flynn was elected chairman of the ILD, a job for which she was qualified, having been secretary of the Workers Defense Union, a similar group, for seven years (1918–1925).*[1]

During the ILD convention, Flynn talked to Charles Ruthenberg, then secretary of the Workers party (WP), about the possibility of her joining the Communist party. He did not give her an immediate answer, and, as a crafty administrator, he felt she could be of more use outside the Party orbit. At this time the Communist party was a small sect torn apart by factions. Ruthenberg's major opponents were William Foster, whom Flynn knew from the free speech movement in Seattle, and James Cannon, whom Flynn called Johnny in this letter. Their faction was called the United Communist party. Cannon had been a Wobbly with a trade union background. In 1928 he was expelled from the Communist party for Trotskyite tendencies and founded the Trotskyist movement in the United States. Alfred Wagenknecht, whom Flynn called Wag, was the national secretary of yet another faction of the Party, the Communist Labor

---

[1]Starting in 1925 Flynn was secretary of the American Fund for Public Services (AFPS), an organization made possible by a donation of a million dollars from Charles Garland, the gift conditional on rapidly spending the whole amount. Flynn said, "I felt like a year round Santa Claus and was appalled at the number of people who deliberately cultivated my friendship." The AFPS financed *The Masses* magazine, the *Daily Worker*, and made large contributions to the Sacco and Vanzetti case, the Sleeping Car Porters Union, and the Passaic strike. By early 1930 the funds were depleted. Flynn Papers, Tamiment. This information came from the manuscript for the second half of Flynn's autobiography.

party. This faction was more humane, friendly, and accessible to American radicals; John Reed was a member of this group.[2]

The Passaic strike is another major topic of Flynn's letter. Passaic, New Jersey, was the biggest woolen worsted center in the United States; half the woolen workers there were women. In October 1926 the mills cut the workers already low wages by 10 percent. The unskilled workers struck, resulting in a bitter and bloody strike that lasted nine months. Police and deputy sheriffs attacked strikers with clubs, fire hoses, tear gas, and guns; injunctions were issued, picket lines broken, and union halls closed. Nearly one thousand were arrested.

The only union in Passaic was the United Textile Workers (UTW), an AFL skilled craft union whose president, Thomas MacMahon, was against the strike. All the factions of the Communist party were ambivalent about the strike, since supporting it meant defying AFL strategy and fostering dual unionism. In spite of this equivocation, the Party dispatched Albert Weisbord, an ambitious and energetic Harvard law school graduate, to organize the strikers. Weisbord was highly successful, and the strike gained momentum and publicity, so the Party sent several other young organizers to Passaic: Smith (her real name was Vera Buch), a recent Hunter graduate and soon to marry Weisbord; Lena Chernenko from the Amalgamated Clothing Workers; Coco, an Italian with anarchist connections; George Ashkenudze, a member of the Russian Federation; and Bob or Robert Minor a cartoonist and later secretary of the Communist party and Mary Heaton Vorse's lover. They were tireless workers and were far more effective and became far more involved in the strike than the Party intended them to.

A United Front Textile Committee of liberal sympathizers was also set in motion. Flynn and Vorse were central to this committee. Flynn raised money for the strike by speaking as well as organizing the women and children, whom she provided with sandwiches and milk every day; the Bakers Union donated the bread. However, policy was decided by the Communist party without consulting the organizers or the strikers. After seven months of hard-fought battles, the Party leadership decided that the mill owners would never agree to negotiation unless the AFL's United Textile Workers took over. After much haggling back and forth, the UTW agreed to represent the strikers, but only if the Party leaders and particularly Weisbord left Passaic. Flynn's status was unclear, but after some mediation she agreed to leave as well. However, the bosses still refused to deal with the UTW, so the strike limped along with minimum leadership. After two more months the wage cuts were restored, but no workers organization was established. The UTW never put any energy or funds into Passaic.

Flynn thought the Party was wrong to retreat. She devoted six hard months

[2]Irving Howe and Lewis Coser, *The American Communist Party: A Critical History* (New York: Praeger, 1957); and Theodore Draper, *The Roots of American Communism* (New York: Viking Press, 1957).

to keeping the strike going, working nonstop. Then, without being consulted, she was moved out. This withdrawal was a betrayal of the workers, organizers, and supporters. Politically, Flynn was wasted and undermined, which undoubtedly contributed to her moral, mental, and physical breakdown in 1926.

The Passaic strike was the first time the Communist party led a mass industrial strike, and they learned a great deal. Because the Party was divided and unclear, its task was difficult. The year 1926 was a bad one for labor and the Left; a clear victory would have been a near miracle even under ideal leadership. In spite of defeat, the strike "demonstrated what massive labor support the party could build up through its subsidiary organizations for defense and relief."³ The Passaic strike is important in that it marked the beginning of an epoch of organizing unskilled workers, culminating a decade later in the formation of the Congress of Industrial Organization (CIO). This important strike is seldom highlighted in labor history books, probably because the strikers were predominantly female and the Communist party led the strike.

Sept. 11, 1926

Dear Mary,

I had intended to write to you as soon as I got a breathing space, but the last few days were extremely hectic and I've had all sorts of trouble.

The convention in Chicago was excellent. I was elected Nat'l Chairman of the International Labor Defense for the coming year. It was very representative as far as localities went, but too much WP [Workers party] as yet. However, all are determined to change that.

I had lunch with Ruthenberg and Lovestone; Albert tried to be included, I understand, but they turned him down. We made the necessary arrangements in line with your suggestions for my future relationships. They were both very nice and made me feel that they appreciated my attitude and myself, which warmed my heart a bit after the large doses of being stepped all over I have received lately. It is all strictly confidential.

After arriving back we went directly to the Workers Party office and met the textile committee. The ranks are still firm and the foreign language organizers are still there. But today's parade marks the turning point with the people, I fear, and the UTW will have to move fast for settlement.

My status was still undetermined. George and Coco still were

³Vera Buch Weisbord, *A Radical Life* (Bloomington: Indiana University Press, 1977), 135. Buch's interpretation of Weisbord's behavior is quite different than Flynn's.

blithely insisting that as long as Bob could go there I surely could. But Johnny was less certain. Wag insisted it be settled one way or the other, so he was authorized to ask MacMahon definitely so there could be no charge of breach of faith. This was done and the answer was that as long as I stayed the mill owners considered the change in leadership a mere form and it was the same as if Weisbord remained, so he [MacMahon] recommended to me not to go any more for the sake of the settlement. It was agreed I was to go last night to tell them about the ILD, which I did, but it was very painful to me and I'm glad the agony is over with at last and I know now I am out.

The people were lovely—but Wag and the organizers were wonderful, Mary. I wish you could have been there. They gave me a beautiful little watch and had a little dinner with wine. Afterwards at which everyone from the whole staff was present—except Smith and Weisbord. He left yesterday altho he knew this was arranged. She was there but did not come. But they [the organizers] all came with me to the ferry, and Lena told me and I felt she spoke for all, that except for the principle involved they were not sorry Weisbord left—but they loved me and hated to see me go. I was deeply touched. It helps to heal my wounds. But the life and heart is out of everything, and everyone from outside is waiting for the end to leave as soon as they can too and the poor people to get to work. The mothers are harassed because they need shoes and clothes for the children to go to school. The strike is dead Mary. The sooner it can be ended with as much dignity and honor, the better. I couldn't bear to go there any more and I am greatly relieved that MacMahon spared me the agony.

Albert on the other hand stepped out as easily as if it never existed. He enjoyed it very much in Chicago and entered into all the discussions with the greatest zest. He thought the invitation to him to come there and the election on the Natl' Committee were *orders* from the Party. He did not know I suggested both to Cannon, and nobody else thought of it at all. I am quite in despair about him. He gets worse, not better.

Everything went to smash between us as a result of our discussion on the train on the way back. It started over an invitation I received from Cannon and a group of IWW friends to a party. They didn't ask him and didn't want him. In fact from the time we arrived in Chicago I completely overshadowed him which made him very peeved. He resented that I went to a party without him and without even asking him. Naturally that attitude led to a discussion of the whole situation. You were quite right Mary, he never told Smith he had come to my place six or seven times and he didn't think it was necessary unless he intended to break with her which he apparently doesn't want to do. He even sent her a telegram, so she met us at the train when we arrived. Naturally I was furious and humiliated. He was so possessive and jealous in Chicago that I thought well at least he will come to a parting of the ways with Smith, but he had no such intention. After the meeting of the textile Committee (during which he had passed me a note to say he couldn't come with me), he asked me aside to talk with me a moment and said, "I suppose you think I am very cruel." I said, "I don't care to discuss the matter any further," and left. I haven't seen or heard from him since. But I understand he left Passaic yesterday and went to the camp in the Adirondacks, and she is trying to get permission to go on a vacation and join him there. I told him I would not stand for such a triangular situation, that I had suffered too much from a similar one. I am sorry I told him as much as I did now. But I thought he loved me and would really understand. I told him he had to make a choice—it was up to him. Obviously he did so—or lacks the courage to do so—I don't know which. But I am terribly hurt, Mary dear. Life surely pummels me pretty badly. I really do love him a lot, yet I see all his faults and realize he probably will never love anyone but himself. Lena tells me the way he insults and abuses Smith is scandalous—but no self-respecting woman would stand it. I can't understand it exactly, because he is so lovely and gentle with me, really the sweetest and most satisfying lover one could have. But it is just as well to have it come to a head now and settled than to drag on the other way, which was really too ghastly. He may calm down and think things out during these few weeks' vacation. But he has insulted me so grossly and seems so unconscious of it, that I don't know if I could forgive him. My pride, my self-respect, were violated.

I reproach myself for permitting myself to become involved to such an extent, especially emotionally. That's where he catches me.

My trip is postponed until after election. But it promises to be a great success. He is going under the auspices of the WP and I fear again I will take the cream and he'll be sore about it. But I can't help my standing in the movement—across the country, can I? He just begins to realize it.

After the Friends meeting on the 22nd I will try to take the much-needed rest. Carlo still wants me to go with him. I really am thinking about it. He's an old dear and to tell him my troubles and weep on his shoulder doesn't seem to bother him and helps me alot. It's a funny situation or else I'm a bit off myself.

I miss you so much, Mary dear. You are my only real friend, the only person I can talk to freely and who really knows me. Do take good care of yourself now. We must both recuperate from Passaic. Other, better fights are ahead.

> With best love, as ever,
> Affectionately,
> Elizabeth

P.S. Write me at home. They often open letters here even if marked personal.

SOURCE: Mary Heaton Vorse Papers, Labor Archives, Wayne State University. I thank Dee Garrison for bringing it to my attention and Dione Miles, librarian and scholar of IWW, for xeroxing it.

Love Poems

FLYNN'S *poetry and letters provide entry into her private, more emotional side. As one of the great American orators and columnists, her public persona was that of a hard-hitting agitator. Her autobiography gives no clue to the depths of her emotional life.*

As a younger woman, most of Flynn's love affairs were with older IWW men, such as Vincent St. John, Joe Ettor, and Arturo Giovannitti, who were unmarried and delighted to have the companionship and the sex. Most of these affairs appear to have been positive and satisfying experiences for Flynn. As an older woman, most of her love adventures were unsatisfying and disquieting. Most were triangles—the men being married and Flynn being disposable. Most of these men tended to be considerably younger than Flynn, but then she was somewhat older than most of her comrades. She was attracted to men who reminded her of her son—large, well-built, masculine types who were neither puritanical nor adverse to drinking and having a good time.

Throughout the 1940s Flynn was in love with a young, rather volatile fireman named Jimmy. As a member of the Party, Jimmy was asked to raise radical issues within the fire department but not to reveal himself as a Communist. Eventually, unable to conceal anything, Jimmy was fired for being a Communist. Party officials disliked Jimmy and felt he was an inappropriate escort for Flynn.[1] The two remained in touch, however, until the 1960s.

Flynn wrote poems about and had romantic friendships with many Communist party officials, including Steve Nelson, Gene Dennis, John Gates, Gran-

---

[1] During our interviews, Peter Martin referred to him. He is also referred to in several letters Kathie wrote to Elizabeth in Alderson.

*ville Hicks, Murray Newberry (a party organizer in Newberry, New York), Art
Young, Eddy Barsky, Al Richmond, Hank Forbes, who was killed in World
War II and gave Flynn his Purple Heart, and John Rossen, a flier killed in
World War II. She hungered for a profound emotional involvement and felt
empty and alone without one, but because she would not settle for a traditional,
subservient marriage or affair, she often did without love or sex.*

*Most of Flynn's love poems were written to Carlo Tresca, with whom she had
her longest, most profound relationship. In this collection, "Pittsburgh" and
"Communist Love Poem" were written to Martin, a Party organizer in Pennsylvania.*[2]

TO CARLO, SOUTH BEACH (AFTER 14 YEARS), 1925–1939

I am alone and being alone am brave!
Gone are the nights of lonely waiting and of tears, of anxious
    worry and a comrade's tears,
To him who did not come, so long ago.

The same tide beats against the waiting sands,
The same moon glides from Coney's lurid crown,
Red Mars nearer yet far, shines peaceful down,
My heart is free—tonite I do not care!

Saint[3] who is dead ten years, lives on for me
Real as the moon, the tide, the great Red star,
Carlo you who still live and move are dead to me,
Died in my heart, died in my faith as well.

I do not miss the kisses or the tears
Only the faith, that died so slow and hard!

(1939)

NOV. 1939

Last month I burned with the sharp hurt of anger
Today I have a dull groping at the bottom of my mind

[2] Possibly his name was Martin Young and he was Jewish; Flynn wrote another
poem to him on Saint Patrick's Day, which is dedicated "to my Jewish friend in
Pittsburgh." Their affair seems to have lasted from the summer of 1938 through
fall 1939. All Flynn's poems are in a loose-leaf notebook in the Flynn Papers,
Tamiment.
[3] Vincent St. John, a leader of the IWW, whom Flynn admired and loved.

Gnawing unceasingly but distantly at my consciousness,
Where is he? How is he? How does he feel towards me?

We know each other better than others do,
Because we are alike—too much alike,
Inside of love, of gentleness, of comradeship
There burns a white-hard core of steel
Which sets us far apart—able to go on alone
Apart from others and alone within ourselves.

How well I know the anodyne of time
That which hurts like a toothache last month recedes,
My mind fills imperceptibly with my work.
I lock my heart against you—throw away the key,
I cannot spend my mind or strength on you or anyone
Everyone has to learn to stand on their own soul's feet—
Alone and unafraid!

To C—

How strange it seems that you are dead
Who were so long the other half of me.
How long it's been that you were dead to me
And now you're dead—you are alive again.
Days, months, have passed without a thought of you
So well I steeled and disciplined my heart,
Pulled out the bleeding roots of love and went far off
Till time had healed and seared the aching wounds.
So when I saw you, you were not yourself to me
Only an old weary disillusioned shadow of the man I knew,
With but a far off glimpse of a glorious past,
Like fading somber echoes of a sun long set.
But deep within the memories long suppressed
Are stored the riches of our young rebellious love,
I saw a melancholy light within your eyes—
As you stood in the doorway the last time we met
And smiling waved goodbye—shortly before you died
Last night I stood upon the pavement where you died
The merciful rain, like tears soft shed
Had washed away your blood—shed by a fascist assassin
In the dimmed out night of war.[4]

[4]Carlo Tresca was assassinated on Jan. 11, 1943.

A COMMUNIST LOVE POEM

To _____

Won't you unlock your warm and tender lips whose kisses are so sweet?

To say some words of love, once in a while?
Why must you be so mute?
Is it a language strange and feared to you, who have no fear?
Have you not heard its nuances and flow?
Why won't you try it now?

Why must love masquerade as servant to a casual need?

Why try to stifle it newborn, in friendship's groove?
Dear comrade, stay a little while with me,
Fold up your tireless wings and light within my arms,
Shut out the world of struggle and of pain,
We will be stronger to return again.

           (August 3, 1939)

PITTSBURGH

I try to keep my dual minds apart,
The mind of reason and the mind of heart,
In parallel grooves, separate and isolate,
Not to disrupt the pattern of my days,
Not to be torn again by gaping wounds,
Not to be anguished by a feverish longing for a most beloved,
Not to possess and therefore not to lose,
Not be possessed and once again be lost,

But taken unawares, how swift I failed,
Furthermost thought upon my reasoning mind,
As if while walking by a deep blue sea,
Hand in hand, with a quietly beloved friend,
Happy and calm, no thought of danger there,
Suddenly he grasped my hand and pulled me far ashore,
Into the warm salt waves, pleasant and oh so sweet,
Stunned and surprised—I ask, "How now return to land?"

Or do I want to go? Love is so strange to me.

           (Summer 1939)

The beauty of love [5]
the duty of love
the tenderness of love
the sadness of love
the joy of love
the pain of love
the oneness of love
the hate of love
the love of love.

Going away from those you love
You are lonely the train rushes,
So fast—the distances become so great
Coming toward then it crawls.

All my life I've had this experience
Always leaving loved ones to go on my appointed journeys.

I lock my heart against you—throw away the key,
I cannot spend my mind or strength on you or anyone
Everyone has to learn to stand on their own soul's feet—
Alone and unafraid.

                                              (November 1939)

SOURCES: All poems from the Flynn Papers, Tamiment.

[5] Untitled poem.

Letters to Mary Heaton Vorse and Agnes Inglis

THESE three letters were written between 1929 and 1936 to Mary Heaton Vorse, Flynn's closest friend, and to Agnes Inglis, an old Wobbly pal. During this period Vorse was anxiously writing as much as she could in order to support herself and her three children, her first two husbands having died. Inglis was in the process of assembling the IWW, anarchist, radical, and feminist papers at the Labadie Library at the University of Michigan, working to save the IWW heritage that the U.S. government had attempted to destroy by raiding IWW offices, burning their literature, and incarcerating their members. In fact, Inglis was singlehandedly responsible for preserving the Wobblies' memory and starting the IWW collection.[1]

These letters were written when Flynn was ailing in Oregon and living with Dr. Marie Equi. Equi was a devoted doctor who spent long hours on horseback, visiting poor patients. In 1915 Equi and her wealthy lover, Harriet Speckart, adopted a child, Mary, Jr. Equi claimed the child belonged to the murdered martyr of the Centralia Massacre, Wesley Everest. Equi was jailed in 1920 for antiwar activities; in 1921 her sentence was commuted and she returned to Portland and her practice. Meanwhile, Speckart, who was never political, had become estranged from Equi during her long trial and moved to Seaside, on the Oregon coast, with Mary, Jr. In 1927 Speckart died of a brain tumor and Mary, Jr., came to live with Equi. However, the two never got along; some said Equi was actually violent with the child. As Equi had no time or patience for Mary, Jr., the child went to live with Anita Whitney, a friend and one of the founding members of the Communist party, in San Francisco.

In 1930 Equi had a heart attack, which left her bedridden for the rest of her life. Flynn blamed the heart attack on the miserable conditions Equi had endured at San Quentin prison and on overwork. Believing Marie Equi was about to die, Flynn sent for the child. While Mary, Jr., was there, Flynn became quite attached to her. In fact she said she stayed in Portland far longer than she might have because of the child. In caring for Mary, Jr., Flynn was perhaps compensating for her estrangement from Fred, her own son, who refused even to communicate with her at this point.[2]

Elizabeth finally left Portland when her brother Tom committed suicide.

Portland, Oregon
March 22, 1929

Dear Mary—

I owe you a most humble and heartfelt apology for not writing sooner. But whether it was a by-product of my long illness or pure laziness, I have the hardest time forcing myself to write letters. I got

---

[1]Much of my information on Vorse (1874–1966) came from Dee Garrison, who has edited a collection of her work, *Rebel Pen* (New York: Monthly Review Press, 1986), and is writing a biography of her as well. Most of my information on Inglis (1870–1952) came from Dione Miles, an archivist at Wayne State Labor Archives, who is writing a biography of her.

[2]Most of my information about Marie Equi came from Nancy Krieger, "Queen of the Bolsheviks: The Hidden History of Dr. Marie Equi," *Radical America*, Jan. 1984, and interviews with Peter Martin and Roberta Bobba.

so bad that actually I only wrote to Mother and Fred for about six months, and that was an effort. At the time I received your last letter I was so uncertain of my plans and so rushed because the Dr. was sick in bed with flu—pneumonia—that I laid it aside, intending to reply shortly. She was so very ill just before X'mas that I was compelled to telephone to Miss Whitney to bring her little girl up at once from California,[3] and we really feared she wouldn't last till the child reached here. I had tentatively planned then to go to Cal. but she decided to have Mary Jr. remain here, so the reason to go was nonexistent.

Tho I have also been a great deal disturbed about Buster. He is a good enough boy from all conventional standards—doesn't drink, smoke, run around with girls etc. I guess he's a reaction from my own wild youth. But my family, as usual, decides what to do—my Father and Mother are too old to quarrel with—but the others should know better. However, they sent him off to the University of Michigan—tho where they expect to get the necessary funds to see him through is beyond me. And they do not seem to realize the importance of him getting a job and helping to pay his own way through. So I've been quite upset by it all. But I suppose eventually it will work out alright. Buster will never be a radical, I fear. He heard too much of it when he was a child and it has no novelty or interest for him. What he heard was mostly criticism, unfortunately, which is destructive of enthusiasm.

But lately, I have begun to feel like myself again. Suddenly, with the coming of Spring, which is very beautiful out here, I felt better. Of course the heart specialists told me two years ago that it would take that long to get the streptococcus infection out of the blood stream, and I simply had to be patient. But I am glad to say I have spoken at two meetings, one in Seattle for the Centralia IWW men and one here for Mooney and Centralia, and did not feel any the worse for it except a little tired.[4] But of course I'll have to take it easy at first and not

---

[3] Anita Whitney, one of the founding members of the Communist party, graduated from Wellesley and went to work at University Settlement in New York City. Later she moved to San Francisco and worked as a social worker. She fought for juvenile courts and became the first probation officer in California. She was also a militant feminist and a vice president of the American Equal Suffrage Association. During World War I she was indicted for "desecrating the flag."

[4] Tom Mooney was an old friend of Flynn's; she had met him in 1910 in Seattle and devoted many months of her life to his defense. He was a member of the IWW and organized streetcar workers in San Francisco. Mooney and Warren Billings were falsely convicted and sent to prison for throwing a bomb that killed many people during a 1916 Preparedness Parade. The Communist party adopted their cause, and finally the governor of California freed Mooney in 1939.

In Centralia the IWW was engaged in a bitter battle to organize lumberjacks, migrant timber cutters in the northwestern forests. The lumber employers who ran the area were determined to stop the IWW organizing drives. IWW halls were

overdo it. And I can never go at the pace I used to—that's certain. I guess it won't delay the revolution any either.

How are you Mary dear? I read a story of yours about the youngster coming home from Europe and was so glad to see that you are writing again. I would be glad to hear from you and to know how you are and what you are doing. I hope you are well and happy. How are your children? Hope you are doing your own work again and conserving your energy.

> With all good wishes and love to you, as ever,
> Your affectionate friend,
> Elizabeth

SOURCE: Mary Heaton Vorse Papers, Labor Archives, Wayne State University.

July 11, 1934

Dear Agnes—

I was certainly delighted to hear from you. I had heard from Lena Morrow Lewis that she had a pleasant visit with you and she was delighted with your work.[5] I had often thought of you and planned to write to you—but Dr. has been very ill and that has kept me very busy.

You ask what I look like today. Well, I am older of course, lots of grey hairs now and *too* stout, probably from a rather inactive, indoor life. Not active at all, at present, though always hoping to be.

My sister is married to Romolo Bobba; they have three children and live in Miami, Arizona.[6] The girls are four and six and the boy is

---

raided, Wobblies were beaten, and newspaper stands selling IWW newspapers were destroyed in mob actions. From 1918 to 1919 a reign of terror existed. Wesley Everest, an IWW member and World War I veteran, was castrated, lynched, and hung. His swinging body was then used for target practice. In a shoot-out on Armistice Day 1919, Everest had shot a man when a Wobbly hall was raided by Legionnaires. The murderers of Wesley Everest, well known to the citizens of Centralia, were never brought to trial. Some Wobblies felt the organization should have gone underground, rather than face the mob and continue to function openly.

[5]Lena Morrow Lewis was the most prominent woman in the Socialist party and the first woman on the National Executive Committee. She ran for Congress in Alaska, having gone there after her divorce and a scandal in which she was accused of having an affair with a well-known free love advocate.

[6]Her sister is Bina, the youngest, with whom Elizabeth was finally reconciled on this trip to Arizona. Bina was so miserable in Arizona that soon after this letter was written she took off for San Francisco with her children. Romolo followed shortly.

eleven. They have had a hard struggle down there; he has been active in the Federal union and in the efforts to wrest a good copper code for the workers of that district. I went down to visit them last summer for a few weeks—it is an arid, hot district and my sister pines for the east.

Fred finally quit college and went home to N.Y.C. I never had a satisfactory talk with him by mail and so [have] postponed all discussion until I get home. Meanwhile he is on the trail of the illusive job. He is a good boy—slow and pedantic—but eventually he'll find himself, I'm sure. Anyhow I've stopped worrying, since I can do nothing much to help him, long distance.

I was certainly interested to hear of Alice Baker—and will gladly write to her. It is good to know she is happily married—when I knew her she had an antique shop in N.Y.C. in partnership with Ruth Albert and they were both desperately hard up. She gave Fred a job but he was about fifteen and so awkward she was afraid he'd break too much. He was heartbroken but very fond of Alice. . . .

I remember hearing my mother speak of Victoria Woodhull.[7] Didn't she run for President?

C. E. S. Wood does not live here in Portland any longer. He is married to Sara Bard Field and they live at Los Gatos, Calif.[8] He has the reputation here of being very egotistical. Several very fine women killed themselves over him, it appears—and he made his money (plenty of it) in land frauds. Maybe it is the case of "prophet without honor in his own country." His daughter, Mrs. Honeyman, is a Democratic politician—especially active for the liquor interests. Women here who know them say that Sara wrote the best parts of the "Poet in the Desert." Well now that's all the gossip I know about C.E.S.

I think the IWW boys did their best in the Centralia case. They never attacked Becker no matter what he said—they took into consideration his state of mind, induced by long imprisonment. Those internal disputes are heartbreaking. Elmer Smith, the lawyer who was disbarred, worked until he died.[9] I went to see him here in a local hospital, where he was operated on twice for cancer of the stomach. He did all in his power for the Centralia boys—died poor, heavily in debt,

---

[7]Victoria Woodhull (1838–1927) was a controversial feminist, free lover, and the first female Wall Street stockbroker, who ran for president in 1872. Her journal, *Woodhull and Claflin's Weekly*, was the first to publish the *Communist Manifesto* in English.

[8]C. E. S. Wood is Charles Erskine Scott Wood, a poet and lawyer who took many IWW cases. Sara Bard Field was a good friend of the journalist Louise Bryant and a Portland celebrity.

[9]Elmer Smith was the IWW lawyer who advised his clients to "defend the hall if you choose to do so, the law gives you the right." For this remark he was charged with murder, and eventually acquitted.

suffered frightfully for years. No use for the new young fellows to criticize those old timers too much until they have gone through the mill themselves. . . .

Last summer Fred Moore died of cancer in Los Angeles—worked to death really.[10] Like Dr. here—she is worn out from overwork in the office and in the movement. No use for fresh, new young recruits to discount it all. Better to take it as a shining example of courage and faith. . . .

A friend of mine from east St. Louis sent me snap shots of E.G. [Emma Goldman]. She surely looked tired, but he said she had a lot of spirit left. Our physical strength goes, unfortunately. . . .

> Best regards—as ever,
> Affectionately,
> Elizabeth

SOURCE: Agnes Inglis Papers, University of Michigan Library. Special Collections.

Sept. 10, 1936

Dear Agnes—

I'm sure you must have wondered what happened to me. I seemed to get marooned out there in Oregon caring for Dr. Equi and her household. Her condition is chronic heart trouble but the time came when I felt I must return home. I am so out of touch with everything and everybody and feel quite at a loss.

But the immediate reason that brought me home is that my dear good brother Tom died suddenly in January. He was forty-two years old, had always lived at home, and it was a terrible shock to my Mother. She is quite old now, of course, about seventy-seven, and very frail and weak, so I am glad to be home with her and able to do for her for a while at least. I fervently hope I will be able to keep her alive a few years more. Her mind is alert and active and she is very gentle and kind—a joy to all around her.

In going over an accumulation of papers etc. here, I found the enclosed material which you sent me at one time and I am now returning for your files. I plan to go through all my material (not much, as unfortunately I never paid enough attention to keeping papers etc.)

[10] Fred Moore was Flynn's lawyer in Spokane and during her World War I espionage trial, as well as the lawyer for the Lawrence strike and the Sacco and Vanzetti case. Flynn's brief husband, Jack Jones, was terribly jealous of him and believed the two were having an affair, which they might have had.

but such as it is. I may find some that you can use and if so will forward it to you. If I ever get to writing anything, which seems a forlorn
hope at present, the material is safer with you and I can have access
to it there. By the way I have a collection of buttons—going back to
Haywood, the McNamaras, Ettor and Giovannitti etc.[11] Would you like
to have it there? If not, it's alright. I could give it to some defense committee to use as a display, I suppose, or to raffle off. But it could be
better kept somewhere for reference—like in your library. Here it's
just packed away in a box—and they are interesting. . . .

My son is employed in Washington at present. We hit it off alright
now. There was too much interference when I was in Portland and he
stopped writing to me, to my great sorrow. But we are alright now, I
am happy to say. . . .

> Your affectionate friend,
> Elizabeth

SOURCE: Agnes Inglis Papers, University of Michigan Library Special
Collections.

Thoughts about Fred (1944)

*"THOUGHTS about Fred" is a meditation, written four years after his tragic
death. In the piece, Flynn referred to the IWO, the International Workers*

[11]The McNamaras were brothers accused of blowing up the antiunion *Los Angeles Times* in 1910; twenty-one union workers were killed. Some IWW members
claimed the explosion was an accident rather than planned sabotage. The brothers
were sentenced to life in prison. Clarence Darrow was their lawyer, and the case
was a cause célèbre in the Left community.

Joe Ettor and Arturo Giovannitti were Italian organizers who were jailed early
in the Lawrence strike. They were accused of causing the death of striker Anna La
Pizza because they had called for picketing in their speeches. After many mass
meetings, marches, and a threatened general strike, they were freed.

Order, a fraternal left-wing benefit society where she found Fred some poorly paid, progressive work. Flynn also alluded to Fred's problems with red-baiting in the American Labor party (ALP), a third-party coalition of liberals, and labor and ethnic minorities, originally founded in 1936 to assure Roosevelt's victory, which Fred joined with his mother's encouragement. The ALP functioned as a party and an independent pressure influencing the selection of candidates and policies by major parties. Fred, who was never a Communist party member, joined the Bronx branch, which was anticommunist.

This was the period of the Hitler-Stalin Pact, and the majority of the ALP delegates sought to remove communists and sympathizers from their clubs. In 1939 a resolution was passed condemning the Nazi-Soviet pact as a "treacherous blow to world civilization" and backing Roosevelt's neutrality. No one seeking political office could receive ALP backing without accepting its anti-Soviet resolution. Mike Quill, head of the Transit Workers Union and up for reelection on the city council, refused to sign the ALP foreign policy statement and lost ALP endorsement and the election.

In early 1940 the Soviet Union invaded Finland, and again the ALP voted to condemn the Soviet Union for its "unprovoked aggression" and called on the United States to send aid to the Finnish people.[1] Fred Flynn was running as an ALP convention delegate in the Bronx and was denied ALP endorsement when he refused to back their resolution on Finland. Finally Flynn could take pride in her politically correct son. Unmercifully, Fred died of cancer just as he was becoming a source of joy and companionship to his mother.

THE wind howls mournfully and mercilessly, and I think of my dear son, gone from me now for four years. How long each hour, each day, each year—yet my grief is yesterday, today, tomorrow, fresh bleeding like a new-made wound, to which each anniversary applies the salt of my despairing grief. I cannot weep, I cannot moan or cry aloud my sorrow and despair. His voice would say to me in memory: "Snap out of it, Mum!" As if he had but now passed through the door I see his dear face, his curly hair, his deep blue eyes, his kind smile. I hear his voice, his laugh, his jokes, his serious discussions, and his songs. Sometimes it all is more than I can bear—I am so lonely and I miss him so. He was my son, my comrade, and my friend. I feel deep sympathy now for mothers in wartime, who must part with sons; whose nights are anguished with uncertainty and whose days are dimmed with anxiety and fear. But yet how proud they are of their brave boys—how happy in their visits and their letters. How strong the hope of their safe return wells up in their mothers' hearts. For me

[1] Kenneth Waltzer, "The American Labor Party: Third Party Politics in the New Deal and Cold War in New York, 1936–54," Ph.D. diss., Dept. of History, Harvard University, 223–240.

as for all other mothers whose sons have died, all this is done. Maybe some have the consolation that there is life beyond the grave and they will see their sons again. I would not take it from them, though I cannot share; my dear son's cool, detached, and scientific mind would scorn such subterfuge from grief for me his mother. I must go on alone, no matter how long or short the road. Death is the end of the beautiful body of youth and the proud clear mind. I cannot believe otherwise, much as I would long to believe that once again I'd look upon his face. I'd give my life gladly for but a moment with my boy again! It cannot ever be.

. . . My son, within whose chest was death, climbed many a weary stairs to win the ALP primaries for the progressives just four short years ago this spring. He came home drenched with sweat, exhausted, falling into a heavy sleep that soon would never end. He left all in good order to pass on to his successor in the work. Today I read of victory of the unity forces against the Soviet haters who expelled him from the club he helped to build because he refused to vote for their vile resolution of attack upon the workers' land. Next day while he was still asleep, their charges, special delivery, were at the door. As he lay gasping out his last breath they attacked him, men he had helped to elect, because he was my son, calling him tool and stooge. They tried to take the votes for his name off the ballot after he had died. The hardest thing I ever did or ever will was vote for my dear son, who was no more. He would have relished the victory today he fought for then. If he had been a member of my party he would have forthright said so. He never denied his principles. He was straightforward, honest, conscientious—never lied. I remember when a store keeper cheated him of change when he was a little boy and said he must have lost it, his childhood indignation. "Why mum he thinks I lied!" And his anger when he found a dog, fed it, and kept it over night, safe and warm, and the man asked stupidly, when he returned him, "Did you take my dog?" This was the fine, upstanding youth—intelligent, hard-working, affective—they fought because they could not control him. When a good old man, a "1905er," said, "Don't Flynn, don't vote No. We're going to elect you. You're going places," my son said "To hell with going places that way!" and walked out. Yes, he would have gone places—maybe to Italy, India, New Guinea. It was not to be. He would have gone places eventually—into our party too. I'm sure. He was deliberate and thought things over well. When he made up his mind the fury of the wildest tempest would not shake him. He was a fighter, cool and bold. He would have come all the way very soon, I know. When a comrade worker at the hospital smiled at him, Fred hardly conscious, whispered, "Mum, he's one of ours." When I told him of the peace the Soviet Union had made with Finland he shook his head, "not enough—she needs more!" he said. When the skunks decided to cut Mike Quill's picture off the campaign literature, Fred gathered it up in his big arms and took it home, distributing it at dawn the next day, before they were awake. He came in white with fury from a neighborhood store. "The damned Nazi!" he said. A Jewish boy had asked for cigarettes and the German owner had cursed him and told him to go to the Jew store. Fred threw his cigars on the counter and said, "I'll go there too." The surprised Nazi tool said, "What's the matter? You're not Jewish!" Fred retorted as he left, "No but I'm an American." Prejudice against Jews, Negroes—any people, made him sick with disgust. He fought for the rights of Negroes in athletics and sports when the IWO sent him as a delegate to the NYC Athletics Association. My pride and joy was great in those few short years, when, after college, he found himself and matured in the labor movement. . . .

All I can do now is to work harder, as I go on alone, to do my own appointed task, then more, yet more   to try to do in a small way what he would have done better as the years went on. The loneliness of the night hours, when we talked together after our separate day, is hardest to face and bear. The radio playing softly, the quiet house, a sandwich, glass of beer, and talk together. My ears are hungry for his voice, forever stilled, to hear him laugh, to see his dear kind eyes. But it is past.

SOURCE: Flynn Papers, Tamiment.

Every Day Should Be Mother's Day for Us (1941)

EVERY year Flynn wrote a column for the Worker *on Mother's Day, International Women's Day, May Day, and Saint Patrick's Day. Being female, Irish, and American-born, she was given these celebrations as her special assignments. Actually she had considerable freedom in the subject matter of her column, and with several to write a week she welcomed an occasional ritual. Al-*

though she was usually full of observations, sometimes she was at a loss and asked her readers for their suggestions.

Americans celebrated International Women's Day until the early 1920s, when the right wing became bothered by its radical implications. In alliance with the florists the Right concocted Mother's Day in an attempt to co-opt the militant International Women's Day, then observed by Socialists and Communists. The Right was successful to a large extent.

THE Philadelphia lady who first proposed Mother's Day meant well. Her suggestion was that everyone should wear a carnation on the second Sunday of May, in honor of their mother—a red carnation if she was living, a white carnation if she was dead.

Out of this modest gesture has grown a million-dollar business. Mother is the least and last beneficiary. The day has been seized upon by telegraph companies, florists, confectioners, and department stores for nationwide exploitation. The universal sentiment which surrounds motherhood is debased by their profane, pioneering hands. Signs are displayed for weeks, "Give Mother This—or That—or the Other!" Leftovers from Christmas are unloaded on dutiful, filial purchasers. Mother's Day becomes a money-making mockery. Real feeling for Mother is smothered in a sugary sentimentality which comes from the radio, drips from greeting cards, and makes of this day a sort of maternal Valentine's Day.

People who love their mothers don't need a special day to be reminded of it. What our mothers have done for us or mean to us should be in our hearts and minds at all times. The trouble is, we're apt to take Mother too much for granted, like the sun and the stars, day and night, she's always there. It's nice to remember your mother with an occasional gift—a few flowers, a pretty scarf, some handkerchiefs, a pair of stockings. But not just once a year, to do penance for indifference the rest of the time. Not just to make a Roman holiday for merchants. It's thoughtful to take your mother to a restaurant and to a show, so she won't have to cook. But not just once and leave her to the tiresome round of monotonous tasks the rest of the year. A good way to neutralize the crass commercializing of Mother's Day is to spread our attentions to Mother. Make every day Mother's Day. It is for her—she's always on duty.

All of the mothers who work in industry carry a double burden— their job and their own work at home. The thousands of domestic day workers who first clean somebody else's home must then do their own. The thousands who work in laundries go home to do their own washing. The thousands who work in hotels rush home to tidy up their own rooms. The thousands who work in restaurants go home to stand several more weary hours to prepare food for their own families.

They do not get equal pay for equal work in industry. Nor is there equalization at home where all domestic work is still "woman's work." Only the most progressive and intelligent men lend a hand at home to lighten this double burden capitalism places on working mothers. On Mother's Day, resolve to do this.

The ones who stay home to care for their children are neither useless nor idle. They handle the finances, do the buying and budgeting. They see the cost of living rise before the statisticians plot the curve. The methods used in the home are antiquated and individualistic. Mother is the last to get modern appliances for her work. On farms with cars and tractors, women will carry water from outdoors.

Mothers need union hours, modern methods of work, relief from worry; peace and security. With the threat of war manacling her, how can any mother enjoy this day under capitalism? Socialism is the way out for mothers when every day will be truly a mother's happy day. Mothers can only be happy when their children are safe and happy.

SOURCE: *Sunday Worker,* May 11, 1941.

International Women's Day (1944)

ON *March 8, 1936, the wives of auto workers at the Flint, Michigan, plant, marching in support of their husbands' strike, revived the celebration in the United States of International Women's Day. However, not until the women's liberation movement of the late 1960s rediscovered International Women's Day and celebrated it with building takeovers and marches did the holiday again become a custom. In this column Flynn reminded her readers of the day's international significance.*

I T is now thirty-six years since an annual holiday was chosen by American working women and mothers, of the East Side of New

York, to hold demonstrations for suffrage. Four years later the 19th Amendment to our Constitution was passed and ratified, extending the right to vote to American women citizens. By that time the date March 8 had been adopted by the international Socialist movement to signalize the universal political demands of women. The names of Clara Zetkin and the martyred Rosa Luxemburg of Germany; of Krupskaya, the wife of Lenin; of Dolores Ibarruri (Pasionaria) of Spain; of our own Mother Bloor and other great women leaders are linked in our memories with this day, and its celebrations over the years.

International Women's Day is identified with a great historical event, the start of the Russian Revolution in 1917, when 90,000 workers downed tools and demonstrated in Petrograd (now Leningrad).

> Women predominated in the crowd. They abandoned the bread lines where they had been standing for hours and joined the strikers. . . . Later, when the Tsar's troops were massed against the workers, they were found to be responsive to the appeals of the people. Workers, and especially working women, would form a close ring around the soldiers. They would seize the latter's bayonets with their hands and plead with the soldiers not to drown the revolution in the blood of their brothers, the workers. (*The History of the Civil War, U.S.S.R.*)

Later in Spain, on March 8, 1936, 80,000 women demonstrated at Madrid, led by Pasionaria, against the menace of fascism, and "for progress and liberty." Later that year, when the fascists started the war against the democratic Republic and the independence of Spain, the Spanish women fought side by side with their men under the courageous leadership of Pasionaria to defend their Republic against Hitler, Mussolini, and their "stooge" Franco. The prisons of fascist Spain are today overcrowded with men and women who are being tortured, starved, and murdered for their defense of their own country. The bloody Franco is still to be defeated. The struggle continues.

A moving description of women emerging from the most backward, medieval conditions into the light of a new world is given by Dr. Fannina Halle in her book *Women in the Soviet Far East,* which is quoted extensively by the Dean of Canterbury. On International Women's Day, 1927, the women poured out into the public squares of Central Asian cities like Samarkand, Bokara, and Tashkent. Determined to break with the past, they gathered around the Lenin statues, tore off the veils which covered their faces, and burned them. "The East was stirred to the depths of its being" at the "common abjuration of a thousand-year-old convention, now become unbearable," the author remarks. Even under new laws, it was not easy for women to free themselves. There were many martyrs, victims of prejudice and fear, in the early days. . . .

In *Battle Hymn of China* Agnes Smedley writes of March 8, 1939: "This was always celebrated throughout China as International Women's Day." In the South Yangtze Valley it was led by Mother Tsai, an old woman with sons in the army. She organized the Women's National Salvation Association. The women till the soil, make uniforms and shoes for the guerrilla fighters, care for the wounded. They ferret out merchants who deal with the enemy, and fight the evils of gambling and opium, fostered by the Japanese. A mass meeting was held in the great courtyard of an old ancestral temple. The front seats were reserved for women. Men leaders were invited to say only a few words of greetings. Posters called on the women to "revive the spirit of Florence Nightingale." In the morning the women carried gifts to the wounded. Mother Tsai always spoke of women's rights to the soldiers. The women organized classes in scouting and espionage. They are "the eyes and ears of the Army" to combat defeatism, uncover spies and traitors, boycott Japanese goods, etc. They question all strangers, and are alert to all dangers.

Behind the Japanese lines, in "guerrilla land," this devoted patriotic service to their country of millions of Chinese women continues today. The Chinese News Service reports of many women fighting in the army and of women in all auxiliary capacities. The "Dare to Die Corps" was a women's unit in Shanghai at the beginning of the war. Girl units of the Kwangsi Army fought in the battles to hold Hsuchow and Kunlunkwen. One brave girl, Miss Huang Chun-cher, doing publicity work, was trapped in a Japanese encircling movement. She took to the mountains and set up a radio station to report on enemy movements. The Japanese closed in on her, but before leaping from a precipice she killed many. Another Chinese guerrilla leader is a short, stout peasant woman named Wang, who helped decapitate six puppet officials and hanged their heads on the city gate. She collects information, acts huge fires, and is the heroine of a hundred battles.

Recently, Madam Sun Yat-sen made a heart-rending appeal on behalf of these guerrilla warriors in *China Today,* that medical supplies and other materials sent from America be distributed to them and asked American labor to support her demand so "that the men who fight fascism behind Japanese lines get a share of its efforts commensurate with the task they are doing." There must be no blockade of these brave guerrillas by reactionary forces. "American labor has a stake in China's democracy," she urged. This noble and devoted woman, widow of the founder of the Chinese Republic, pleads for the armed miners, and railroad workers, farmers, villagers, women and little children who fight behind the lines.

Louis Adamic in his book *Native Land* tells of the participation of women peasants and professionals in the valiant struggle of Tito and his guerrillas to expel the fascist invaders from Yugoslavia. The book is dedicated to a boy and a girl, medical students who gave their lives for their country and who symbolize millions of such heroic youth who fight for their countries against the fascist hordes.

SOURCE: *The Communist,* vol. 23, Mar. 1944. *The Communist* was the Communist party's theoretical journal; it is now called *Political Affairs.*

Foremothers

Mama, sister Kathie, and Elizabeth (left to right), 1910

Unionists in Poke Bonnets (1942)

As a foremother, Flynn took special pride in reminding male Daily Worker *readers and trade unionists of the important contributions made by women to the labor and socialist movements.*

I T would be excellent for the *men* who lead labor to take a little time out to read up on the history of women in the labor movement. It would help them today to organize women. All too many leaders of strong progressive unions have blind spots where this job is concerned. They are behind the time because they have not yet accepted as a finality the permanent role of women in the labor movement.

There is a consistent, continuous, and encouraging activity on the part of women workers in industry for the past 120 years. "Flare-ups and turn outs," the capitalist press derisively called the first strikes of women in the New England textile mills against wage cuts and lengthening of hours, but 102 women and girls in Pawtucket, R.I., made history in 1824. They were the first women to strike and to have a woman's labor meeting in America. The papers reported there "was little noise and scarcely a single speech."

In the next two decades women figured in strikes in Lowell, Mass., Paterson, N.J., Philadelphia, Dover, N.H., Taunton, Mass., New York City, Baltimore, Boston, and even as far "West" as Pittsburgh. An outstanding strike was in Lowell, Mass., in support of a discharged girl. Two thousand marched out of the mill and paraded through the town. They placarded the mill with rhymes of protest. One of the leaders used a pump for a platform, which the *Boston Transcript* described as having so "powerful an effect on her auditors that they determined to have their way if they died for it!"

Here in the "City of Spindles" the first union of women alone was organized in 1834, called the Factory Girls' Association. The word *union* had not yet come into general usage. The women's first attempts had very lady-like designations, such as Female Society of Lynn and Vicinity, for the Protection and Promotion of Female Industry, the Philadelphia Female Improvement Society, and the Daughters of St. Crispin (shoe workers). Finally in New York there came a Female Union Association in 1835.

In the pioneer industries which employed women—textile, needle trades, and shoe—they were particularly militant. It is inspiring to look back over the passage of a century of parades of women workers in hoop skirts, waving their poke bonnets and chanting: *"American ladies will never be slaves!"* And to Lynn, Mass., where nine hundred women stitchers struck in 1862, asserting their "need of protecting our rights and privileges as free born women and *our interests as working women.*"

The first state investigation of labor conditions occurred in Massachusetts. Sarah G. Bagley, president of the Lowell Association, appeared before the legislation committee in 1845. She was the first union organizer of women, sent by the Lowell women to organize the New Hampshire women workers. As a result of their joint agitation, New Hampshire passed the first law regulating the length of working hours to ten for both men and women. But in spite of these commendable efforts of overworked, underpaid, and inexperienced new workers, there was little encouragement given to them by any except the most progressive and farsighted leaders.

Such a man was William Sylvia, President of the National Labor Union, which first advanced the slogan Equal Pay for Equal Work. His insistence that women must be organized was far in advance of the policies of the then existing craft unions. Out of thirty unions only two admitted women. There were four women delegates to the Congress of the National Labor Union in 1868 (more than there are in too many trade union conventions today, I am sorry to say). He appointed the first official woman labor organizer in the United States, Kate Mullaney, who was President of the Collar Laundry Working Women's Union of Troy, New York. It had a membership of four hundred and had contributed $1,000 to the locked-out molders in 1867.

Now with millions of new women workers to organize in present unions, labor leaders should emulate Sylvia by the appointment of hundreds of women organizers. Let us have locals of women workers named in honor of such pioneer women as Sarah Bagley, Kate Mullaney, and Leonora O'Reilly, who was later appointed an organizer of the Knights of Labor in the 1880s. Let us remember and honor likewise such brave women as Lucy Parsons, who fought for the eight-hour day; "Mother" Jones, who organized the miners in spite of injunctions, troops, and company thugs; Fanny Sellins, who was shot in Pennsylvania, on August 26, 1919, when she was organizing both the miners and the steel workers. In the South the workers remember the textile woman leader Ella May Wiggins, who was shot to death in Gastonia, N.C., in 1929.

Samuel Gompers, who was for twenty-four years the president of the AFL, referred in 1900 to women as "unorganizable." Within the next ten years thousands of women and girls did organize, however, especially in the needle trades of New York City. Twenty-thousand girl and women shirt waist makers were out on a general strike in 1909. The International Ladies Garment Workers Union was founded on these revolts of girls. But the skepticism of men like Gompers has left its scars on the labor movement in the serious lack of recognition, placing of responsibility, training, election to office, acceptance and adequate organization of women workers. We women are still in the category of second-class citizens in the labor movement.

SOURCE: *Daily Worker*, Aug. 19, 1942.

Women in American Socialist Struggles (1960)

IN this article Flynn established that the leading suffragists were radical militants and that the socialists had an impressive tradition of women's rights activism.

IN 1910, when International Women's Day was born, many devoted and courageous women were active in the Socialist Party. . . . While they were all staunch fighters for "Votes for Women," they did not confine themselves to this single issue. In this respect, they followed in the path of the two giant pioneers for women's rights—Susan B. Anthony and Elizabeth Cady Stanton, who had passed away at the turn of the century. For approximately half a century, these names had been linked as the intrepid and militant leaders of the women's movement.

They actively associated themselves with all the freedom movements of their day—the abolition of slavery, the early building of unions among women, and for legal, social and human rights for women, as well as the vote.

They came in conflict with the more conservative suffragists, who wanted to disassociate suffrage from all other popular causes. These women preferred to work quietly to gain the vote state by state, and did not favor the nationwide campaign for a federal amendment to the U.S. Constitution, as advocated by Miss Anthony and Mrs. Stanton. They disapproved of women who refused to pay taxes or who attempted to vote, as Miss Anthony did in 1872. (She was fined $100 which she never paid.) The first federal amendment was proposed in 1868, as a sixteenth amendment to repair the damage of the word *male* inserted in the fourteenth amendment. The women said that the word *sex* should have been in the fifteenth amendment, along with other reasons why the right to vote should not be abridged. It was a sore disappointment to these women, who had so long identified their struggle with the abolitionist movement, that Negro and white women were left behind without the vote. Southern Negro men then, and Negro women later, were actually enfranchised but only theoretically, as we well know today—ninety-two years afterwards. The federal amendment, granting the vote to American women, was proposed in 1878 and passed as the nineteenth amendment in 1920.

By 1910 the Conservative wing of the suffrage movement had another headache—the increasing activity of Socialist women in the suffrage organizations and independently. The Socialist Party, conscious of the growing upsurge among women, set up a national committee of women, at their 1910 convention. At that time there was only one woman member of their national committee—Kate Richards O'Hare. The founders of the international Socialist movement, Karl Marx and Frederick Engels, had written many times on the exploitation and injustices suffered by women, as for example the famous statement of Karl Marx, in commenting on the presence of women delegates at the American National Labor Union Convention, in 1868, "Anybody who knows anything of history knows that great social changes are impossible without the feminine ferment." But mere lip service had been paid to women by many Socialist parties until conditions forced a change.

The hardships and handicaps suffered by women speakers and organizers of that period are hard to realize today. Leaving home on speaking trips meant arrangements for care of children. Families were antagonistic. Divorces often ensued. Travel was difficult, in trains and wagons. There were no loudspeakers for open-air meetings. Women speakers met with ridicule, abuse, and sometimes violence. These early Socialist women were truly pioneers. *We Are Many*, by Ella Reeve Bloor, gives a graphic account of the difficulties. The first Marxist Socialist American woman in our country was Mrs. Florence Kelley. In the 1880s, she corresponded with Frederick Engels, under her married name Wischnewetsky, and made the first English translation of Engels' *The Condition of the Working Class in England*.

She was a resident at Hull House, Chicago, and chief factory inspector of Illinois, 1893–97—the first in the country. She was an active suffragist, member of the Women's Trade Union League, and of the NAACP. She was a founder of the National Consumers' League and active in the National Child Labor Committee. She toiled untiringly—until her death in 1932, at the age of seventy-three—for a child labor amendment to the Constitution. Her granddaughter, Florence Kelley, has recently been appointed a judge in New York City.

The secretary of the New York Women's Socialist Committee in 1911 was Mrs. Margaret Sanger. I recall speaking at a laundry workers' strike meeting, with her and with Sylvia Pankhurst, the British suffragist. The Socialist women were helping the strikers. In 1912, Mrs. Sanger was in charge of a group of Lawrence strikers' children brought to New York City. She testified, as a nurse, before a Congressional hearing in Washington on the bad physical condition of these children.

Later she organized the Birth Control League to which she devoted herself exclusively. In its early days she was arrested in Brownsville for opening a free clinic for working class mothers. It was a long, hard struggle before her ideas finally attained acceptance as "planned parenthood."

Harriet Stanton Blatch, daughter of Mrs. Stanton, was a Socialist. She had witnessed militant tactics in England and felt the suffrage movement here was stodgy, lacking pep and drama. In 1907 she gathered forty women together, in a small hall on 4th Street near the Bowery, to organize the Equality League of Self-Supporting Women, later the Women's Political Union. This organization held the first open air meetings and parades for suffrage. They mobilized delegations of working women to go to Albany before committees. I recall meeting Mrs. Blatch at early Socialist meetings; she was a dynamic personality. Her organization canvassed union officers, spoke at factory gates and helped create support in labor and Socialist circles for the campaign for "Votes for Women." Her purpose was to reach women in industry and the professions, not just the women of leisure. Her daughter, Mrs. Nora Stanton Barney, is an architect, and although quite elderly is an active and consistent supporter of all progressive causes today.

Kate Richards O'Hare was the outstanding woman of the American Socialist Party. She had been a member of the Socialist Labor Party in 1899 and later transferred to the Socialist Party. Born in Kansas, she was a teacher and social worker. It was estimated that she had covered more territory and delivered more Socialist lectures than anyone else in the country. She was active in the suffrage movement, editor of the *National Rip-Saw*, a founder of Commonwealth College, in 1923. She was International Secretary for the Socialist Party in 1912–14—the only woman in any country to have held that position in the 2nd International. Mrs. O'Hare was chairman of the committee at the St. Louis Emergency Convention of the Socialist Party in 1917, which wrote the famous anti-war resolution. Every summer for many years, Mrs. O'Hare organized and spoke, sometimes twice daily, at Socialist Encampments in Oklahoma, Arkansas, and lower Missouri. They went on for several days, people coming from miles around to hear folk-songs, speeches and to socialize. She was one of the first persons convicted under the war-time Espionage Act and served fourteen months of a five-year sentence, in the Missouri State Penitentiary. Her sentence was commuted by President Wilson after the Church Federation of Chicago exposed it as a frame-up based on perjury.

After her release, this gallant woman, mother of four children, organized the Children's Crusade for Amnesty in 1920, which secured the release of a group of tenant farmers of the Southwest. She shifted her activity to prison reform, touring the country, under the auspices of the AFL union labor leagues, exposing prison conditions and prison labor. As a result of her efforts in enlisting many women's organizations, modern federal prisons, like Alderson, were built for women and prison goods were taken off the open market. Federal Industries, Inc., was set up in 1934 and goods manufactured in the prison shops are now made only for departments and agencies of the U.S. government. So the last years of her life bore fruit in benefits for women, prisoners, and workers.

Ella Reeve Bloor's life work spanned nearly three-quarters of a century. She learned to speak as a prohibitionist, decided she was a Socialist in 1896, took courses at the University of Pennsylvania after she had four children, and joined the Socialist Party in 1900. She ran for office in three states, was state organizer in Pennsylvania, Delaware, Connecticut and Ohio. She worked in suffrage campaigns, organized unions, led strikes, travelled tirelessly across the continent, spoke at funerals of workers killed by gunmen, visited prisoners and was herself arrested numerous times. She belonged to the Left Wing of the Socialist Party which in 1919 became a part of the newly-formed Communist Party. From then until shortly before her death in 1952, at nearly ninety, she eloquently carried its message everywhere. Full of boundless energy and determination, she scorned old age. At sixty-three she hitch-hiked from coast to coast for the *Daily Worker*. At the age of seventy-five she made her last trip to the Soviet Union. At seventy-eight she ran for office in Pennsylvania, and said: "It has been a privilege and joy to carry the torch for Socialism."

Another pioneer woman Socialist was Lena Morrow Lewis. Her life followed the same pattern as many others—lecturer for temperance, suffrage, and for Socialism. She was the first member of the National Committee of the Socialist Party, from 1900 to 1910. She was the first woman to enlist the support of the Chicago labor unions for suffrage, in 1899. From 1916 to 1918 Mrs. Lewis was the Socialist Party organizer in Alaska. She edited the Alaska *Labor News,* and the Seattle *Daily Call* in 1918. She was not as well known as Mrs. O'Hare and Mother Bloor nor as broad in her views. But in her quiet, unobtrusive way, she served as an organizer and educator for Socialism in many obscure and remote corners of this country.

A Socialist woman I met in Montana in 1909 was Ida Crouch-Hazlitt, editor of the Socialist paper, *Montana News,* published at Helena. She had been a national organizer for the Women Suffrage Association, from 1896 to 1901, when she joined the Socialist Party. She ran for Congress on the Socialist Party ticket in Colorado in 1902, and was reputed then to be the first woman parliamentary candidate in the world. Before, she had been a local candidate on the Prohibition and Populist tickets. Montana was then a rugged place for a woman to edit a Socialist paper. But she did not hesitate to endorse the cause of the hated and feared IWW. She issued a special edition on our behalf and helped us to win free speech in Missoula, Montana.

Rose Pastor Stokes was a gifted Polish immigrant girl living on the East Side in New York, a cigar-maker and self-educated. She became a Socialist speaker, writer, poet, playwright and artist. Her marriage to the "millionaire Socialist" J. G. Phelps Stokes in 1907 created a sensation in both Jewish and Gentile circles. When World War I was declared, a group of Socialists, including Robert Hunter, John Spargo, William E. Walling and Stokes, left the Socialist Party and endorsed the war aims of Woodrow Wilson. For a short time Mrs. Stokes joined them. But after the Russian Revolution of 1917, true to her working class instincts, she repudiated this stand and returned to join the Left Wing of the Socialist Party. She was sentenced to ten years in prison in 1918 at Kansas City, Mo., for a speech against the war and indicted twice later for Communist activities. She died in 1933 of cancer, as a result of a blow of a policeman's club during a demonstration.

Other Socialist women who were candidates for public office in these early days were Anna Maley, who ran for Governor of Minnesota; Emma Henry of Indiana, who ran for state treasurer, state representative and secretary of state; Mrs. Louise Adams Floyd, who ran for secretary in Massachusetts. Frieda Hogan was state secretary of the Socialist Party of Arkansas, 1914–17, and a member of the National Committee. Kate Sadler Greenblagh was the outstanding Socialist woman in the northwest, a truly great orator who was arrested innumerable times, especially in the war period. She had joined with C. E. Ruth Enbey in proposing the anti-war resolution in the St. Louis convention and belonged to the Left Wing of the Socialist Party.

There were many fine writers and editors among the pioneer Socialist women. Mrs. Mary Marcy was a scientific Socialist, a Marxist. She was the editor of the *International Socialist News,* published by the Kerr Company in Chicago. She was the author of a popular pamphlet, *Shop Talks on Economics,* which was a model of clarity. There was a women's magazine published in Chicago about 1908–09—*The Socialist Woman,* edited by Josephine Conger-Kaneko, an American woman married to a Japanese Socialist. Also there was a Socialist women's publishing company in Girard, Kansas, where the *Appeal to Reason* was published. When Joseph Medill Patterson, a wealthy Chicago pseudo-Socialist, wrote a book called *Little Brother of the Rich,* they issued a book called *Little Sister of the Poor.*

Next to Bebel's *Women under Socialism,* a book on my shelf I treasure is *Women and Economics,* published in 1898 by Charlotte Perkins Gilman. She was one of the few women theoreticians in the Socialist movement of long ago. She lectured, and published a magazine called *The Forerunner.* Her views were extremely radical for that day but would readily find acceptance today, especially in the Socialist countries. She argued that women would never be really "emancipated" until they were no longer economically dependent upon men and until they ceased to be "housewives." She advocated self-support for women, state care of children and mothers, the abolition of the kitchen in individual homes, and collective nurseries, kitchens, dining rooms and the like.

Mrs. Gilman built her arguments for Socialism around the inequalities, exploitation, dependency, and degradation of women under capitalism. When she discovered she had cancer, she committed suicide, not to be a burden upon her daughter. Too bad she could not live to see the new Socialist women!

Meta Stein Lilienthal was a Socialist woman writer. Her two pamphlets, *From Fireside to Factory* and *A Woman of the Future,* were extremely popular in 1916. They were published by the Rand School for Social Science, a school endowed by a rich Socialist woman, Mrs. Carrie Rand. Mrs. Lilienthal was dissatisfied with the De Leon translation of Bebel's *Women under Socialism* and translated her own version of it.

A militant suffragist, who belonged to no suffrage organization but was a Socialist, was Maud Malone. When I first began to speak she was a stormy petrel, causing the official suffrage organization much embarrassment. In a day when such a thing was unheard of, she went to political meetings and interrupted candidates to ask where they stood on "Votes for Women." Even more shocking, she paraded up and down Broadway like a sandwich man, wearing "Votes for Women" placards fore and aft. She lost her job as a librarian in consequence. For a number of years before her death, she was in charge of the files at the *Daily Worker* office.

Anita Whitney, a daughter of pioneers, became a Socialist in 1914. As President of the College Equal Rights League, she led to victory in 1911, when California became the sixth state to grant woman suffrage. She was second Vice-President of the National Equal Suffrage Association, with Dr. Anna Shaw as President. She was on the executive committee of the NAACP. She had been a social worker in Alameda County for fifteen years, and was a relief worker in the San Francisco fire, in 1906. She finally resigned from the profession because she felt a fundamental political change was necessary to abolish poverty.

She became a member of the Communist Party when her branch of the Socialist Party joined in a body in 1919. Subsequently she was arrested under the state criminal syndicalist law, for membership in the CP. The case dragged through the courts until 1926 when the conviction was upheld by the Supreme Court. However, due to her tremendous popularity, especially among women and in labor circles, she was pardoned by the Governor of California. In her person she symbolized, as did so many of these wonderful Socialist women of yesterday, all freedom causes—for the Negro people, for labor, for women, for peace, for socialism.

In all my contacts with the Socialist Party and the IWW, I met only one Negro woman speaker—Helen Holman. She came from Philadelphia and was extremely eloquent. In 1919–20 she was the Secretary of the Kate Richards O'Hare Defense Committee with an office in the Rand School, and did extremely effective work in this capacity.

The foregoing are but a few of the women Socialists of yesterday— many more could be mentioned—devoted and indefatigable, struggling under great difficulties but resolute and firm in their faith in a Socialist world of tomorrow. They helped to sow the seed. Others will reap the fruit, but they must not be forgotten.

SOURCE: *Political Affairs*, Apr. 1960.

The Hotel Workers Union and the Children (1958)

THE *Children's Crusade, a march of women and children from St. Louis to Washington, D.C., hoped to call Pres. Warren G. Harding's attention to the less-well-known political prisoners remaining in jail after World War I. The crusade was originally suggested by Kate Richards O'Hare, herself pardoned by Harding.*

Flynn raised enormous sums of money for this successful activity and secured the Fifth Avenue mansion of a wealthy woman for the participants—the women and children of the cotton fields and factory towns of Arkansas and Oklahoma. Although Flynn had a real sense of herself as a historic figure, part of an American radical tradition, she often effaced herself from the events she participated in. For example, in this column, "The Hotel Workers Union and the Children," she did not mention that she was in charge of the New York City reception for the Children's Crusade.

WHEN I read in the papers about the Hotel Workers Union bringing the Negro high school children from Little Rock, Arkansas, I was deeply touched. Their noble action in tendering them a testimonial and an award for their steadfast courage in the struggle against racial segregation in the schools is consistent with the history of these organized workers.

It is not the first time that this union honored a group of children, and strangely enough, many of them were from Arkansas, in a former unique demonstration.

It occurred twenty-six years ago, in 1922, and was known as *The Children's Crusade. . . .*

The dramatic climax of the movement for amnesty in the 1920s came unexpected out of small groups of friendless and poverty-stricken families in Oklahoma and Arkansas. They became the center of a Children's Crusade to the nation's capital, a long trek for back-woods folks who had never been but a few miles from their little farms.

The idea of a living petition, one that could not be pigeonholed or thrown into a wastepaper basket, originated with resourceful and determined Kate Richards O'Hare. She had just finished serving two years in Jefferson City, Missouri, Prison for an anti-war speech.

A Women's Committee to Free Kate Richards O'Hare had been set up in the Rand School building in New York City. A talented and eloquent young Negro woman Socialist, Helen Holman, was its secretary. Thanks to the tireless efforts of these Socialist women, her sentence has been cut from five to two years.

As a Socialist agitator, working out of St. Louis, Mrs. O'Hare had made many speaking trips into the Southwest and knew the barren, hard lives of the tenant farmers and their wives and children.

Now a group of the leaders of these people were in Leavenworth Prison for opposing the war and resisting the draft. Some were Socialists, all were members of an organization called The Working Class Union, and their anti-war movement became known as the Green Corn Rebellion. With their shotguns in hand, they went up into the hills to barricade themselves against being drafted.

The families left behind by these political prisoners were in dire poverty, unable to visit their men in prison for lack of funds. Kate was aroused to great indignation by the story of the wife of Stanley Clark, a Socialist lawyer, whose only "crime" was that he had collected funds to help the families of the Bisbee miners who had been deported into the desert in 1917—during a strike. Mrs. Clark had gathered affidavits to prove that her husband was actually pro-war and had sent all the material to Washington but heard nothing of it. Kate decided to gather up all the families in that part of the country, to make a tour on the way to Washington, and tell their stories in every city.

Several IWW families joined en route, and there were thirty-three in the party when they reached New York City. They had visited Cincinnati and Detroit and had stopped off at Terre Haute, Indiana, to see Eugene V. Debs, who was quite ill at the time. Their meetings collected over $4,000 for their expenses on the crusade, a large sum in those days.

Everywhere the Crusade was greeted with deep emotion. . . . Over three years had passed since the Armistice and there had been great disappointment that at Christmas, in 1921, President Harding had pardoned only a few of the political prisoners and had refused to see delegations to discuss the matter further. The families had expected a general amnesty. The vociferous opposition of the American Legion slowed the President down after he released Eugene V. Debs.

The Crusade left St. Louis on April 16, 1922, and arrived in Washington on April 29. They remained until after July 19.

When they arrived in New York City from Buffalo, on an early morning train, they were a forlorn yet valiant little band of eager, wide-eyed youngsters, sleepy babies and anxious, tired mothers. As they came off the train, they efficiently unfurled their signs and marched proudly through the Grand Central Station.

This extraordinary "Army with Banners" created an immediate sensation among all spectators.

"A Little Child Shall Lead Them" was out in front. Then came "A Hundred and Thirteen Men Jailed for Their Opinions," and "My Daddy Didn't Want to Kill"; another said, "Eugene Debs Is Free—Why Not My Daddy?" A young girl, Irene Danley, carried a sign that read: "My Mother Died of Grief." A young mother walked with a three-year-old child carrying a banner: "I Never Saw My Daddy."

An elderly woman, Mrs. Hough, mother of an imprisoned IWW youth, marched proudly along. Our first destination was the nearby headquarters of the Amalgamated Food Workers (the hotel workers of that day). The police asked me if I had a permit for a parade. I said, "No, it's not a parade. We intend to take these women and children to a place where they can eat and rest." They looked at them and gruffly acceded to our plan, and we were soon there.

Here, at last, were not strange people staring at them and their banners. Here were comrades and friends such as they found in other cities. Few local people dared to speak to them or come near them at home. But now their circle of friends grew ever stronger and wider. They were not alone on a bleak farm on a lonely hillside.

Big handsome bearded French and Italian chefs from the most exclusive hotels and restaurants in New York were there, wearing their white cooks' hats a foot high. The most skilled waiters in the world, with tears in their eyes, tenderly served these hungry children. The tables were decked with flowers. Each child was given a souvenir, a small replica of the Statue of Liberty. The children sang "My Country, 'Tis of Thee," for their hosts. It was heartrending to hear their childish voices sing "Sweet Land of Liberty!" under the circumstances.

SOURCE: *Sunday Worker,* July 13, 1958.

A Comrade's Memory of Rose Pastor Stokes (1943)

FLYNN was a loyal friend and remembered and honored her comrades with obituaries and columns on their birthdays. She wrote several columns about Rose Pastor Stokes, the poor Jewish cigar maker who shocked New York City by marrying Socialist millionaire J. G. Phelps Stokes. The marriage broke up in 1917 over the Russian Revolution, which Rose Pastor cheered and Phelps Stokes feared. Rose Stokes died penniless, of cancer, having to go to Germany for treatments she could not afford in the United States.

S OME rare personalities are so vibrant and vivid, like a flame, that death and the ever-lengthening passage of time cannot efface them. They continue a living force in the memory of those who knew them. Their beauty and warmth in passionate defense of the rights of the people, their tenacious courage in the struggle to find the clear path towards freedom, remain in oft recalled scenes from our earlier days.

. . . Such a personality was Rose Pastor Stokes, who died ten years ago today. . . .

Rose Stokes died at fifty-four, in a hospital for the treatment of cancer in Germany, driven there by a desperate search for health. Her presence there was unknown to the Nazi tyrants. The blow of a policeman's club on her breast, at a City Hall demonstration on behalf of the unemployed, was responsible for the cancer which caused her death, after a long and painful illness.

Her real and purposeful life as a revolutionary Socialist and Communist was unfortunately obscured and distorted by the Cinderella-like glamor of her marriage to the "millionaire Socialist"—J. G. Phelps Stokes. I first met her in 1910, on Carites Island, which was a beautiful secluded spot in Long Island Sound, off Stamford, Conn., where they sought escape from the flood of sensational publicity let loose upon them because she was a poor Jewish immigrant girl from the slums,

and he was a Christian, son of a rich banker, one of the socially "elite."
She was attacked by the orthodox Jews and he was equally attacked by
the orthodox Christians. He belonged to a group of serious-minded
young social workers in an East Side settlement house, who were concerned with "How the Other Half Lives." . . .

Immediately after their marriage they toured together under the
auspices of the Socialist Party. Large audiences animated by curiosity
came to gaze upon a millionaire Socialist and his "Rose from the
ghetto." But he hemmed and stammered and made grotesque gestures. He had nothing to say worth listening to, and the listeners
might well have left in the midst of his painful effort. But their interest in her held them. She was beautiful and talented. The oldest of a
large family who were Polish immigrants via London, self-educated
after only a year and a half of primary school, a cigarmaker by trade,
she knew by bitter experiences and deep sympathetic understanding
the lives of the poor. She was in her twenties—a dynamic personality.
Her clouds of red-brown curly hair shook loose as she spoke, forming
a lovely frame for her large expressive brown eyes and her clear-cut
cameo-like features. She had a tiny scar on the tip of her nose from a
cut when she fell as a child, sliding down the banister of her tenement
house. It gave her a piquant, retroussé effect.

Her poems and articles, contributed to the Jewish press, had attracted much attention by their charm and originality. With moving
eloquence and passion she made her convincing appeal for Socialism,
to end poverty and inequalities. Her faith in and love for the plain
people of the earth were the steel core of her being. It saved her from
becoming softened by or submerged in a luxurious, secure existence.
It finally pulled her away from the ranks of the bourgeois liberals,
back into the fighting ranks of the people, to find poverty more comfortable than doled-out riches. It caused her to be unhappy among
the self-centered, idle·rich, and happy to be back on Second Avenue in
a humble apartment among hardworking, sorrowful, anxious people,
who fought for life and happiness. No travail or tragedy of the poor
was alien to her. I remember a fastidious lady saying to her: "But
Rose, the poor could at least keep clean!" and her fiery, scornful retort: "Did your mother ever look at a nickel in her hand and have to
decide whether to buy a cake of soap or a loaf of bread? Well, mine
did and she bought bread!"

. . . Her basic class consciousness and revolutionary spirit rose to
the clarion call of the Russian Revolution in 1917. As a daughter
of the working class, she rejoiced in its victory. Her feet were again on
the straight path, as happened then to thousands of sincere American
Socialists and IWWs. The same bourgeois world which had smiled
upon and patronized her as the rich lady dabbling in art and politics,

now snarled and bared their fangs, when she made her final, irre-vocable choice and joined the Communist Party in 1919, at its birth. She was already under indictment in Kansas City, Mo., for opposing the imperialist war. She was indicted in Chicago, Ill., in 1919 and in Michigan in 1922, during the Palmer Red Raids and the vicious reac-tionary attacks upon American labor at that time. Rose Pastor Stokes was also a member of the Women's Trade Union League and carried a retired card from the Cigarmakers Union Local No. 11. She was a member of the Poetry Society of America and in the last years of her life discovered she possessed an aptitude for painting. When I was very ill in Portland, Oregon, I received a loving, cheerful message from her with a little sketch of trees, which was excellent, and a poem, equally good.

The last time I saw her, she had undergone an operation and was expecting another. She was in great pain, her face flushed and her eyes agonized. This was shortly before she left for Europe. I was home on a visit and far from well. Her great concern was when I would recover and be able to work again. For herself she had little hope. She had read many volumes on cancer and accepted her terrible condition as a death sentence. As I left, she drew me over to kiss me goodbye and said softly, so the person with me could not hear: "Be good to the Party, Elizabeth."

SOURCE: *Daily Worker*, June 20, 1943.

A Woman Who Died for Labor in August 1919 (1942)

FLYNN had a warm spot for miners and visited mining towns as often as she could, often staying in miners' homes. She devoted many columns to their heroic battles and organizing drives. Flynn felt more at home on the industrial fron-tier than she did in sophisticated New York City Communist party offices, bat-tling sectarian bureaucrats in internecine squabbles. She often asked to be sent to the hinterlands.

TWENTY-THREE years ago on August 26, 1919, a woman labor organizer, Mrs. Fanny Sellins, received a mysterious telephone call to
come at once to West Natrona, Pa. She lived in New Kensington, across
the murky Allegheny River. She was tired and wanted to stay home
that hot afternoon. Her favorite grandchild was having a birthday
party and she had walked a long time around town until she found a
toy horse and wagon which he had expressed a wish to have.

But this Irish-American widow, forty-nine years old, was a good
soldier of labor—one of the very best. Her maiden name was Mooney.
Her husband had been killed in a strike. She went to work as an organizer of the garment workers in St. Louis, Mo. Then she moved to
Western Pa. to be with her married daughter and there became a pioneer organizer of the United Mine Workers of America. It was a
tough territory to work in—this notorious anti-labor Black Valley, but
she earned the undying hatred of the operators by organizing many
thousands of poor miners.

In August 1919, the great organizing drive was on in steel. Later, in
September 1919, there was a nationwide steel strike which lasted
three and a half months and involved 365,000 men in fifty cities of ten
states. Mrs. Sellins was loaned by the miners to the National Committee for Organizing Iron and Steel Workers.

William Z. Foster, the leader of the campaign, described her as "an
able speaker, possessed of boundless courage, energy, enthusiasm and
idealism who worked indefatigably." He attributes the organization
of the workers of the U.S. Steel Corporation Mills at Vandergrift,
Leechburgh, and New Kensington as well as those of the so-called
independent Allegheny and West Pennsylvania Steel Companies of
Brackenridge, as due to Mrs. Sellins' splendid work.

The Allegheny Coal and Coke Co. was located in Natrona, Pa. It is
situated in the mill yard of the Allegheny Steel Company and furnished the coal for it. This is what is called "a captive mine," completely subsidiary to another industry. The miners were on strike and
a few were picketing this sultry August afternoon. They had not sent
for Fanny Sellins. Suddenly a group of drunken deputy sheriffs who
were stationed there on guard duty rushed out and began shooting at
the pickets. One, a Polish miner, Joseph Strzelcki, fell to the ground,
mortally wounded. Mrs. Sellins rushed to push some children nearby
through a fence and out of danger. Then she came back to try to stop
the deputies who were clubbing the prostrate pickets.

In 1939 I met a miner who had witnessed the horrible tragedy.
A mine official struck her with a club and she fell to the ground. As
she arose and dragged herself towards the fence, three shots were
fired, each mortally wounding her. As she lay unconscious on the
ground a deputy emptied his gun into her body. A deputy then

crushed in her skull with a club, before the helpless little group of miners, their wives and children.

One deputy grabbed her hat, danced around her body and said: "I'm Mrs. Sellins now!" So died this martyred woman organizer.

SOURCE: *Daily Worker*, Aug. 28, 1942.

The Feminine Ferment (1960)

FLYNN praised the Communist party whenever the occasion arose, as in her article "Feminine Ferment." However, she failed to mention in this article that she was the only woman on the National Executive Board, the highest ruling body of the Party.

IN 1868 Karl Marx wrote: "Anybody who knows anything of history knows that great social changes are impossible without the feminine ferment."

In our recent 17th Convention of the Communist Party, U.S.A., it was obvious. I was happy to see a large number of women delegates; in fact, they were well represented in practically every district delegation—old and young, Negro and white. They were designated on all committees, a large number spoke during the four days' sessions, and a special resolution was submitted on the problems of American women by a committee. It was adopted unanimously by the convention.

It is called "Resolution on the Work and Status of Women" and stresses the disastrous effects of a cold war economy on the family and on education. It points out the power women voters have in the 1960 elections and the necessity to fight for the rights of Negro women to vote, especially in the South, and of Spanish-speaking women in the North and West.

The tremendous political power exercised by women *"can take a war budget and change it into a peace budget."* It points out the special exploitation of women in capitalist society and reminds the Communist Party of its unique responsibility to educate on "the status of women, the rights of women, and the role of women," as well as to popularize the achievements of women under socialism. . . .

When it came to the election of a National Committee for the Communist Party, I am glad to report that ten women were elected. Five were new members and five were re-elected. Four are Negro women and six are white (which proportion could be improved). Five are women who work directly for the Communist Party, nationally or on a state level. Five are employed otherwise.

An interesting development was the election of three couples. It used to be said this "couldn't be done," and occasionally a frustrated woman would say to me: "You're lucky you're not married to a party leader! You'd never get elected to a top post!" Well, this old notion went out the window at the Hotel Theresa last week. . . .

Lenin once said: "We must root out the old 'master' idea to its last and smallest root, in the party and among the masses." It runs deep. But I do believe, though I may start a debate here, that Communist men are superior to others, in this respect.

SOURCE: *Sunday Worker,* Jan. 3, 1960.

Women in War and Peace

New York Communist party members leaving the Federal Court House after being indicted under the Smith Act, July 1951. Front row, left to right: Jacob Mindel and his wife Ann Mindel, Elizabeth Gurley Flynn, Betty Gannett, Claudia Jones, and Pettis Perry. From the New York Times, *April 16, 1972.*

Women in the War (1942)

THE World War II period was one of the most productive in Elizabeth Gurley Flynn's Communist party career. She felt at home in the now respectable, expanding Communist party and was in demand as a speaker and writer.

The following document is taken from Flynn's Women in the War, *a compilation of some of her articles and speeches.*

W AR creates extraordinary demands for labor. . American women will accept it [conscription] as gallantly as have the men in our people's army. Local registration has been completed in Seattle, Detroit, Akron, Connecticut. In Oregon, 99,000 women volunteered for the fruit harvest; 116,532 women of Detroit signed as willing to take war jobs. The Manpower Commission announces that 80,000 will be needed in Detroit, 50,000 in Seattle, 12,000 in Syracuse, and 40,000 in Buffalo, N.Y., in the near future. . . .

. . . Prejudices break down in a national crisis. Women and the Negro people must be given the right to show their mettle as workers. Work is not *man's* versus woman's, any more than it is *white's* versus Negro's, or *native-born's* versus foreign-born's, or *Christian's* versus Jew's. Such a characterization as "*Male, white, Christian, native-born*" is typically Nazi, repugnant to American concepts of democracy. Women's role in industry, like that of the Negro people, is not of a temporary nature. War emergency accelerates the entry of women into industry. But there were ten million women employed in 1930, two and a half million more than in 1920. Many more will remain in industry after this war than were there before, especially in new industries. . . .

Any job, except some very heavy types of physical labor, can be undertaken by women. With mechanical assistance, most of these can be handled, too. "Can Women Do the Job?" is being answered by demonstrations from Brooklyn to Seattle. A "Consolidated" engineer in California told a reporter recently: "There are more than one hundred and one thousand separate and distinct parts in one of our bombers, not counting rivets, and most of them are so light in weight that women can assemble and test them as easily as men. Better in most cases."

Ten months ago when the first women went to work at "Consolidated," the foreman growled, "The factory is no place for a woman!" Today the industrial relations director of North American Aviation says, "Women do approximately 50 per cent of the work required to construct a modern airplane."

Women are proving best adapted to jobs requiring patience and alertness, keen eyesight, and finger and hand dexterity. They use blueprints, micrometers, gauges and other precision tools expertly. Because they are anxious to learn they are easy to teach. The labor turnover has decreased, accidents diminished, and damage to tools and materials is less. Employers and male fellow workers agree that the women, if they are treated merely as "new workers" without prejudice or favor, and are given proper guarantees for health, safety and sanitation, are able to carry on efficiently.

A lively interest in the mobilization of women is sweeping the country. It is not only a recognition of their importance but a campaign to stimulate larger numbers to enter plants. The "soldierettes" of the home front are interviewed, featured on the fashion pages of newspapers and magazines in their snappy uniforms, are the heroines of movies. The glamour girl of today, the woman in the news, is the working woman. Every day brings a thrilling account of a new difficult or delicate job mastered by a woman; every such accomplishment lays low some ancient superstition about women. They are not afraid of heat, electricity, noise, lights, gas, smells, high, dark, or dangerous places. They do not worry about their appearance. "Feminine vanity" does not balk at dirty faces, greasy hands, hair plastered down under a protective cap, severely tailored uniforms, shoes conditioned for safety, and a lunch box instead of a fancy purse. Our women measure up to the stern requirements of modern industry. Why not? Their maternal ancestors were immigrants to New England and the Atlantic Coast and pioneers in covered wagons to mid-America and the far West. Our country wasn't built the soft way. Women worked hard on farms and in households. They carried on in every war while their men were on the battlefields. Privation, sacrifice, work, are in the blood of American women, whose ancestors cleared the wilderness, built railroads and cities, tamed rivers, dug mines, made homes in log cabins, and taught their children by candlelight.

Employers are accepting women in new and strange jobs as a necessity, some gracefully—some in "die-hard" desperation. New industries, such as Pacific Coast Aircraft, are giving women the greatest opportunities. Their skillful feminine fingers are carrying out President Roosevelt's assignment for 60,000 planes in 1942 and 125,000 in 1943.

Pacific aviators gratefully dub them "angels with dirty faces" who "keep us flying." In reply to a questionnaire sent out by *Modern Industry* to 1,000 plant executives, 74 per cent reported present or contemplated employment of women. It is encouraging, too, to hear that their experience condemns "all women" departments. Men and women working side by side is more satisfactory, once men overcome their fear of women as rivals. A preference for young married mothers, whose menfolks are already employed or are in the armed forces, indicates a discrimination against older women which must not be tolerated. They foresee the need of improvements in the plants to accommodate women. *I wonder if a questionnaire sent to 1,000 labor leaders would indicate a similar alertness to women workers' needs and problems?* Frankly, I doubt it. Recent trade union conventions have either not discussed the requirements of these millions of new women workers or disposed of them with the customary general resolutions, a hangover of their past bad practices. A pat on the back does not suffice today, brother trade unionists. Intelligent understanding and prompt action are needed.

A scrapping of past prejudices, underestimation and antagonism to women is imperative. The needs which these 1,000 employers list should have been a *must* long ago, especially of unions of war-production industries, where women are flocking to the plants. These requirements are special lockers, washrooms, rest and recreation rooms; first-aid equipment, medical and sanitary supplies; stools, chairs, benches and tables; special material-handling equipment; safety shoes, goggles, and work uniforms; lifts, platforms, ladders; increased feeding facilities; special transportation for night shifts and child care facilities. Employers may recognize the need of all this. But their replies do not indicate a too great readiness to furnish them. Labor will have to insist upon them, as union demands, in many places. The Woman's Bureau of the Department of Labor (Mary Anderson, director) is publishing an excellent series of pamphlets and bulletins on the standards required for women in war industries. I recommend a careful study of them by special committees in every union. Address the Bureau, Washington, D.C., for further information.

These are the minimum needs which labor unions should press for women workers. The success of the unions in organizing the twelve million women, who are as yet unorganized in our country, depends upon the promptness and firmness with which they take up such demands as basic union issues. In addition and equally important are adequate training; housing facilities—especially in the boom towns of mushroom growth; equal pay for equal work; protection against all forms of discrimination, especially as practiced so generally against Negro women. *Proper child care is the crying need of many women workers. . . .*

. . . The labor movement must include women as full and equal members, encouraging them to active participation in its affairs, electing them as shop stewards, chairmen of locals, to executive boards, to grievance and other committees, as delegates to central bodies and to conventions.

That there were less women delegates (21) at the recent convention of the United Auto Workers than at the previous one is deplorable. True, excellent resolutions were passed. One was to hire capable women organizers *"as the necessity arises."* But thus far, there have been less than a half-dozen women organizers added. The necessity is here now with thousands of women entering the industry. There is no time to waste. Why did the Auto Workers lose the Labor Board election to the company union at the important Buffalo Curtiss-Wright plant? There was not one woman among one hundred organizers. The same thing happened at Thompson Products in Cleveland. Later, at a conference, one of the men said, "It was the damned dames that did it!" He was undoubtedly correct in both instances. But a good squad of woman organizers, including some bright, peppy girls right out of the shops, could have turned the tide. I wonder if this brother knew that Curtiss-Wright had opened up a nursery and that Thompson Products had promised one and had made special appeal to women by establishing rest rooms, buses, and a cafeteria? Many of these new women do not know that the trade unions have successfully fought for all these improvements, in other places, and that the eagerness of the employers to grant them is to forestall and offset the union demands.

A resolution was passed at the Auto Workers convention affirming their adherence to equal pay for equal work. In the two instances, General Motors and Olds Motor Company, the union won test cases for women employees,upholding the constitutionality of the equal pay law. There was an excellent discussion by women delegates. Delegate McKernan warned the men against classifying women's demands as "women's problems." She insisted correctly, as did Delegate Alma Anderson, a crane-operator delegate to the United Steel Workers Convention from Weirton, W. Va., that equal pay for equal work is a union issue, not a problem of women alone. Miss Anderson pointed out that men's wages would ultimately be lowered if women accept less pay. President Murray assured her that she was correct, and union membership and protection will be afforded to all new women workers entering the steel industry to secure equal compensation for them.

On September 26, the War Labor Board decided in the case of Brown and Shays Manufacturing Co. of Providence, R.I., that women who perform the same work as competently as men must be paid equal rates of wages. The company had insisted upon a 20 per cent differential on the theory that women are of inferior physical strength.

The War Labor Board stated uncompromisingly, *"There is no real proof, scientific or otherwise, that women are 20 per cent less capable than men all the time."* Dr. George W. Taylor who wrote the opinion said emphatically that American women should not be discriminated against in compensation. This is a real victory for women and organized labor. It means that women cannot be used as competitors to beat down wage levels established by collective bargaining, after years of struggle on the part of labor.

When women delegates at auto, steel, and other conventions insist that women's problems are today the concern of the whole labor movement, they are absolutely right. *There are over twelve million unorganized women workers in America today. This figure nearly equals the total membership of all existing trade unions put together.* In other words, organized labor could double its strength and influence by organizing all the women workers now outside its ranks.

Why are these millions of working women unorganized? Is it because American women are adverse to belonging to organizations? Far from it. There are actually twelve million women in various organizations in this country—political, cultural, patriotic, religious, educational, farm, consumers, and what not. Women's clubs are peculiar to America. They indicate a high level of progress and intelligence. Margaret C. Banning, in her book *Women for Defense*, remarks: "You have to be very poor or very stubborn not to belong to something if you are an American woman." The General Federation of Women's Clubs totals about two million. They are not a solid bloc, but they are serious, sincere, and honest. Many are already discussing, as a part of the national defense, the very issues to which labor should be giving its earnest attention. Up to recently, the YWCA had more working girls attached to its industrial section than were in trade unions. It is evident that American women are organizable. Let the labor unions launch a campaign with the vigor and enthusiasm with which the CIO was started, with women organizers, special literature, posters, conferences, meetings, and results would follow immediately. Discuss shop issues, the needs of national war production, the history and value of labor unions, the particular interests of the women workers, and have top-ranking leaders of American labor take part in this campaign, and the women will gladly enlist in organized labor. The militant struggles of women to organize the textile and needle trades unions demonstrate this. Sixty per cent of the 150,000 in the Amalgamated Clothing Workers and 75 per cent of the International Ladies Garment Workers' 200,000 members are women.

If women workers remain unorganized the labor unions will have themselves to blame. The dire results of neglect will most directly affect the women. It will lower their standards, deprive them of the strength to defend themselves, and weaken their morale as workers in a war period—and after. It will make them ready prey for anti-union schemes such as company unionism. In addition to the disastrous effects upon the women workers, labor unions must face the reality that the security of already established standards, the guarantee of hard-fought gains, the very existence of some unions depend upon enlisting these new workers. As the labor composition changes it must either be absorbed in the union or the union is thereby weakened. Several million male trade unionists are away in our armed forces. More will follow. Not only the jobs they vacate but the unions they build will depend upon the women they leave behind them.

. . . It is a likewise disgrace that some AFL and independent unions adhere stubbornly to their bars against Negroes as members. This automatically excludes them from occupations where a closed shop or union contract exists. Or they are denied equal status, discouraged from joining, or "Jim Crowed" into separate locals, deprived of the right to hold office or to be delegates to conventions. Jurisdictional rights are invoked by the offending unions to resist efforts of the AFL Council to remedy the situation—just as Southern states invoke "state's rights" to resist abolition of poll-tax restrictions on voting and national anti-lynching legislation. The CIO has taken a strong position opposing all forms of discrimination against Negro workers. It encourages Negro membership on an equal basis, and has many Negro organizers and officials. CIO contracts in iron and steel, maritime and mining industries, among others, have eliminated wage differentials between Negroes and whites on similar jobs. The result is that the CIO has a large Negro membership, and Negroes have proven themselves efficient workers, loyal and intelligent members, and capable leaders.

. . . Despicable and widespread discrimination still prevails in spite of President Roosevelt's Order No. 8802, which specifically bars discrimination against Negroes in plants working on war orders. I heard in Lancaster, Pennsylvania, of Negro high school graduates applying for work at the Armstrong Linoleum factory, now converted to war purposes. They were told: "We don't need any domestics or porters here!" Negro girls of Oakland, Calif., fruitlessly apply for war jobs and are told: "No help wanted."

Katherine Hoffman, Administrative Secretary of the Greater Newark (N.J.) Industrial Council, charged that "the employment of Negro women at any kind of work is still non-existent." Ku Klux Klan and fascist elements in Detroit created a demonstration against Negro women in the Hudson Plant last June. The U.S. Army ordered that the white women either work with the Negro women, who were specially trained at the Ordnance Training School, or forfeit their jobs. Just as trouble was fomented by defeatist elements over the occupancy of the Sojourner Truth Houses, so 3,000 workers were made idle at the Dodge Truck plant in June. The United Auto Workers Union ordered the few malcontents either to work with the Negroes or get out of the shops. A struggle has been going on against the Ford Motor Company since last winter. Before the Ford Plants were unionized, Henry Ford employed Negro men workers, as if he were their only friend. Now he tries to set the Negro people against the union by claiming that union members are unwilling to work with Negro women. He has an "Uncle Tom" Negro personnel director—Willis Hard, who refused to hire Negro women, because he said race hatred would be engendered. White women are admitted at the gate to apply for work and Negro women are barred. In protest, five hundred Negro women marched to the gates of the Ford Rouge plant to apply for jobs. Detroit employers announced the wife of a drafted man would be hired in his place. No Negro woman has been given her drafted husband's job. Eight hundred Negro women received defense training but none has been hired. Ford union men and some wives of Negro workers organized Women's Industrial Jobs Committees. Mrs. Mattie Lee Woodson is secretary and Senator Charles Diggs is chairman. Their efforts secured wide community support among progressive Negro and white citizens. But they are having a hard struggle to drive "Jim Crow" out of Detroit. (Note—Press dispatches of September 27 state that Ford Motor Company has at last hired twenty-seven Negro women who, after training, will act as instructors for other Negro women, according to Lawrence W. Cramer of the Fair Employment Practices Committee. If this really means *equal work for Negro women* and no Jim Crow, then congratulations are due to the local committee, which has won a real victory for the Negro people. But why not hire those already trained?)

Allen Industry has hired Negro women. Through the alertness of James Walker, shop steward, Murray Body hired eleven—but not on the belt line. Packard promised to hire some. Later they announced a "Jim Crow" plant will be opened for Negroes with Negro instructors. This is a rank violation of government and union rules. It is an insult to thousands of Negro union members and their families. To bring the industry, capabilities, loyalty, and intelligence of the great masses of Negro people into the main channels of war efforts requires that they be treated as equals. . . .

. . . The best resolution on Child Care Centers passed thus far by any labor convention was adopted unanimously by the Auto Workers Convention. Unfortunately there was no discussion. It often happens that splendid resolutions meet the unhappy fate of being buried away in archives and are not read by the membership of the unions which fathered them. I hope the Auto Workers Union is aware of the importance of making this a live issue. It is the key to organizing millions of women. We must not be deterred by reactionary opposition. "Breaking up the home!" say some old fogies, as did their forerunners about kindergartens and public school. "Mothers with children should not work," cry others, as if they never heard of thousands upon thousands who work in peacetime and for whom there should have been child care provisions made long ago. The most stupid recommendation I have heard yet is that mothers should work nights so they can take care of their homes and children in the daytime. I suppose they can sleep at odd times like horses or elephants—standing up!

. . . Child care is a major political issue in our country today. The unions who sponsor it and the Congressmen who fight for further appropriations will win the ardent support of women. Funds can be secured under the Lanham Act. Six million dollars of WPA funds are already allocated for this purpose. More must be made available.

There are thirty child care committees in various places. The first wartime Child Care Project was approved by the President and opened up in New Haven, Conn., in August. It is for pre-school, kindergarten, and school-age children, and is open from 6:30 A.M. to 6:30 P.M. Hundreds more are needed. Juvenile delinquency is on the increase to an alarming degree in our country. Proper care, feeding, and supervision of children will help to overcome it. Every industrial community should apply for government child care projects. Let Uncle Sam mind the children while mother works to win the war. Indifference and neglect of their children may reap a whirlwind of resentful feeling among working mothers, against the government, unions, and the war.

Housing is another major need of workers in war production centers. The Manpower Commission could far more readily move labor forces around the country if this problem were adequately met. New workers coming into cities like Oakland, San Diego, Buffalo, Bridgeport are worn out by the search for a place to stay. Many cannot bring their families for lack of accommodations, and their cost of living is doubled.

Women are even more sensitive to bad housing conditions than men because they carry the burden of domestic duty after a day's work. Homes are working places to them. Let a women worker come home to a modern, comfortable, government project house with all the facilities for a quick bath, a dinner already prepared in the frigidaire or partly cooked in an electric stove—and the world looks different to her. Workers who live in these houses are happy. The only trouble is, there are too few of them, just samples to satisfy the lucky few and aggravate the disappointed many.

To summarize—the vital needs of American women workers to help win the war are as follows:

1. Equal opportunity to work for all women (Negro and white) at all occupations.
2. Adequate training for jobs, under government and union supervision.
3. Equal pay for equal work.
4. Safe and sanitary shop conditions.
5. Equal membership, protection by and participation in labor unions.
6. Child care centers, with federal funds and supervision.
7. Adequate modern housing.

What is being done to realize these imperative requirements for millions whose labor is manpower today? Many excellent local conferences have already been held—as in Seattle, Massachusetts, New Jersey, and Los Angeles. Most recent was the Bay Area Regional Conference on Women in Industry, held in San Francisco with more than three hundred delegates from AFL and CIO unions. Labor's Unity for Victory Committee sponsored it. Qualified experts in various fields of war work were invited. At the Newark Conference on Home Front Co-ordination, labor, management, government, and the community participated. Josephine Petrucelli, organizer of the United Electrical and Radio Workers Union, CIO, presented the forthright demand of women workers for nurseries to solve the problem of labor shortage, in reply to some who opposed women working. A national conference is needed now, as proposed by the Auxiliary and endorsed by the Maritime Workers Union.

Two tendencies must be guarded against in relation to local conferences. First, they are much more effective if they are not just "women's conferences," but are the "Win-the-War Conferences" of both men and women, to discuss the needs of women, as the concern of all-labor leaders, government officials, etc. Preliminary get-together conferences of the women will help to formulate their demands, to increase their self-confidence and ability to express themselves. But we must insist that the *new issues raised by the presence of women in industry be on the order of business at every affected union meeting, central council, and convention.* Paul R. Porter of the War Production Board announced that 150,000 women will be recruited to work in shipyards during the next year. Jack Murry, personnel director of three Kaiser yards, declared recently that "30 per cent of the posts could be held by women." At the recent Shipbuilders Union, CIO, convention there were no women delegates, no resolutions, and no discussion on these new workers. Is this progressive union missing the boat?

Secondly, we must counteract a tendency to lump all "women's problems" together—auxiliaries, new members, etc. The unions cannot drop the campaign "to organize the unorganized" into the laps of the auxiliaries. They will gladly help, as they have in all organizational drives. Auxiliary members (women relatives) are not in the shops. The function where they excel today is primarily in civilian defense, to serve on rationing boards, and to act wherever labor's interests and consumers are concerned. The Office of Price Administration counts upon their active cooperation in price control, the Oil Workers' Auxiliary was told by a representative at their recent Texas convention. The Montana and West Virginia miners' auxiliaries are busy at First Aid and Red Cross classes, as air raid wardens, in raising relief funds, selling bonds, in salvage and scrap iron campaigns, as members of the American Women's Auxiliary Service. The Auto Workers' Auxiliary in Detroit wear their UAW insignia on their sleeves. There are splendid auxiliaries attached to both AFL and CIO unions whose war work in support of the President's foreign policy, especially to open a Western Front, and whose political activities to elect only "Win-the-War" candidates to back him up here, reflect the greatest credit to organized labor. In fact some unions have to step fast to keep up with their auxiliaries. They deserve far more cooperation, financial support, and appreciation than they receive. A sort of "Oh well—Ma's always there!" attitude prevails toward them in many of the unions. The trade unions themselves must undertake and give full-time attention and leadership to a conference on the enormous job of organizing twelve million women. I commend the splendid resolution passed by the Maritime Workers' Auxiliary this summer and endorsed by the union, calling for such *a national conference.*

Women are rare on the decisive committees of all but a handful of national unions. There is one woman, Eleanor Nelson, on the Executive Council of the CIO and none on the AFL. Mr. McNutt followed this example, I fear. In selecting an advisory committee of twelve women, he appointed only two union women and neither of them from the new wartime industries. No woman was selected from any auxiliary or from the Women's Trade Union League. This is partly due to the fact that the unions did not recommend or insist upon any of their appointments.

. . . Speak up and act now. Victory is at stake.

SOURCE: *Women in the War* (New York: Workers Library Publishers, 1942).

Street for Playground While Mothers Work (1943)

UNLIKE most Daily Worker *columnists, Flynn often wrote about her family and childhood. Perhaps this is the reason her columns were so popular.*

WHEN I was a child, the hot streets of the South Bronx were our playgrounds, except when we scared up a few nickels and went to see our Aunt Mary, at Sheepshead Bay.

Camps were unheard of then. Once a year, the Tammany district leader chartered an excursion boat up the Hudson River for an "outing" with free ice cream and beer. Exhausted mothers dragged their excited offspring to a distant pier, crowded on a dangerously jammed boat, and for a few hours gazed on green hills and cool waters, only to return, as similar excursionists do now, to the fetid tenements at night. . . .

In wartime, with over 16,000,000 women working in industry, safety and recreation should be provided for these stay-at-home children through playgrounds. I wish I could boast to out-of-town readers that my home town is in the vanguard. But it wouldn't be true. The great city of New York is a laggard, disgracefully indifferent to the needs of its young children.

The Board of Education asked for $347,000 to finance 342 playgrounds for July and August. The Board of Estimate cut the request almost to half. This allowed for 260 playgrounds, for half a day only. New York City has facilities for 700 playgrounds. The very least a great metropolis can do in the hot summer months is to keep all her available playgrounds open all day, and take the children off the streets. Not a single one is open all day.

SOURCE: *Sunday Worker*, Aug. 8, 1943.

Love Is Grand but We're at War (1943)

"LOVE Is Grand but We're at War" was part of a controversial series of Daily Worker *articles and letters Flynn wrote, from fall 1942 through summer 1943, on the duties of wives during wartime. Flynn showed little compassion for the lonely, overburdened women who wrote letters to her complaining of the extra work they were being bludgeoned into taking on by the Party and the overtime they were forced to work in industry. Flynn made it clear that the fight against fascism came first, before family and love. She condemned women who moved to military bases to be near their loved ones. Usually on the hedonistic, sensual side of most debates on the responsibility of Party members, during World War II Flynn was uncharacteristically stoic and stodgy.*

To the indignant womenfolks who protested that I was unkind, cold, even cynical in my recent column on the subject of soldiers' wives leaving their jobs to go where their husbands are stationed, permit me to make a few further remarks.

Of course, you feel sad and lonely when your menfolks are away. It's natural and human. And I'm not questioning the sincerity of their love letters to you, in which they express similar feelings.

I am a strong believer in love, and approve of love letters. I wouldn't mind getting some myself!

But I allowed for a certain poetic license in personal and private expressions which are not of a public political character. I'm not criticizing them or you for loving each other strongly and hoping that you will be together again in a peaceful world.

Undoubtedly, all soldiers' wives and mothers feel the same way, women on farms, women way back in the hills in mining camps all over the United States—not just us Communist women, but women.

We have duties and responsibilities, to set an example of how women should behave in wartime, no matter how hard it is to do. We talk considerably about "our vanguard role." This is it, or a large part of it, right now.

I am somewhat astounded to be accused of being hard-hearted. But there is a necessity for all of us, no matter how warmhearted we are, to be coolheaded. If I wrote in what seemed a sharp manner, it was to emphasize a truism that needs little argument, namely, that in our country at war, everybody belongs in the place and on the job where they can do their best to help win the war.

There may be exceptional cases where a woman can do this near where her husband is located. But the danger is that each couple will want to believe and will therefore argue that their case is the exception.

Recently I read that the Army and Navy authorities are seriously concerned about what they call "gypsy wives." They clutter up transportation, they aggravate the housing problem, and they affect the morale of the men *adversely*—distracting them from their routine and causing them worry as to the future of the wives when they leave for the front. Orders have already been issued excluding them from some military zones.

Wives are strongly advised by Uncle Sam to stay at home. If the situation should become acute, they will be ordered to stay home, as a military necessity.

Communist women should exercise self-control and self-discipline, and not have to be ordered by the government.

I am not arguing against visiting where it is convenient, but against pulling up stakes and settling in a camp community or nearby. One goes to Florida, another to Nebraska, another to Arkansas—all convinced that their situation is different from everybody else's. How can there be planned production and rationing of materials, labor, etc. . . . if such individualistic, impulsive, planless, selfish treking around the country becomes widespread?

I say "selfish" advisedly. When we act on our own personal feelings, regardless of the serious consequences if such actions become general, no matter how we try to rationalize it, our act is selfish. We certainly cannot encourage all wives of all soldiers to do likewise. Imagine the chaos and confusion such a migration would create. Yet each wife has as much right to be "near my husband" as you have, and you can only persuade her against such reasoning by your example. . . .

. . . Undoubtedly, a chance to see America would broaden a lot of New York folks, if I may say so without starting another row, but now is hardly the time. We are at war. We must strain every effort to win the war. We must produce, we must save, we must plan. We must ration food, materials, labor. We must be economical of time and effort.

I say again—and hope it will carry the weight it deserves—can you imagine the Soviet women, who love their men dearly, dropping the work that supplies those men with the sinews of war? They dare not allow themselves the luxury of personal desires. Neither can we.

SOURCE: *Sunday Worker,* Jan. 17, 1943.

We Thank Uncle Sam for Training Our Boys (1943)

THIS article is an example of Flynn's humorous, feminist side. None of the men she lived with—her father, brother, son, or Carlo Tresca—did any housework, nor did most men at this time.

TRAVELING around the country as much as I do, I see and hear a great many soldiers. They are a pleasant, polite, cheerful, happy lot—at least when they are going places. Their principal topic of conversation is "beer," which is a safe and harmless subject, devoid of military information. But when they do groan or moan about any aspect of their transformed lives it is about "KP"—or "Kitchen Police."

In his entertaining sketch of army life, Private Hargrove observes wisely that when the army gets through with him he'll be a good wife for some girl at home. Soldiers learn much besides the manual of arms—to make their beds, to wash their clothes, to keep everything in order in their quarters, to scrub floors, to wash pots, pans and dishes, to peel vegetables (especially spuds), to clean up around the yards, etc.

To hear them tell it, the drills, carrying the heavy packs, the long marches, the target practice—all these are mere trifles that any one of them can do without a murmur. It would be unmanly to complain! But KP is the bane of their soldierly existence. If mother or wife were only around to do it for them, plus sewing on a few buttons, life would be serene.

But in spite of their resentment, the routine is affecting them considerably and for the better. A friend of mine came to see me when he was on furlough. Soldier Joe looked my room over with a military inspection glance and said, "You know, Gurley, this floor wouldn't be considered clean in the Army." . . .

. . . But to get back to KP, I wondered why they consider it so distasteful. Soldier Joe suggested that if it were not made a form of punishment but were included as a regular part of camp routine, it would not be resented so much. Undoubtedly this is true. But it is more than that. Certain work has probably been identified in their minds with "woman's work," considered drudgery and below their male dignity. Many of them never washed a dish or scrubbed a floor in their lives.

Some Southerners of the more prosperous groups resent KP bitterly because it isn't even considered white folks' work in their part of the country. Their idea of a perfect army would be to have the Negro soldiers do all the work while they rehearsed to be heroes.

But Uncle Sam says in effect: "Look here, soldier! Who sleeps in that bed, walks on that floor, eats off that dish, wears those clothes? You do. Therefore, it's your job to keep them clean just as much as it is to shave your own face and wash your own teeth." It's a lesson in personal responsibility.

In fact, if households were run on a similar system, especially now in wartime when mothers are working outside the home, much drudgery could be taken out of "women's work." If all members of a household did their share, at least took care of their own effects—the house would not be such an overwhelming burden on one person—usually the mother. Uncle Sam is showing us a good example, except that it should not be considered punishment, in sharing work which must be done if common quarters are to be clean, healthful, and pleasant.

Housework, like any form of work, should be organized on a schedule, to be done properly. But this is difficult if one person carries the load. One also needs proper equipment, and here women are apt to scrimp or to use makeshifts. Men usually insist on the right tools to get a job well done. Today women are learning this too in the shops. . . .

. . . Maybe our soldier boys will come back with a new appreciation of all the work done cheerfully and uncomplainingly by Ma, Sis, and Friend Wife. If our style of housekeeping doesn't measure up to theirs, maybe we could turn the job over to them, at least part time. We'll even promise not to inspect with white gloves to see if there's a spot on the plate or the bed railing.

We are grateful to Uncle Sam for the training our boys are receiving and promise to keep them in practice in the future, by gladly and generously sharing our home front KP jobs with them.

SOURCE: *Sunday Worker,* Apr. 11, 1943.

Hitler's 3 K's for Woman— An American Rehash (1947)

GETTING women off the production line and back into full-time mothering and consuming was a major theme of postwar popular literature. The best-selling book, The Modern Woman: The Lost Sex, *written by Marynia Farnham and Ferdinand Lundberg and syndicated in the* Ladies Home Journal, *was the most influential book of this period, helping to create and reinforce the "feminine mystique." With the authority of science, Lundberg, a sociologist, and Farnham, a psychiatrist, blamed women's penis envy for provoking war and called on modern women to come to the aid of their country by returning home to nurture their sons. This book so distressed Simone de Beauvoir that she was inspired to write her feminist classic,* The Second Sex.

It was unusual for Party magazines or newspapers to review such popular tracts. Flynn herself did not write many reviews, and the dozen she wrote were mainly reviews of books written by friends. Her review of Modern Woman *indicates that she understood this reactionary, misogynist tract might even have an impact on CP readers.*

THIS book, purporting to idealize home and mother, is 487 pages of chicanery, comparable even to the obscene arguments of maudlin drunks of a half century ago on "women's rights." It is a vulgar rehash of every slander and misrepresentation of women, of every argument for the home as a ghetto and for depriving women of political, social, legal and economic rights. It is on the lowest imaginable level. You can't laugh it off. It is hateful and contemptuous of women, snarling and mean in tone, downright lewd in language. It has the ugly face of fascism. Hitler is its logical forerunner. Many who laughed at him are dead. Fascism is no laughing matter. Every claw mark of the Nazi beast is here—nasty gibes at Jews, Negroes, labor, the Communists and women, who are their special target.

FASCIST IDEOLOGY

To ridicule or ignore such books is to ignore fascist ideology in our midst. It masquerades here as psychiatry, with a smattering of alleged science, history and sociology, a neat camouflage. In the Nazi concentration camps, bestial women doctors tortured their own sex in the guise of "scientific experiments." Their aggressive hatred of women is in this book.

The Nazis destroyed all rights and organizations of women, driving them out of the professions and public life. In 1932 there were thirty-eight women in the Reichstag. By 1933 there were none. The Nazis did what Lundberg and Farnham advocate.

Hitler said: "The aim of feminine education unalterably has to do with future mothers." They say: "We propose that women should attain status and prestige through motherhood."

Hitler said: "Her sphere is her . . . home." They say women must be "attracted into organizing their lives more closely around the home."

Hitler said: "The problem of our women's movement contains really only one single point—that the child must come into being and thrive" (fathered by Nordic supermen, of course). The authors advocate "a government supervisory agency devoted to serving women who live as women—that is, women as mothers. Its first general task would unquestionably be one of propaganda, with a view to restoring women's sense of prestige and self-esteem as women, actual or potential mothers."

This sounds suspiciously like the Mother Service Dept. of the Nazi "Frauenwerk," established in 1934, to educate women over eighteen for the duties of motherhood, regardless of marriage. Prof. Clifford Kirkpatrick, in his book *Nazi Germany: Its Women and Family Life,* quotes from an official German medical journal of 1933: "An unmarried mother, who rears a healthy and worthy child, is immeasurably more valuable to the nation than a childless married woman."

In Nazi Germany, women teachers were excluded from even girls' high schools. Single women teachers were ruthlessly demoted. These authors, not to be outdone, advocate "that all spinsters be barred by law from having anything to do with the teaching of children on the ground of theoretical (usually real) emotional incompetence."

In 1933 Frau Silber, a Nazi, accused the older leaders of women's organizations of "a dangerous and perverted aping of men." These authors accuse early feminists of "imagining they have male organs." They sneer at existing American women's organizations: "Many such organizations will fight rather than support a rational program to reorient women towards satisfying goals in life."

Women's organizations did fight in Germany. The Association of

Academic Women, the Federation of German Teachers, the Federation of German Women's Clubs, and the German Association of Women Citizens refused to join the Nazi Frauenschaft and were forcibly dissolved in 1933, as these authors would undoubtedly like to see happen here. Women were forced out of governmental and educational posts. Many were imprisoned or executed, others driven into exile. What of the danger of over-population if all women are specialized to breeding? The Hitler-like reply of Lundberg and Farnham is brutally frank:

"If it should ever arise, its solution would probably be in imposing public controls to prevent the breeding of certain strains. With a full population a country could afford to be more selective, could discourage certain types of people from propagating."

The infamous Nazi Sterilization Laws of July 14, 1933, were such imposition of controls, and were used wholesale for racial and political persecution in unrestrained sadism against Jews, Communists, and other victims of the Nazis. I hate to think of this pair deciding which "certain strains" or "types of people" should be sterilized. Their contempt for women and "inferior men" active in "causes," for Communists and workers, indicates plainly where the knife of such "experts" would fall. They also comment: "We are rapidly becoming a population of the aged." The Nazis took care of that too, in their fiery furnaces.

This is not the language of science, but of Nazism.

Why Is Modern Woman "Lost"?

Why is modern woman "lost," a neurotic, "one of modern civilization's unsolved problems"? Because she is unhappy, they charge. To them unhappiness is a monstrous offense. But what is there to be happy about? Is it not fantastic to expect adults who have experienced two world wars within three decades to be universally happy? Wounds are not yet healed, tears not yet dry, the grass not yet green on millions of graves of youth who died to free us from fascism. Can we forget so easily the six million murdered Jews of Europe, nameless orphan children, ancient cities destroyed? Fellow human beings die of hunger in many lands. Resolute people stack the rubble and labor to restore their ravished countries. Prisons are full in Greece, Spain, and Palestine. Atomic bombs piled in the U.S.A. menace the peace of an uneasy, fearful world. But women are "neurotics" if they are not happy in the midst of all this!

The authors reject objective conditions as causative factors. "Unhappiness caused by poverty, disease and war," they say, "will be left to one side in this discussion." And again: "Modern large-scale war and economic boom and depressions . . . we leave to one side, as not directly germane to the sort of obscured induced unhappiness we are discussing."

Lundberg and Farnham are anti-Marxists, of which their anti-feminism is a part. They oppose material progress. They yearn for the medieval home as "stimulating and satisfying," though it lacked toilets, bath-tubs, running water, lights, heating, refrigeration, a laundry and a modern mattress. They are nostalgic for hand tools; they deplore the machine age. "For centuries on end the symbol of womanly power had been the cradle, the distaff, the spinning wheel. . . . With the loss of the self-contained traditional home women's inner emotional balance was disastrously upset." They scorn the modern woman worker. "Every shop girl, steam laundry slavey and canning factory robot might now become the DuBarry of the local tavern on Saturday nights," they sneer.

Their main thesis is that "contemporary women in very large numbers are psychologically disordered." The remedy? Restoration of the medieval home. "The original rich content of the home was lost," they wail, because weaving, spinning, serving, cooking, preserving, baking, and washing is now done outside the home. "If then three-quarters of the canning plants and commercialized baking establishments were to close overnight and food and baking were to be restored to their one time state in the home, the nation would leap forward about one hundred years or more, nutritionally or in food enjoyment."

They trace the dissolution of the home as follows: First, father left to go to work outside. Then the children left to go to public school. Then labor-saving devices took one job after another away from mother, until she finally emerged to find interest outside. The day nursery took the baby out! They disapprove of it all—the industrial revolution, the school system, even the automobile which to them is "neurosis given wheels." In olden times there were fireside neighborly visits, quilting bees, log rolling. "Can anyone point to anything of equal satisfaction that has arisen to take its place?" they ask. Try that question on the young people in your home!

Mussolini Anticipated Them

The authors' main enemy is "feminism," a term which they use indiscriminately for all but "the nutritive activities," as distinguished from the "masculine exploitive activities." Even in this they are not original; for Mussolini also referred to "the emancipated women—the women in masculine professions." Sarcastic, cheap gibes at women pepper this book. "The world is still waiting"—for a woman genius, they remark. On John Stuart Mill's claim that women are capable of doing everything that is done by man, they wisecrack, "Such as impregnating another woman?"

Describing early women's righters, they say, "a more grim-faced crew never faced mortal eyes, on or off a battlefield," and again, "the rape fantasy, a wishful projection, played a large role in feminist literature and speeches." They reveal their contempt for labor also in the following: "Great was the satisfaction of the feminists when [in wartime, EGF] women appeared as house-painters, railroad signal-men, chimney sweeps, and grave diggers." They make a vicious attack on the WACS and WAVES, and seek to present them in a farcical light.

A constantly reiterated vulgar term intended to mean female sex-ual inferiority is used to characterize women like Mary Wollstonecraft, Elizabeth Cady Stanton, Anna Shaw, Charlotte Perkins Gilman. Twenty pages spew forth the most hateful attack on a woman dead 170 years—Mary Wollstonecraft, wife of William Godwin, mother of Mary Shelley, friend of Thomas Paine, and author of *A Vindication of the Rights of Women.* In an alleged psychiatric analysis, her tragic life is torn asunder and her death in child-birth is not spared ridicule.

If you are disgusted thus far, consider this: They take "the magic word *equality,* a fetish of the feminist movement" and define it as "*identity.*" They ask, "Physiologically . . . what did this mean?" They answer, "It meant that society was being asked to accept as identical two similar but decidedly different and complementary organisms." They then list on page 147, all the male and female sexual organs. After said anatomical listings, they conclude: "It meant that society was to accept as identical the functions of these different sets of or-gans . . . and was to act as though the social consequences of their functioning or not functioning was identical." Is that not an all-time bar-room low in argumentation on the woman question? Such "logic," *à la* Nazi, would infer that black cannot be "equal" to white because it is not "identical."

There are two male villains of this psychiatric melodrama—Coper-nicus and Karl Marx. Before Copernicus wrote *De revolutionibus or-bium coelestium (On the Revolution of the Celestial Spheres)* man was the center of the universe. Copernicus dislodged him and placed the sun there. The authors say it was "psychologically cataclysmic and cata-strophic" to man's complacency. He fought to conquer nature through technology and industry, to reassert his importance. Capitalism is the result of man's struggle to conquer his inferiority complex induced by Copernicus' taking the center of the universe away from him.

In the chapter "This Phallic World," they attribute a sexual signifi-cance to machinery—levers, pistons, torpedoes, etc., and—to the atomic bomb explosion.

ANTI-SOVIETISM

Their sociology is equally "scientific" and is charged with aggressive anti-Sovietism. "The fullest flower of the creche system has been seen in the Soviet Union. It is a system that guarantees beyond doubt a new crop of fresh neurotics." (Odd, isn't it, that the USSR has the lowest rate of mental illness, according to William Mandel's *A Guide to the Soviet Union?*)

They state that feminism has been most fully realized in the USSR, although its underpinnings are swept away now since easy divorce and abortions are no longer legal. "The official Russian propaganda hymns the virtues of family life as eloquently as does the Roman Catholic."

They continue:

"The political agents of the Kremlin abroad continue to beat the feminist drums in full awareness of its disruptive influence among the potential enemies of the Soviet Union. The Women's International Democratic Federation was therefore launched in Nov. 1945 in Paris. This organization will, outside Russia, probably continue to promote the theories of feminism and what it can of neurotic disorders in the already neurotic capitalist world." . . .

"For them the lack of woman suffrage was but another count to be charged against capitalism. . . . They were fishing in troubled water and had for women no higher destiny than making them equal partners and workers in the socialist factory system."

Here, in one sentence, is their five-point, anti-feminist gripe against the Soviet Union, that women are *equal, partners, workers,* in a *socialist, factory system.*

They include in the organized movements—"of hatred, hostility and violence"—Communism, Socialism, National Socialism, anti-Semitism, and feminism. To quote:

"Marxism preached irreconcilable hatred to all who opposed it and prescribed for them very simply extinction, death. . . . The principal upthrust of Marxism to date has come in Russia where it proceeded to put its theories to work." . . .

GOSPEL OF HATE

It is difficult to give a clear picture of this jumbled book. It is ugly, distorted, anti-Soviet, Nazi-minded, and disquietingly full of sexual references. In summarizing, they list as forces contributing to undermining the stability of the home the following: the idea of progress; that human welfare is to be sought in material and physiological pathways; the emphasis on work and endless production of goods; the primacy of rationality over emotions; the desirability of human equality in all things; the idea of freedom.

These concepts, they say, have disorganized the feelings of women. Their unbridled hatred of the Soviet Union stems from the fact that it stands for the progress they repudiate. Anti-Semitism is revealed in their pseudo-history.

"The Hebrews in the beginning were a small culturally inferior group that aspired greatly to superiority and nationhood. . . . Hebrew leaders in every possible way created and stressed *differences* between themselves and surrounding people."

And further:

"The Germanic tribes of Europe in particular were psychically healthy and free of inner conflicts when first exposed to Greco-Roman-Judeo-Christian culture."

What could be more reminiscent of Hitler's ravings?

There is a veritable flood of such books and articles attacking the modern American woman. The stench of fascism arises from them. This happened in Germany when Hitler came to power. Back to the kitchen, the brothel, the menial tasks, breed the master race—are the degrading concepts of women inherent in fascism.

SOURCE: *Political Affairs*, Apr. 1947.

Woman's Place—In the Fight for a Better World (1947)

THE CP women were in the forefront of the fight for peace and nuclear disarmament.

W OMEN *want lasting peace!"* Mothers and young wives of veterans, mothers of growing children, youth facing the future, want a world free from the fear of war, and everything that breeds war.

Wars have been horrible enough in the past. The development of the atomic bomb by American scientists has unleashed a force that can destroy all life on our planet. To save humanity from such a fate, the mothers of the race must demand that the manufacture of this monstrous weapon be outlawed forever. All existing stockpiles in our country must be destroyed.

. . . Our statesmen act like excited schoolboys playing "hide and seek" with a deadly toy. "Spy! He peeked!" they shout at another country. We women are not interested in "me first" in a game of world suicide. The scientists and engineers who developed the bomb are worried. They know how dangerous it is. Dr. L. W. Chubb, Director of the Westinghouse Research Laboratory, worked with the atomic bomb project from its beginning. In *The World within the Atom* he says: "Man has entered the age of atomic energy—we are faced with the greatest challenge of all times. Will we use this power to blast civilization from the earth, or will we learn to apply it usefully in a world where each of us is the next door neighbor to everyone else?" Mr. E. V. Murphee, vice-president of the central research organization of the Standard Oil Company, also connected with the atomic bomb project, discussing "how will nuclear energy be geared into our industrial and social system" (*The Lamp,* June 1946), warns against "misuse of atomic energy by troublemakers anywhere." He concludes: "When man's philosophy and statesmanship catch up with his science, the atom can go to work for him safely." Scientists generally want the bomb outlawed.

It is stupid for our statesmen to assume that we can long have a monopoly on atomic bombs. Scientists for years have worked on the atom and how to release its energy for industrial and scientific uses. The atomic bomb was a by-product. It can be abandoned without stopping peaceful uses of atomic energy. Can we expect other countries will wait for us to show them the atomic bomb in another war?

. . . American women have the power to help stop it. Women are 50.6 per cent of our population. Let the voice of American women be heard. Let every organization of women speak out quickly and emphatically to the President and State Department, to our delegates to the United Nations, to Congress, for international disarmament. Let us re-affirm, on International Women's Day, our determination to achieve "an enduring peace for many generations to come," as our spokesman Franklin D. Roosevelt pledged at the Big Three meeting, which led to the United Nations. American women have tremendous political power. We must use it intelligently; to place our country in the vanguard for peace.

. . . From the baby in the crib to grandpa, everyone is a consumer. But women usually have the unhappy job of making ends meet. There has been a 68 per cent rise in prices since 1938. Has there been an equal rise in wages? To hear the employers, and their mouthpieces in the press, on the radio, and in Congress—it's all the fault of the unions. Government figures of the Department of Commerce show that workers' wages and salaries rose only 6 per cent in 1946 while "business incomes"—salaries paid to corporation officers, etc. went up 10 per cent and dividends and interest payments to owners and stockholders of companies went up 24 per cent. Corporation profits are now between fifteen and sixteen billion dollars a year, which is divided among a comparatively few people. This is an all time high in the U.S.

The Congress of Industrial Organizations (CIO) has shown (in the Nathan Report) that the excess corporate profits are so great that a general wage increase of 25 per cent could be granted without raising prices or without reducing profits below the 1936–39 peacetime level. The average weekly earnings of workers in manufacturing industry have declined from $47.50 in January 1945 to $39.24 in October 1946. Wartime overtime and bonuses stepped them up temporarily. In every industry where there was a wage increase, the actual price increase was far more than would offset it. In food, where 1.3 per cent would equal wage increases, the price rise was 26.2 per cent in 1946, according to OPA [Office of Price Administration]. In textiles, where 4.5 per cent would equal wage increases, the price rise was 26.2 per cent. In hides and leather the wage increase could be offset by 3 per cent, the price rise was 20.1 per cent. These figures speak eloquently to women. Big Business, not the unions, are responsible for price increases on food, clothing, and shoes.

SOURCE: *Woman's Place: In the Fight for a Better World* (New York: New Century Publishers, 1946).

Where is Korea? Soldier's Mother Asks (1950)

WHEN the Communist party was against a war it considered unjust, like the Korean War, Flynn became a pacifist and called on women, almost using the biological imperative of motherhood, to protect their sons. When the Communist party was pro war, as in World War II, she became a hawk, appealing to mothers to encourage their sons to enlist in the heroic cause.

The waitress Flynn referred to in this article had the FBI baffled. Because Flynn chatted with her often, they assumed she must be a dangerous subversive and therefore followed her. Her clandestine activities alluded them, and they could not figure out the relationship. It never occurred to them Flynn was simply interested in ordinary folks and enjoyed smoozing.

I met a woman, a young woman, English-born, whose story gripped me, so I have to write it. She is a waitress in a place where I eat my meals. She works, therefore tips are important. She is youthful looking, blond, blue-eyed, slender; she jokes and laughs with the customers; she sings with the juke box; she knows how to jolly children so they'll eat their cereals for breakfast; to tell the reducers how to count their calories; to kid the men, old and young, who invariably try to show what Don Juans they are, in her presence. There is something so efficient, so cool and competent about her, yet friendly and pleasant, that everyone expands and feels more in a holiday mood.

Little by little, as a week passes, I learn details of her life. She is a widow, she has three children. They live nearby and are in the care of a good neighbor, while she works. Her husband died seven years ago. She has lived, after her terrible grief, for one purpose, to raise her children. She used to go to Miami in the winter and to Northern resorts in the summer. But as her children grew older she decided to keep her growing family together and with her, so is settled now in the North. There are two boys and a girl. This I learned at first. She showed me their pictures, two beautiful, healthy children and the oldest son, nineteen, taller than she is.

Later we talked some more. She told me she does all her own housework, washes and irons her uniforms and her daughter's dresses. How she goes home in the evening to find her two young children in bed, but usually awake to bid her good-night. Then one cold rainy night when there were no customers I asked her to join me in a glass of wine while she had her late-night sandwich and coffee just before closing.

Suddenly all the jolly front of her occupation fell away and she told me about her oldest son. He is in the army, in the South now, in combat training. He felt she was doing too much in taking care of the whole family, so he joined the army to learn a trade. She said, "His best friend was just killed in Korea. I thought we were at peace. I would never have consented to him joining the army if I thought there was any danger of more war! I'm so worried they'll send him."

So eating at the heart of this gallant working-class mother is a terrible fear for her son. "If anything happens to him, I'll be finished," she said, "I can't go through that shock twice."

This woman did not know me. To her I was just an elderly woman on vacation, possibly a retired teacher, because I read all the time. I had mentioned that I had lost my only son. This unlocked the emotions she keeps so well concealed and under control all day long. But she asked me, "What is it all about? Why do American boys have to be killed? Is it a war?"

When I suggested it would be better to let the Koreans settle their own affairs and run their own country, this working class woman who knows nothing of world politics agreed. What she knows is that she wants peace in the world and her young son returned safely to her.

"How did your son die?" she asked. I told her, "In a hospital in 1940, in New York, after an operation." She replied sympathetically, "Maybe you were luckier than a lot of other mothers. You were there and you know what happened to him."

SOURCE: *Daily Worker,* Aug. 1, 1950.

Women and Politics

Elizabeth Gurley Flynn at a Communist Party rally, Pittsburgh, 1939

The Bogus Amendment (1939)

ELIZABETH *Gurley Flynn wrote nine* Daily Worker *articles and gave many speeches attacking the Equal Rights Amendment (ERA). Most progressive feminists attacked the amendment as well. Why did these progressives until the 1970s prefer protection over equality? Although aware of women workers, most socialists and labor union activists assumed that woman's primary responsibility was child rearing. If women worked, Flynn and most liberals advocated special laws (such as limits on the weight they could lift, guarantees of no overtime) that they believed would eliminate exploitation and protect women. The differences between men and women, rather than the similarities, were primary for those who, like Flynn, proposed protective legislation.*

The notions of equal opportunity, comparable worth, cooperative parenting, and affirmative action were not suggested until the 1960s and 1970s as alternatives to achieving equality. From the late 1920s until World War II, the lack of jobs for women and their heavy family responsibilities restricted women's access to work. Even though Flynn chose the public over the private sphere for herself, she assumed other women were unlike her and preferred protection and domesticity to a lifetime career. Only a few militant suffragists and feminists in the nineteenth century campaigned for equal rights legislation.

By the 1970s a majority of women were working, and there was a clear need for all-encompassing new legislation. When Title 7 of the Civil Rights Act passed in 1964, complaints of sex discrimination flooded the federal government and caused backlogs in the courts. By the 1970s feminists and labor advocates understood that protective legislation in fact prevented women from job advancement and restricted them to inferior, low-paid, dead-end work. In the 1970s feminist organizations mounted a huge campaign to educate people about the need for the ERA. This campaign influenced the Communist party and the AFL-CIO to change their anti-ERA position. By 1976 all progressives finally endorsed the Equal Rights Amendment. However, in 1982 the ERA failed to be ratified by the necessary number of states and was defeated, this time by a small margin.

WHAT is the Equal Rights Amendment? In the past sixteen years the Women's Party has proposed an amendment to the Constitution: "Men and women shall have equal rights throughout the United States and every place subject to its jurisdiction."[1] These eighteen words are an unsuccessful attempt to summarize the needs of American women. They are misleading.

Who composes the Women's Party? From 1912 to 1920 they did a good job to which they owe their present prestige. As militant fighters for Votes for Women they picketed the White House, were arrested, went on hunger strikes. When suffrage was won, Equal Rights became their slogan. Their first program was twenty-eight points. All progressives gave enthusiastic support to twenty-seven, as a necessary mopping up job, to remove all vestiges of old English common law which still deprives women of many legal and civil rights.

One point caused a storm of protest, which still rages today, their opposition to all special labor legislation for women wage workers, as sex discrimination. The Women's Party has done a bad job since 1923. They have sullied their past. They have become a spearhead for reactionary employers.

Who opposes the Equal Rights Amendment? Their stand against labor legislation has alienated old-time suffragists, progressive women's organizations, and organized labor. All the non-controversial issues on equality which could unite women today are neglected by the Women's Party. They have split the forces of women and held back real equal rights for sixteen years.

Seven large organizations of women who opposed the amendment originally stand firm today. They are the YWCA, the National Council of Catholic Women, the Jewish Women's Council, the Consumer's League, the American Association of University Women, and the Women's Trade Union League. They objected to "blanket legislation which may aggravate existing inequalities or substitute new ones," and cited as necessary hours and wage laws, rape penalties and mothers' pensions. Believe it or not, the cockeyed "feminists" of the Women's Party replied that rape penalties and pensions should apply equally to both sexes. They advocate "Parenthood Aid" instead of "Maternity Aid." If man could give birth to babies this would make sense, not before. (A drink is all the aid daddy needs before a birth.)

Who supports the Equal Rights Amendment? The Women's Party have had solid Republican backing for the amendment from the start. It was introduced in 1923 by Senator Curtis of Kansas, later Vice President under Hoover. The Republican National Committee with T. Coleman Du Pont a member endorsed it. Wm. Randolph Hearst is "a resolute feminist" to the Women's Party. Their contributors sound like the social register—Hearst, Belmont, Du Pont, Havemeyer, Goelet, Pell. Their present sponsors are Senator Burke, foe of the Wagner Labor Act, and Congressman Ludlow, foe of WPA.

[1] Flynn is paraphrasing the actual wording of the Amendment.

What can we do to stop the Amendment? Expose this group of well-fed, well-dressed, well-housed, well-financed ladies, who call night laws for mothers in a textile mill "coddling laws." Repudiate women who applaud when the Supreme Court declares a Minimum Wage Law unconstitutional. They are not fighting for women. They are not "above the battle" of the class struggle. They are for Big Business. On guard against a counterfeit Equal Rights Amendment.

SOURCE: *Sunday Worker,* Apr. 9, 1939.

Why Women Should Vote Labor and Communist (1942)

FLYNN had never spoken on the radio before 1936. When she returned from her long illness, she feared her orating ability would be made obsolete by the new technological wonder. Obviously she overcame her fear and adjusted to electronic methods of speaking her piece. However, being a Red, she did not have much opportunity to become a radio personality and develop this talent to its fullest.

"Why Women Should Vote Labor and Communist" is a speech Flynn gave over the radio in 1942 in support of Peter Cacchione, the Communist candidate for city council from Brooklyn. The talk was given during the Popular Front period, when New York City had proportional representation—a European electoral system allowing the voter to rank the candidates. It was only with proportional representation that minority candidates could possibly win elections. Pete Cacchione was elected three times to the city council. In 1947, with the cold war approaching, proportional representation was defeated and with it Communist representation in government.

B RAVE women fought for 133 years to win this right for us in 1920. We should exercise it with intelligence and effect. We must not waste our votes. It is a chance to say publicly where we stand on the vital interests of our city. Women are not experts in political theories. But women are very close to the real needs of the people. For this reason, I am addressing my appeal particularly to women—to defeat Tammany, to vote Labor and Communist. Now don't turn the dial at this point, sister, and say, "Oh, just another political speech!" This speech won't be that kind of politics. It will be about us and our lives. So listen a while longer. Don't go away!

Why don't women want to listen to "politics"? Because in the past, politics was men's business—not all men's, just the politicians! And a fine mess they made of it, didn't they? Politics meant Tammany and Tammany meant graft. It meant incompetent job holders, a badly run city; a dirty, disorderly shameful city. The poor live in slums. Babies die. Children play in crowded streets. Accidents happen daily. A Tammany inspector passes an overcrowded firetrap as safe. The next day people are burned to death. Or a house tumbles down in a storm and kills poor women and children, as happened in Staten Island recently.

. . . There are so many issues which go direct to the hearts of women. The high cost of living for example. Women do the daily buying for the homes. The cost of milk, bread, meat; rent, clothes, shoes continues to increase. The Milk Trust, Bread Trust, Meat Trust try to trick the consumers into accepting this as unavoidable. They say: "It's on account of wage increases!" Friends, wages went up 2% in one year; food prices went up 42% in the last four years. Clothes went up 26% and rents went up 10%. They just use a small pay increase, which workers had to organize and fight for, as an excuse. They try to prejudice you against labor unions. They want you to think it's all the working man's fault. But they carefully conceal their own fat salaries and huge profits.

. . . Women hate poverty. Persons who glorify poverty have never endured it. They profit by it. Many women have joined organized labor, especially the CIO. The laundry workers and girls in the five and dime stores have already bettered their conditions. The domestic workers, beauty parlor operators, store clerks are building their unions. The Women's Auxiliaries are flourishing everywhere. "Ma and the girls helping Pa" they called it during the steel and auto strikes. Thirty auxiliaries are affiliated with a council in N.Y. City. I am glad so many daughters of our fighting Irish race are in the Transport auxiliary. Now textiles are organizing. 40% are women. The Communist Party co-operates in all this. It urges special labor legislation for women. It exposes hypocritical use of the slogan Equal Rights to steal legislative gains from women toilers. It exposes the triple exploitation of Negro women, as Negroes, as women, as workers discriminated against, segregated, underpaid, insulted. It exposes the shame of child labor—over two and a quarter million children working in industry and agriculture, while grown-ups look for work and Big Business fights a Child Labor Amendment.

. . . Our immediate responsibility is to vote Labor and Communist. There are four Communist candidates for City Council—Peter Cacchione in Kings, Israel Amter in Manhattan, Isidore Begun in the Bronx, and Paul Crosbie in Queens; I urge you to designate the one in your county as number one choice. Then vote the labor party candidates as your further choices. Each Communist candidate has been selected by our Party for his particular fitness as a fighting councilman. He will co-operate with all progressives. He will be the voice of workers' experience. He will fight for men and women and children; for the unemployed, for the labor unions. Every Communist councilman will raise the political level of our city.

SOURCE: WMCA Radio Address, Oct. 24, 1942. Flynn Papers, Tamiment.

A Tip to Candidates—Watch Your Jokes (1944)

DURING *the Popular Front period, Ben Davis, a black lawyer from Harlem, was elected to the city council. It is Davis Flynn referred to in "A Tip to Candidates." In private she also criticized him for his treatment of women and his womanizing. She believed other Party members tolerated Davis's chauvinism because they had a double standard for blacks.*

I recently attended a dinner. I won't say for whom because I don't want to identify it. A win-the-war candidate for an important office jeopardized votes before my very eyes, as the saying goes. I wished I could have stopped him from ruining an otherwise excellent and eloquent speech by pulling an offensive and tactless joke about the alleged proclivity of women to talk a lot, as if men were all silent clams! It so happened that the shortest and best speeches were made by women.

This candidate is a popular man, yet a murmur of resentment that threatened to be audible protest rippled through the hall, especially among the women guests. I hope he reads this column or that somebody will show it to him. I admire him greatly, but I implore him, if you want to get elected, don't joke in a chauvinistic manner about women. Women won't take it. In fact, this is a good tip to all progressive candidates.

Mr. Candidate, you do not rely on cajolery and witticisms to win men's votes. Treat women voters as seriously and assume that they are as intelligent on political issues as are your own men constituents. The days of kissing babies and kidding women are past—if they ever existed.

Women are not sensitive plants. They don't mind joking of the right sort in the right time and place. But they are fed up with what the younger generation rightly calls "corny jokes" about their loquaciousness, irrationality, lack of logic, extravagance, and lightmindedness— just as the Negro people are. The stage Irishman with his "Be Jabbers" and the Jewish comedian with a derby hat pulled over his ears were eliminated long ago by popular protest. Similar caricatures of Negroes and women are passing. I notice that jokes about WACS and WAVES fall flat with vaudeville audiences. Jokes that tend to feed the fire of prejudice against others on account of color, nationality, religion, or sex should be rebuked and discouraged. The Negro people despise the Stepin Fetchit and Mammy types and demand serious and dignified treatment on the stage, and an opportunity to express their rich cultural development. No candidate in his right mind would dare to crack jokes in Harlem about the Negro people. Women are entitled to the same consideration.

. . . The remark of Dr. Samuel Johnson, English essayist of the eighteenth century, that a "woman who makes a speech is like a dog who walks on its hind legs, a marvel that it can be done at all"—is a measure of the progress that has been made. It would be considered a pretty low remark today.

SOURCE: *Daily Worker,* July 23, 1944.

Votes for All Negro Women (1959)

On the whole the Communist party was aware of the damaging effects of racism and was in the forefront of the fight for integration in sports, schools, housing, and employment. Flynn herself wrote many Daily Worker *columns on the evils of racism. In the early 1960s she celebrated the revived spirit of activism in the civil rights movement and believed the student protests had some of the strengths and weaknesses of the IWW. She was far more enthusiastic about the sixties activism than most Party officials, who had made alliances with more conservative civil rights groups, such as the National Association for the Advancement of Colored People and the Urban League, and who dismissed militance as an infantile disorder.*

As an IWW member, Flynn had been against any participation in the bourgeois democratic process: elections, collective bargaining, or contracts. However, even before she officially joined the Communist party she had begun to think that to be effective in American life, Communists had to participate wholeheartedly in electoral struggles, to create independent political forms, and to take full advantage of every avenue open for talking to people about socialism.

MILLIONS of Americans in the South are denied the right to vote, by force and violence, poll taxes, so-called character tests, and literacy tests full of tricky questions. Over two hundred local laws have been passed in Mississippi, Georgia, Alabama, Tennessee and elsewhere, deliberately planned to prevent Negro citizens from voting.

Half, at least, of those who are barred from going to the polls are Negro women. The 19th Amendment is a dead letter for them. They remain disenfranchised in fact.

When I was in the Women's Federal Reformatory at Alderson, W. Va., I never met a single Negro woman from the South who had voted. They did not even know they had a right to do so. When the question was sometimes discussed among the inmates as to whether one had lost their vote, they would say: "We never had it where I come from!" and would tell what terrible things had happened to Negro men who had tried to vote.

The NAACP is carrying on a campaign for three million Negro voters in the South by 1960. It is a hard, up-hill fight and needs widespread publicity and support.

I was glad to read that the League of Women Voters is interesting itself in this drive. Several members attempted to answer the questions that are posed to Negro voters and found that they could not pass the test set up for so-called illiterates. So they realize what a fraud it is.

The struggle for woman suffrage began at Seneca Falls, N.Y., over one hundred years ago. Among those present there, with Elizabeth Cady Stanton, Lucretia Mott and Susan B. Anthony, was Frederick Douglass, the eloquent Negro anti-slavery lecturer. In fact he was the one who urged women to include "the right to vote" among their demands for equal rights, so bold a demand for that time that they hesitated. A new suffrage movement for the right of Negro women to vote is called for today, to finish the unfulfilled task of four decades ago. The 14th Amendment specified "male," thus excluding both white and Negro women from voting in 1868.

The federal Civil Rights Commission has recommended that federal registrars be appointed for the 1960 elections, to help guarantee the vote to Southern Negro citizens. Today white trickery in the states cheats them of their right. White primaries were outlawed by the Supreme Court in 1954. But the South flouts these rulings, by token integration and token voting. The recommendation of the Commission would help, no doubt of that, to overcome fear and encourage Negro people to come forward with some assurance of protection from the Federal government. Some suits are now pending brought by Negroes.

We who live in the North little realize the tremendous courage displayed by Negro people in the deep South—to set up branches of the NAACP, to become candidates for public office, to register to vote, to send their children to desegregated schools, to buy a house out of the Negro ghetto area, to break down discrimination in stores, luncheons, soda fountains, libraries, on beaches and tennis courts. Negro women are in the forefront and giving leadership in many of these hard struggles. An eighty-three-year-old woman, Mrs. Nettie Dicksen, gave $10,000 to the NAACP in San Francisco last year "in God's name to fight against the disgraceful abuse of American democracy."

Mrs. Daisy Bates, editor of the Arkansas State Press of Little Rock, Arkansas, led the fight there to open up the schools to Negro children. In Louisiana the state chairman of the NAACP is a woman, Mrs. Dorothea Combre; Mrs. Margaret Belafonte is co-chairman with Duke Ellington in the Freedom Fund Drive. Many branches are headed by women in many states. Several Negro women doctors are on their national health committee. Departments are headed up by quite a few women. Negro women are organized in churches, societies, and in several large national associations.

Sojourner Truth, a powerful orator, was a pioneer Negro woman advocate of votes for women. Her memory and tradition should be revived today, in a united effort to guarantee full suffrage for all women.

SOURCE: *Sunday Worker*, Oct. 25, 1959.

What Price Housework? (1941)

IN "What Price Housework" Flynn was responding to articles that others had written. In 1935 Mary Inman, inspired by Clara Zetkin's pamphlet Lenin on the Woman Question, *wrote* In Women's Defense, *a book about housework as productive labor. For various reasons the Party refused to publish Inman's work, but the San Francisco Party newspaper, the* Peoples World, *serialized it; when finally published as a volume,* In Women's Defense *sold well and was favorably reviewed in the* Daily Worker.

Ruth McKenney, an editor of New Masses, *in late 1940 wrote two articles for the magazine, criticizing Inman and refocusing the debate. Harrison George, an old Wobbly and editor of the* Daily Worker, *replied to McKenney, in early 1941. He supported Inman's position, although he never mentioned her; Flynn, in her article, generally agreed with George, but she only summarized his ideas.*[1]

There is a real contrast in Flynn's articles from her IWW period and those

[1] Sherna Gluck has done research on Mary Inman and shared her material with me. In Flynn's FBI Files No. NY100-1696, May 5, 26, is a letter that states, "I did not see them, as the discussion was going on in re the Secretariat letter and I did not feel it wise to interfere in any way, particularly as there is no love lost between [Harrison] George and myself, over the Inman affair." In this letter, copied by the FBI, Flynn was informing Party officials of her talks in California in 1947.

*from her Communist party period on the subject of housework. In her IWW
period she initiated discussion of housework, whereas in the Communist party
period she mainly responded to articles that others had written. In Flynn's "The
IWW Call to Women" (in "The Wobbly Years," this volume) her ideas resemble
McKenny's rather than George's (and Inman's). In 1915 Flynn wrote that the
machine made housework obsolete and therefore the home produced a conservatism and selfishness in women. In the Wobbly period Flynn saw joining the
IWW as a solution for women; McKenney recommended joining the CIO and
Communist party. McKenney's article claimed boldly that "nobody can write
about the woman question today in good faith without stating the fact that
women have been completely and unconditionally emancipated in the Soviet
Union."[2] This assertion Flynn did not dare tackle.*

*Inman had argued that housework was labor and that housewives should be
treated as other workers and organized as a special group, as blacks were. This
notion was heretical to the Party; it implied that women were a unique, special
group, and that current Marxist terminology and structures did not adequately
address women's oppression. It is unfortunate the Communist party suppressed
Inman's work, although as it turned out, many of her ideas were discussed by
the women's liberation movement of the 1960s.*

To New Masses; I agree with Harrison George that Ruth McKenney
has done a grand service in discussing the position of women.

The friendly dispute between them (*New Masses*, Feb. 11, 1941) is
whether a mother's work in the home is "unpaid labor" without ex-
change or use value, unproductive and not socially useful. Ruth argues that we should not insult women by pretending that we think
housework is useful or appealing to their interests as housewives.
Harrison double damns housework as gruelling, monotonous drudgery. But he insists that it is useful and is paid for "in keep," subsis-
tence, food, clothing and shelter. He argues that a man's wage is a
family wage. "Petty domestic economy" as Lenin called it, is a hangover of the handicraft period of home industry; machinery has taken
a large part of "woman work" out of the home, such as textile, needle
trades, soap-making, beer, butter, and cheese making, food preserving, etc. Machinery could do considerable of what's left if we had
"large scale socialist economy" as Lenin said. The collective way of life
in the Soviet Union illustrates this.

. . . Marx and Lenin condemned both the breaking up of the family under capitalism and the stultifying and crushing drudgery forced
upon poor mothers. Whether they are "paid" is not essentially impor-

[2]Ruth McKenney, "Women Are Human Beings, No. 2," *New Masses*, Dec. 17,
1940, 9.

tant, although Marx states in *Capital,* in *Wage-Labor and Capital,* and in *Value, Price and Profit* that wages include what is necessary to perpetuate the race of laborers. That man, like the machine, will wear out and must be replaced by another man. Besides the amount of necessaries required for his *own* maintenance, he wants another amount of necessaries to bring up a certain quota of children that are to replace him on the labor market and to perpetuate the race of laborers (*Value, Price and Profit*). John comes home on Saturday night and hands his wife the pay envelope. She pays the family's bills. They all subsist, including mother. But suppose John decided to go "equalitarian" and pay Mary wages—say half his earnings. Under capitalism it would become an immediate absurdity. They'd both pay the same bills with the same money and be broke just as quickly. It's six of one or half dozen of the other.

I think Ruth is wrong when she argues that housewives do not perform *useful* work. It is drudgery for WPA workers who dig with hand shovels instead of steam shovels.[3] Still, it's useful work Housework is far more useful than a lot of jobs for which good money is paid under capitalism. We all agree that it should be reorganized, mechanized, socialized to eliminate waste, duplication, and drudgery. We cannot abolish diapering babies, wiping their noses, feeding them, keeping them clean, teaching them to talk and walk. To free the individual mother from a twenty-four-hour job, and put it on a professional basis, to have collective nurseries, kitchens and laundries, is a belated recognition of just how socially necessary and useful is all the work she has performed so long and laboriously under capitalism.

There's always danger of generalization in discussing the subject "Women." Ruth's title "Women Are Human Beings" seems somewhat outmoded to me. With the winning of suffrage, the rapid growth of labor unions, and general public activities of women, it is practically axiomatic in America. Exceptions in backward areas are where men are not human beings either.

That women are human beings is a true statement, but it leaves me cold. It isn't enough to be a primate mammal in the world as it is today. What class you belong to, and what you do are more important. The term *women,* like *men,* is too general for political discussion. Women cannot be lumped together as a sex. *Women* is not a term defining an age, racial, national, or class group—as are *youth, Negro, Irish,* and *labor.* Women are approximately half of all of them. There are no problems common to all women. Ruth's first article, in the Dec. 17, 1940 issue, oversimplifies, I fear. The problems she poses, such as "career or home," are probably important to some women, though plain "get-

[3] The WPA was the Works Progress Administration of the New Deal.

ting a job" is not a choice but a necessity with most young women. "Fear of not getting married" is not the bugaboo today it once was. Certainly few women give up their jobs and expect to be supported. They are lucky in this period of unemployment if they don't find themselves with a husband to support.

The problems of women are as varied and complex as the categories of women. There are women of the capitalist class, rich, idle, secure. Their "problems" are not our concern. There are women of the working class, wage earners, employed or unemployed; wives who work in the home and the "white collar" salaried groups. Capitalist women and working women are divided, as men are, by the chasm of conflicting economic interests.

SOURCE: *New Masses*, Mar. 4, 1941.

Letter to Al Richmond (1964)

IN her later years, Flynn was an inveterate letter writer, often writing three and four letters a day.[1] Most of her friends lived outside New York City, and, especially after Kathie died in 1962, Flynn was lonely, but busy. Many of her letters were filled with news of sick, dying, or dead friends. One of the themes in her letters was aging and her fear that the Communist party was filled with old, tired men who refused to step down and give youth a chance. As she wrote to Al Richmond on approaching seventy-five,[2]

[1] The Department of Justice opened Flynn's mail. I have a great deal of it due to the Freedom of Information Act.

[2] Al Richmond was editor of *People's World*, the West Coast CP newspaper, which was considerably more controversial and lively than the East Coast *Daily World*. He is author of *A Long View from the Left: Memoires of an American Revolutionary* (Boston: Houghton Mifflin, 1973) and no longer a Party member. He gave the Tamiment Library all his letters from Flynn. The two wrote frequently during 1963 and 1964, as Richmond was writing an article on the IWW. Richmond helped me with background to this document.

It seems incredible to be that old. One's bones may feel it and wrinkles reveal it, but strangely enough one does not feel old inside, or in spirit, tho I hate all that pollyanna stuff about really being young—which isn't so at all.
. . . It has its political significance. I'm strong for older people withdrawing to leave room for the young—but unfortunately they are still scarce in our ranks. When I said to Gus [Gus Hall was party chief at that time and still is] maybe I should retire to set an example for others. I could name for you at least a half a dozen who should not hold on so tightly but let go. Gus replies "Don't do it. You'll be the only one. They won't follow your example." They really don't trust the youth to take over. Nor do they see their shortcomings—some of which you suggest in your letter re *self-delusion*.[3]

The following letter was written at the beginning of the student movement; Flynn sensed that both students and women were on the move and the Communist party had better seize the day. Her reasons for capitalizing on the woman question were not merely opportunistic; as she observed, male chauvinism had increased, and she was critical of herself for not having previously taken up the issue in the Party. Nothing seems to have come of her concern with the status of women, probably because she was too busy fighting the McCarran Act and securing her passport to go to the Soviet Union, where she hoped to finish her autobiography.

March 11, 1964

Dear Al:
    Your cheerful and inspiring letter came this a.m. I'm going to read it to my colleagues at our next session. I wish the youth here (close to us at least) could be infused with a like spirit. Here they are infatuated with "theory" but not inclined to action. Mary Kaufman, as the lawyer for the Advance group,[4] told me confidentially they are nice kids but utterly inept. Marvin and Sue are going out there. She is very good but he is an imitation of all the worst features of "a leader." I hope he will change in a different atmosphere. Bettina wrote me a fine letter on her experiences.[5]
    It's a year ago today that Behan came to this hotel.[6] I fear we will

[3] Letter to Al Richmond, Sept. 24, 1963; Tamiment and R. Baxandall have copies.
    [4] Advance was a CP student organization indicted under the McCarran Act for failure to register. Marvin Markman and Sue Witcofsky were members.
    [5] Bettina Aptheker was a leader of the Berkeley free speech movement, and an active member of the Communist party, to which she no longer belongs. I was helped by Aptheker with information from this period.
    [6] Brendan Behan, poet and playwright, lived at the Chelsea Hotel, where Flynn was also residing at this time. In fact, Flynn was right; he died in 1964. They were

never see him again. His condition does indeed sound very serious. Too bad drink had such a terrible hold on him. The curse of the Irish it's called. Not too many of us can take it in moderation. Not much news from here. Ben is out of the hospital—after two weeks or so of tests.[7] He had kidney stones and Drs thought it might be a growth, necessitating an operation. But apparently that is not the case, Louis came back, well tanned, but still looking sick; he should have stayed longer in California.[8] He can hardly resist getting caught up again in tensions here, I fear. Winny is busy as can be—with appointments day and night.[9] Later he will go to the mid-west to see his mother and still later plans a trip across the country. He spoke very well at Carnegie Hall—saved the occasion as a matter of fact; I wish our editor had your modesty.[10] Both speeches here and in Chicago were disappointing but he insists on *protocol* as editor to be the main speaker. A lovely Latin American program helped lighten the occasion. But the crowd will not come another year if there is a repeat of speaker. Our passport case will probably be argued before the Supreme Court in April. The Government has not yet indicated if it will appeal the Party case, but probably will. It looks as if Bobby may be on his way out. I feel we'll defeat the [McCarran] Act finally but not until after the election and the [Department of Justice] has a new head.[11] He carries vendettas against Hoffa, against us, and *possibly* against the Pres. He's what the Irish call "black Irish"—no reference to color but to the *heart.*

---

pals. When Behan was asked about the Irish Americans on television, he said, "which, McCarthy or Elizabeth Gurley Flynn?" (*Daily Worker*, Mar. 15, 1964).

[7] Ben Davis was a black lawyer, congressman, and leader of the Communist party.

[8] Louis Weinstock was head of the Painters Union and on the CP executive board.

[9] Henry Winston was a Party executive and Smith Act defendant, whose sentence John Kennedy commuted in 1961. Winston, who was black, lost his sight as a result of a brain tumor prison authorities were slow to treat while he was in the federal penitentiary in Terre Haute, Indiana. Flynn was very fond of him. He was more open and less doctrinaire than many Party leaders.

[10] James Jackson, then editor of the *Daily Worker*.

[11] Robert Kennedy, then attorney general. The Kennedys had an ambivalent attitude toward government prosecution of Communists and radicals. They believed the Communist party was not a threat to the United States and wanted to erase all tints of McCarthyism from their administration (Arthur Schlesinger, *A Thousand Days*, Boston: Houghton Mifflin, 1965, 699–700). Right wingers called for Robert Kennedy's impeachment, saying he was dragging his feet in prosecuting Communists (*Saturday Evening Post*, May 19, 1962, 17–23).

The McCarran Act, called the Communist Control Act or Internal Security Act, was passed in 1950 and then upheld by the Supreme Court in 1961. However in 1965 the Court ruled that the government could not compel Party members to register.

I plug a little now and again on the book but get deflected alot.[12] If I can get the material organized and an outline under way, I'll try to take off June, July, and August and leave NY to be able to concentrate on it. We got a few good sized contributions from Calif. to date, thanks to the ad and your endorsement of it. Did you get yours—first they sent three and later one—when I got over there to autograph some more. Now I've autographed one hundred ahead, to avoid delay. The books here already brought in over $200 for defense. Besides they are going out. I sent ten to top labor leaders including Harry, Joe Curran, Mike Quill, Randolph, etc.[13] If you want one to go to any particular labor guy out there—let me know. Old timers especially.

I've been pulled off center of defense and the book by another matter—old but terribly neglected by all of us—"the woman question." The Pres's action demanding a talent search for fifty women to appoint to high Govt. posts, set me off. He got ten so far—but he insists. It's more than we do. I feel quite self-critical and have sent for the report of the Pres.'s Commission on the Status of Women—the Women's Bureau material and the latest from the League of Women Voters. Also have ordered *The Feminine Mystique*—recently published and some say very good too. Helen Lima wrote me that she is reading Eleanor Flexner's book, which was very good too.[14] But we have nothing in the last ten years. I'm jogging the elbow of International Publishers to at least get out a pamphlet, tho I suppose they'll ask me to write it. I wish some of the young women students would get interested in it as a thesis. Of course it's probably politics with L.B.J. but it's good politics, considering the women's vote in the USA. . . .

As ever—affectionately,
Elizabeth

P.S. My niece is stuck in Egypt.[15] They can't get her car on to a boat there. It's too heavy.

---

[12] Flynn was referring to her autobiography, covering the second half of her life.

[13] Harry Bridges was a West Coast leader of the Longshoremen's Union. Joe Curran was an East Coast leader of the Longshoremen's Union. Mike Quill was the leader of the Transit Workers Union. Philip Randolph was the leader of the Sleeping Car Porters Union, and a friend of Flynn's from the International Labor Defense days.

[14] Helen Lima was a California Communist party activist. She and her husband, Mickey Lima, were good friends of Flynn's. Eleanor Flexner's book, *Century of Struggle*, is an important feminist history (Boston: Harvard University Press, 1959).

[15] Roberta Bobba, an inveterate traveler, journeyed around the world in a Volkswagen camper.

Talent Search (1964)

FLYNN could have included the Communist party in her list of organizations guilty of tokenism toward women and blacks.

THE National Broadcasting Co. took a whole page in the *N.Y. Times* of March 8 to show the pictures of their newscasters who will cover the 1964 campaigns and elections. It is a large group. But conspicuously to be noted, there are exactly one woman and one Negro. I suppose even this is to be considered progress in such a conservative outfit.

Token representation is not yet obsolete.

In the same paper is news from Washington that President Johnson is determined to end "stag government." Weeks ago he had pledged to place at least fifty women in top government jobs.

The "talent search" was begun by the White House and government departments. At the dinner at which the Eleanor Roosevelt Memorial Award was presented, the President announced the appointment of a woman Ambassador; a woman as director of the Women's Bureau of the Dept. of Labor, to succeed Mrs. Esther Peterson, who is now the President's advisor on consumer affairs, and eight others, who are named to important posts in various government departments. The award was presented to Judge Anna M. Kross, Commissioner of Correction, who has tried hard to improve the jails and penal institutions in our city.

I am sure it was not difficult to find these ten able and qualified women nor will it be hard to find forty more if the men delegated to this talent search really look around. In many departments, not only in government but in industry, organizations, the professions, schools and colleges, which are headed by men, women do a large share of the actual work behind the scenes.

The role of women secretaries, who carry a tremendous responsibility, is well known yet seldom honored or recognized. Many of these women are as capable, if not more so, than the boss himself.

Apparently our President recognizes this fact when he says the promotion of women is sound policy as well as good politics.

Like an echo out of our own past of the last century is a story in the same *Times* of March 8 (International Women's Day) of a women's conference of women university graduates in Beirut, Lebanon, the first of its kind ever held in the Arab world. Their resolution calls for complete emancipation of Arab women in political, economic, and social affairs, wider job opportunities for women, and the elimination of illiteracy. More than one hundred delegates, representing the United Arab Republic, Syria, Lebanon, Jordon, Iraq, and Kuwait, were present.

Many conferences of African women have been held in the last few years since the liberation of their countries. A magazine *The African Woman* was long published in England.

Among the deep-seated abuses of women in the Middle East and in some African countries are slavery, polygamy, child marriages, the isolation of women to the household, and the veiling of their faces in public.

The right to vote, to obtain an education, to practice a profession, join a union, make contracts, own property are among the demands of the women's movements in these countries. They are aware of what their grievances are, and their demands are explicit.

Here we flatter ourselves that all is well and the boast is that compared to all other countries American women are in "a favorable position." But this can bear investigation. A few questions will point it up.

How many Negro women eligible to vote will be allowed to vote in the South in 1964?

Why is there not a single labor international body in the U.S. with a woman president?

Why is there not a single woman in the President's Cabinet or on the Executive Board of the AFL-CIO?

What local unions of any size, especially where women members are in the majority, have a woman president?

What women's colleges have women as their heads?

Why is there such a small percentage of women doctors and dentists in the U.S. compared to the USSR? Or women architects, engineers, congressmen and Senators? Are there any women State Governors?

These are disturbing questions after a century of a women's rights movement in the U.S., especially when women are forging ahead so rapidly in other lands.

Source: *Daily Worker*, Mar. 22, 1964.

Reflections on the Life of a Communist Organizer

Elizabeth Gurley Flynn awaiting sentencing under the Smith Act, summer of 1952

Memories of Oregon, Leaving West Virginia (1939)

THE *country, as well as Flynn herself, changed dramatically during her years of recuperation and hibernation in Oregon. In ten years she aged, mellowed, and put on weight. She was no longer the feisty IWW sweetheart; she feared becoming a middle-aged dinosaur, unable to adapt.*

Labor, now part of the New Deal's Democratic coalition, did not demand gutsy, individual, rabble-rousers as leaders; instead the CIO required administrative wheeler-dealers, a role Flynn never managed, even within the Communist party. To be a leading force in the IWW had required a dynamism that connected to the rough and ready working class. Communist party leadership entailed organizational acuity and connections with Moscow. Flynn possessed neither. She feared, as she stated in "Memories of Oregon, Leaving West Virginia," the brave new Communist party world, and entered it with trepidation.

TEN long years, conquered by weakness, silenced by sickness,
Dangerous delirium, bordering on madness, rushing of angels wings,
Unnumbered days, passed like a feverish nightmare,
Escaped at last from out the house of heartbreak,
Out of the darkness into the light again,
Life was sweet to my lips, my heart sang joyously,
Days were too short—time not enuf for me.
Sleep I begrudged, revelled in papers, meetings, books;
People after solitude, places after loneliness.
Work—after idleness, twice chosen my beloved work.
Happily I plunged—saturated myself in the thick of it,
Joy was in my words, they poured from my eager lips,
Rushed from my pent-up aching throat!
How I rejoiced at their flow. A brave new world, my dear old world to me!

Often I prayed—will I be whole again?
Will I conquer the deadly germ, renew the red corpuscles

Mend the strained and leaking heart?
Make whole the distraught mind?

New York was good now because it was "home" to me,
Dear family who love and tolerate and abide with me,
The streets, the subway, the great crowds were bearable
Because I was free happy home at last
But frightened—how to pick up the shattered pieces of my life again?
My ten lost years, the broken thread of work.
Forget the old, outworn, betrayed, swept out,
Step in the new, the young, the ever moving stream?
Next travelling short journey Boston, Phila, Baltimore, Passaic,
Hartford, Paterson and Lawrence again! testing my strength,
Feeling my way, learning to speak again,
Frightened—was I a ghost a passing legend?
"Veteran" out of the past, soon to be discarded?
How would I know true answers to my dread?
How known if I could serve again my cause?
Pittsburgh—city steel and coal, city of life,
After ten years of *death* you gave me back my world.

                                          (June 18, 1939)

SOURCE: Flynn Papers, Tamiment.

Notes from Train (1944)

WHILE *Flynn joined the Communist party and struggled to make the United
States socialist, she adored America, in an almost cornball way. Unlike many
Communist party leaders, she did not look to Europe or Russia for models. She
had deep roots in the American traditions. "Notes from Train" conveys the
pride she felt in America. For Flynn, those who looked to the Soviet Union and
Europe undermined and underestimated the American, radical, working-class
potential.*

THIS country is breathtaking in its sheer beauty and impressive in the conquest of nature by man, great struggles and heroic personalities without becoming bogged down in mere reminiscences no matter how entertaining. Two dangers are involved. First that we of the older generation will unwittingly romanticize the past, ourselves, and our associates, forgetting that we were not veterans or "old-timers" then, but a younger generation which made many mistakes along with our good work. Unless we are ready to indulge in a considerable degree of self-criticism, we are apt to paint a distorted picture which will leave the present younger generation cold—like brass statues in the parks do—of bearded sages in frock coats and dignified statesmen, who were once politicians. The other danger is endowing our old-time associates in retrospect with propositions they actually did not attain and super qualities they did not possess, and thus giving young people today a sort of inferiority complex—that try as they will they can never measure up to a Debs or Haywood, a Fanny Sellins, a Mother Jones. Yet these people, except that there were fewer of them then and they were more conspicuous, were not possessed of such exceptional organizing ability nor courage, were not made of such a unique mold that they cannot be duplicated, rare and strong though they were. But our movement has always been one of youth and good stuff is all around us today in the CIO and in our Party, as made our leaders of yesterday emerge in the struggle of their day. JLL [John L. Lewis] is a better labor leader, an easier man to work with, more ready to listen and to learn from others, than was individualistic rough and rugged Bill Haywood.

Deb's style of oratory would be old fashioned and outmoded by the loudspeaker and amplifier of today, would be flamboyant and sentimental to the extreme I fear to the youth of today. To my mind they are a great improvement on youth of yesterday. When I was young (1906–1916), youth was closer to the age of rugged individualism; too anarchistic, too uncontrolled, too violent in language and headstrong in having its own way. Bohemianism, free love, trappings of adolescent rebellion were too marked . . . the youth today is far superior, more scientific, cool, controlled, more disciplined, more collective in its thinking and acting, far more capable of concerted planning and execution. We talked more; they do more and will go further.

No use to glorify the good old days. The best thing about them is that they are no more. Take what is best, what teaches and inspires us, lessons of determination, examples of bravery, but don't live in the past. The "old-timers" turned over ground, sowed seed, pioneered. But as log cabins, wooden sidewalks, and covered wagons passed and great modern cities grew—so out of the Knights of Labor and SP

[Socialist party] and LA [Labor Alliance], IWW, etc. grew the modern CIO—its auxiliaries, its youth, Negro, farmer, affiliations, its political sagacity, and its peace program. The hodgepodge of radical "intellectuals," ex-preachers, lawyers, and misfits of the old SP has passed. They advocated everything from vegetarianism to astrology and called it socialism.

We have today a real party of American Socialism in the CP, inheriting the best traditions of the fighting past, sloughing off its follies and freakishness and identified with mass immediate needs and problems as well as a vanguard party of socialism.

SOURCE: Flynn Papers, Tamiment.

A Speaker Looks at Meetings (1939)

FLYNN hated New York City, seeing it as the center of smug, sectarian bureaucrats. She looked forward to touring the United States, which she did until the age of seventy-two, giving talks in strange towns, as she described in her column titled "A Speaker Looks at Meetings," and meeting ordinary folk and hearing about their victories and defeats. She believed Party leaders would have a more accurate idea of the American political climate if they got out from behind their desks and mixed with the mighty multitude.

I arrive in a strange town. Sometimes no one meets the train; I'm lucky to have the address, and after wandering through a maze of unfamiliar streets, find the hall. Sometimes I have only a P.O. Box or an office number, and find it closed on Sundays. A nice nerve-racking puzzle, fit for a hunting dog, to find the meeting, the picnic (somewhere out of town), or the committee then!

There are the dismal meetings that never get started. I've arrived at the appointed hour, found only the janitor who opened the hall. Everybody, including the committee, struggles in eventually and the meeting drags to a wearisome late hour in consequence. Tired workers fall asleep. It looks like an endurance test.

Ancient halls that are fire traps, up two and three rickety flights of stairs, alarm me, especially if there is only one exit. They are so depressing and funeral, it's hard to warm an audience up even on a summer day. A nice cheerful modern hall, well lighted and well aired, with comfortable seats and a big pitcher of water for the speakers and children, gives any meeting a good atmosphere.

"What's the subject, please?" I inquire, apprehensively. It's like reaching into a grab bag. I am handed a circular—sometimes a whole speech is printed thereon; sometimes a series of topics, which would require a dozen lectures to properly elucidate. But worst of all is a long list of questions which "she will answer." How relieved I feel if a simple timely topic is advertised which approximates what I have prepared to say and is elastic enough to allow me to answer my own questions and elaborate on my own subtopics. But the worst isn't over. There's still the chairman—always an uncertainty. There is one who covers the high points of the subject neatly and completely and leaves you like a fish out of water, gasping for breath. There is one who talks forty-five minutes about local conditions and then asks you to be brief. Mother Jones used to pull their coat-tails and say, "Don't forget, the people came to hear me." I feel like doing it, I confess. Then there is the one who gives you such a flowery effusive introduction that you are embarrassed to even attempt to live up to it. My ideal chairman is like the old German Socialist who was rebuked for his long-windedness. So he got up the next time and said, "I am here to introduce Comrade So-and-So, who will speak on Socialism. I have done it and he will do it," and sat down.

The literature salesman who obviously hasn't read what he's trying to sell and peers surreptitiously to see the price; the haughty young lady who looks right over the heads of people holding up bills for collection and passes the box as if she dared anyone to put money in it; the long-winded resolution nobody listens to; the "friend" who asks the most difficult question, not germane to the subject, which would require a whole speech to properly answer; the ushers who chat with each other all through the meeting, all these are seen by a speaker.

SOURCE: *Sunday Worker*, Oct. 1, 1939.

Sexual Politics (1939)

"BRAIN of a Woman" and "Equality," which Flynn scribbled in a notebook and never published, indicate that she got more sustenance from work than she did from love and sex. Men, she observed, preferred docile, insecure women who made them look larger than life; they had no room for strong, proud, intelligent Flynn types. She felt more in control of her intellectual life and feared her turbulent, irrational passions. In a notebook of poems she penciled these lines:

> My mind and not my heart remains my living core,
> Resisting colder heat and weaker flame,
> It holds me even to my course, it drives me on,
> It saves me from my wild tempestuous heart.[1]

Flynn's emotional needs seemed inexplicable to her. She probably wrote this poetry as a way of understanding her sexual surges. The following poem is entitled "A Poem to a Scornful One."

> Here is a poem then, for you alone, yet not for you to scorn,
> Out of my crowded solitude, my loneliness and pain,
> Lately I spilled my reckless halting words at your feet,
> Inarticulate and confused, I anguished to explain,
> I to whom words are as the breath of life.[2]

Perhaps Flynn would not have felt so needy if she had had more friends. However, most of her colleagues in the Communist party were married and had children. They hardly had enough time to spend with their own families, so they seldom invited Flynn along. By the late 1940s much of Flynn's family support and friendship network were gone; her sister Bina and her father had died, and only Kathie and her three nieces and a nephew remained. Flynn's "fa-

---

[1] Undated, in Flynn Papers, Tamiment.
[2] Summer 1938, Pittsburgh, in Flynn Papers, Tamiment.

vorite," as she jokingly referred to her only nephew, Peter Martin, lived with Kathie and Elizabeth in between his marriages and lovers. Flynn visited Roberta Bobba, an energetic niece, once a year in San Francisco and wrote proudly to her friends about Roberta's daring feats. These contacts with family provided her with warmth and a feeling of belonging, but they could not compensate for the deeper loneliness she often felt.

In the late 1950s, as the Party became smaller, there were fewer celebrations, picnics, and events; the social world of the Party shrunk. Although Flynn loved good food and drink, low brow movies, and music, she did not have the money to go out; Communist party functionaries were paid bare minimum wages. Her time was taken up with organizational chores and she felt needed by the Party, but she still longed for a lover-companion.

BRAIN OF A WOMAN

One thinks about my schedule, my letters, my articles, my speech tonite

The subject, the place, the people, the results.
It is calm, methodical, it directs my work, my conversations,
It asks questions, sorts answers, absorbs information, seeks to know more,
    learn more, be useful,
Soaks up what I must know to give guidance, and clear answers to patient
    eager workers who listen to me.

This is the brain that likes to work, to write, to speak, to act,
This is the brain of the cool collected me,
The core of me, the unshakeable, unchangeable, dependable, reliable
    me.
That directs my speech, detects the moment of detachment from the
    audience,
The lessening and loosening of the electric current between speaker and
    listener,
Here there is no sex no double standard
No difference.

                            (Undated, perhaps 1939)

SOURCE: Flynn Papers, Tamiment.

EQUALITY

How can a man refuse a flame and huddle to a spark?
How they love "yes" women. They fear to be outshone.
Afraid to be overshadowed, possessed, dwarfed out,
Only a brave man, mentally sufficient and strong can be calmly
   equal with a proud intelligent passionate woman.

(Summer 1939)

SOURCE: Flynn Papers, Tamiment.

I Love My Comrade Organizers (1940)

FLYNN had made it in a man's world. She worked at a man's job and lived like a bachelor, eating most meals out and spending a great deal of time away from home, either at the office, at meetings, or on the road. True, she did not have a "wife," but in later years her sister Kathie served almost that purpose, working as her secretary and general helpmate. Elizabeth, however, was the more domestic of the two; she loved to cook and had a creative flair for sewing and a green thumb. She was compulsively neat and was "always going about folding things up, putting things in order."[1] In most ways, however, her life-style was not representative of most women's. As she aged, her ideas on housework and motherhood changed. She no longer saw the home as a prison, but as the preferable place for raising children. Flynn's respect for homemakers grew over the years.

I love my comrade organizers and speakers,—but I don't envy their
   wives,
I've been a wife myself and I'm a comrade too,
I know the strain we are!

[1] Virginia Gardner, "The Cab Driver Told Kathie," *Daily Worker*, Jan. 30, 1955.

The skipped meals, the broken dates, the unpaid bills, the hard lives
The clothes you can't have, the worries you do have,
We come late or not at all! You wait and watch
Are we in jail or mobbed or just the car broke down?
The endless meetings, trips, committees, calls,
To go here and run there, this comrade needs advice, this one is fired—
    the Party must attend.

I love my comrades—but, dear wives, I don't envy you
At home, alone, and waiting for your men,
I know them in their work, I talk with them, laugh meet, eat drink, travel
    day and night, with them,
Sleep in the same houses, run risks together, have endless discussions
    with them
They are great and I admire them tremendously and collectively,
But you wash their shorts and shirts, lay out their ties and socks,
You pack their suitcases, and have their shirts pressed,
I see your loving care in their nice blue shirts and matching vest and
    clean handkerchiefs!
I don't envy you!

I love my comrades 'deed I do, I love them one and all,
But I don't envy you dear wives, the care they are,
How good they are, how uncomplaining, devoted we know well,
But careless of their health sleep and food and rest,
Now impatient to stop a while and think of self,
So you must do it for them; make them dress warm, take a pill;
Put on their rubbers and their mufflers, make them get a hair cut and a
    shave.
They love you, you should hear them tell what grand girls you are!
But they forget to tell you, I'm afraid. NO—I don't envy you!
But I do envy them the comradeship of understanding love you give to
    them
Because you so unselfishly serve our cause in taking care of them,
You forget self to keep them free from personal tasks and fit, healthy
    and strong
And I do envy them the sweetness of your love,
Don't worry their devotion to their task absorbs and consumes them
Keeps them true to you, dear wives, beyond all other men,
Yes I do envy them having someone to really care so much,
I fear I envy you one thing only dear wives,
Their love when I am lonely!
and some one man—to do all that for me!
I guess I need a wife!

SOURCE: Flynn Papers, Tamiment.

I Like a Hotel (1939)

FLYNN'S daily life contradicted her later ideas on housework and motherhood. She never stayed home to care for her child, nor did she ever do much housework. In fact, when she and her sister Kathie lived together, they hired a maid to clean once a week. When Kathie died, Elizabeth moved into a hotel.

WHEN a committee puts me up at a hotel, I don't say "Bourgeois," scornfully. Not me! I luxuriate, because it doesn't happen often. I think "Well, this is a sample of the future, what every woman ought to have, a room to herself and release from domestic tasks." I hope to see the day we banish washtubs, kitchen stoves and straw brooms to the museum, as relics of the past.

It's a grand feeling for a woman (I can't speak for the men) to get up in a warm room, no worry about the furnace; get dressed in your street clothes, not in an apron or housedress, go down to a breakfast you didn't cook. I return to a well-stocked desk, pen, ink, writing stationery. This has a little house on it, "Where Washington refused a crown, 1776" (Newhigh, N.Y.). It inspires me to write.

The telephone doesn't ring incessantly, no doorbell, bill collector, laundryman, grocer, or peddler interrupts my thoughts. No lunch to worry about. (Is there bread in the house? Is the sugar all gone?) The bed is unmade—at home I'd stop to tidy my room before I start to write. My mother used to laugh when I'd clean the apartment, then rush to my desk and say, "Now I must get to work!"

In a hotel room I read the *Daily Worker* and the *Times* thoroughly. I collect my thoughts. I do some neglected reading. I work on a special article. I get an early start on the column. I catch up on my correspondence and surprise my friends with letters. I do my work.

Somebody else will make the bed and wash the dishes. Service in a well-run hotel is professional, not menial. Work in homes is amateur by comparison. You can eat in the restaurant or in your own room. This room is clean, comfortable, yet bare of non-essentials.

I see lots of old ladies in hotels. People pity them. It's quite unnecessary. They enjoy it immensely. It's a sort of "sit-down strike." Many say frankly they are tired of households.

They don't want a place where the grandchildren are parked. Lots of grandmothers feel that way. Few can afford to avoid it. These always look happy, like little grey pussy cats, purring with contentment. They read, go to shows, play bridge—all the things they wanted to.

It's the way all old people should be able to live out their last years. Today it's only possible for a few. A comfortable hotel is a glimpse of the future rest homes for the aged and for mothers, when capitalism is no more. How heavenly it would be for tired, overworked mothers! It gives us another incentive to socialize the world.

If I ever actually write the story of my life I think the publishers will have to stake me to stay at a quiet hotel. Page the International Publishers!

SOURCE: *Sunday Worker*, Feb. 19, 1939.

Letters to Anne K. Flynn and Muriel Symington (1956)

FLYNN was aware that her positions on housework and motherhood sounded conservative. In her prison letters she attributed her changed views on child rearing to the wrecked lives of her prison mates. However, close contact with the victims of poor, broken families could have led her to believe that society, rather than the family, should bear more, rather than less, responsibility for raising children. In fact, during World War II Flynn campaigned for nurseries, but this was because women were needed in the work force, not because nurseries were best for children.

Flynn's position on housework seemed to have altered slightly during her illness, in Oregon, and again after her son's death. Also after Fred died she developed a deepened appreciation of mothers and saw their work as reward-

*ing, rather than harmful and wasteful. Tragically it took the loss of her son for
her to realize the satisfactions and benefits of motherhood. Even though Flynn
said that children benefit from a nurturing, full-time mother, she cautioned her
sister, in her letter from Alderson, not to quote her; in case this was not the
Communist party line, Flynn did not want to cause trouble.[1] Her son's death
and illness made her more sympathetic to housewives and mothers, but also less
secure and sure of her own feminist vision and voice. She seemed to fear speaking her own piece and perhaps felt she no longer spoke for women since she was
no longer a mother.*

May 18, 1956

Dearest Kathie,[2]

On the housework argument, I've concluded long ago it's a futile
one. I like it as a recreation but doubt I would as an occupation. Women
in homes, especially mothers of family, do work terribly long hours, if
they are counted up. The electrical appliances and gadgets are wonderful, but everyone doesn't have them, especially in rural areas and
even big cities. The middle class and higher wage group do, of course.
I think it's all wrong to consider the work of women in their homes for
their families as menial and treat it with contempt. Children are entitled to proper care, a good environment and direction as to character building. The real mother gives this as well as her labor. It's amazing how many people land here from broken homes and neglectful
parents or institutions in cases of orphans. The home is not to be un-
derrated. If I may speak frankly to you (not to be quoted) I don't think
an erratic person who lives in a furnished room, does not even pay
due regard to her own clothes and has a genius and martyr complex,
is any authority on domestic problems. It is true lots of women do prefer their home and all its multitudes of tasks to working in an office, in
mass production factory, etc. So what? Somebody has to do the *work*
for all these career people, regardless of where it is done. Of course
lots of it could be reduced from drudgery and simplified. A well-
rounded person should not scorn doing things. Look at Marion,[3] how

[1] Flynn wrote this letter after the Twentieth Party Congress and Khrushchev's
revelations about Stalin. The Party line was in flux, and Flynn was in jail and unable to read Party papers or talk to colleagues.

[2] Anne K. Flynn, Elizabeth's middle sister, was always called Kathie, from
Katherine, her middle name.

[3] The "erratic person" refers to Elizabeth Lawson (see n.5). Marion Bachrach
was one of Elizabeth's best friends and also the sister of her lawyer, John Abt.
Bachrach was a Communist party activist who was indicted under the Smith Act;
however, because she was dying of cancer she managed to get her case severed.

competent she is and yet she can think rings around the ladies you mentioned. Well you sure get me started. Yes, on the sheets, the better grades are heavier and last longer. Glad to hear the younger generation are so attentive. But you deserve it or you would not get it. Glad you liked Roger's review.[4] Maybe you are more objective than I am. It seemed so cold and unfeeling from a one-time close friend and so fearful of the Communist issue, which does not figure in those long ago years. His letter sounds better. . . . I saw these tables I mentioned advertised from Wanamakers (Sunday Trib), 6 feet 2 inches $27, 8 feet $33. Watch for them.

Love,
Elizabeth

SOURCE: Flynn Papers, Tamiment.

June 16, 1956

. . . I'm not terribly impressed by Elizabeth L. writing on the women question.[5] A great deal can undoubtedly be done by the application of collective mechanization to household tasks—but there is a certain amount of unavoidable routine connected with *all work,* whether industries and or the domestic field, unless we return to handicrafts. Eight hours' work at a typewriter, in a factory, on a farm, as a painter, plumber or bricklayer are all monotonous and repetitous to a large extent. But the work of the world has to be done by someone. E.L's own manner of life, living alone in a furnished room, eating alone, in a restaurant with a book propped up against a sugar bowl—indifferent to her appearance, all this is not conducive to understanding the life of a typical wife and mother who *enjoys* her life. Personally, I do not mind housework—it's a form of rest and relaxation for me. Of course I don't get too much of it, true. But I wonder if a mother working to pay somebody else to care for her children is any solution? I doubt it. There is a lot to the argument of *security* for children in the home, built around the mother's presence and influence. Sounds con-

[4]Roger Baldwin was once a lover of Flynn's, but they were not on good terms after he was instrumental in having her expelled from the ACLU. He reviewed the first edition of Flynn's autobiography, *I Speak My Own Piece,* for the *Nation* (May 12, 1956).
[5]Elizabeth L. was Elizabeth Lawson, author of dozens of books on black and abolitionist heroes and an organizer in the South. While I could not find the Lawson piece in the *Daily Worker* files, the article seems to have appeared in a special *Daily Worker* International Women's Day supplement that was not microfilmed.

servative, eh? I learn as I go. Of course large numbers of women work because they *must,* to support or help support a family, parents, etc. Biologically women are the most important sex certainly. But there are "handicaps" (if so considered) naturally to doing a lot of other things, for the childbearing woman, at least for a number of years. I'd like to say some more on that topic later. It's a difficult problem, saw where an Australian woman leader spoke out on it recently, to favor mother's staying home.

Love as ever,
Elizabeth

SOURCE: Flynn Papers, Tamiment.

What Do I Miss—You Ask (1955)

FLYNN *wrote "What Do I Miss" in a letter dated August 21, 1955, from Alderson prison, to Clemens France. France "was a teacher, a lawyer, a social worker, at one time Director of Social Welfare for the State of Rhode Island and a leader in prison reform. . . . I did not know Clemens France very well when I went to Alderson. I had met him occasionally at public functions. He impressed me as a man of strong courage and convictions. My problem in prison was to secure correspondents who could pass an FBI check. I suggested to my sister to ask Dr. France. He accepted immediately."* [1] *Flynn's other correspondents were her sister Kathie, Muriel Symington, Alice Hamilton, the famous occupational health expert, Dr. Lovett, an old friend from the 1920s, and her nephew, Peter Martin.*

[1] Elizabeth Gurley Flynn, "In Memory of Clemens France," *Sunday Worker,* June 28, 1959.

Besides freedom, work, my friends and life, I'm sure you mean. To
    faithfully answer? The list grows—both great and small.
I miss the fog horns on the river at night and the pictures on the wall.
I miss the children playing on the sunny street, and the corner candy
    store with good neighbors whom I meet.
I miss my sleepy cat, my ugly cactus, my treasured books, and a long
    leisurely talky breakfast under Kathie's kindly looks.
I miss sleeping until I wake up and getting up when I can't sleep.
I miss turning on the light at my ease and turning off the radio when I
    please.
I miss walking alone at night and seeing the stars and returning to an
    open door, a window without bars.
I miss a key on the inside of the door and a soft wool rug, not rag, to
    cover the floor.
I miss a large bureau with capacious drawers and a long, wide mirror
    without flaws.
I miss nylon stockings and a colorful dressing-gown and leaving the
    house at will to take a bus ride 'round the town.
I miss grapefruit and real hot coffee in my big blue French cup and eggs
    and strawberries and cream to sup.
I miss sardines, cheese, olives and beer with the "early bird" edition at
    midnight and Giovannitti and other friends, to cheer.
I miss real movies—unexpurgated—with an audience of men, women,
    and lively children, and soft voices and low pitched laughter.
I miss talking to men—talk about politics, trade unions, families and
    friends.
I miss soft dresses and underwear and gay, bright scarfs and my wrist
    watch, my zircon ring and fountain pen.
I miss my firm, wide bed, my thick walls, my privacy to sleep, unheard to
    read aloud, to sing a little—even to weep.
I miss my full name spoken with a proper prefix because it is a long time
    since I was or felt like "a girl."
I miss the beauty parlor on University Place and Sonny asking "Wave or
    curl?"
I miss the Hudson River and East River Drive and the U.N. at night and I
    miss dear old Brooklyn Bridge and the skyline all alight.
I miss New York Harbor and the Statue in the bay, and LaGuardia
    airport, Idlewild and Union Square in May.
I miss travelling—I miss America—the Mississippi, the Rocky Mountains,
    Puget Sound, the Pacific Ocean, and Philadelphia, Detroit, Pittsburgh
    and ever-lovely San Francisco.
Nothing and no one can take my country away from me. It is ever in my
    mind, my heart, my eyes. But most of all I miss people—my own kind
    of people—people with ideas, ideals, dreams, hopes of tomorrow.

I miss real talks, natural laughter, jokes, persiflage, a sense of humor;
  people who are objective, who can discuss without prejudice, debate
  without anger, reason without rancor.
I miss people who know what they believe, are willing to suffer and
  sacrifice for it cheerfully and be true to it, come what may.
I miss good plain workers, who go to work, belong to unions, help their
  fellows, love their kids and wives—fur and steel workers, miners and
  auto workers who lead normal, useful lives.
Yes, in this strange hiatus, this temporary withdrawal from a living
  world—I miss still more the intangibles, hard to define—personal
  liberty, the search for happiness, the right to speak my mind.
But in my memory I have all I miss and in my thoughts—all I seek, so
  fear not that their loss should make me sad or weak.

SOURCE: Flynn Papers, Tamiment.

Letter to Clemens France (1955)

IN Alderson Federal Reformatory, Flynn met women whose paths she would otherwise not have crossed: drug addicts, thieves, habitual criminals, and degenerate youth. She was unaccustomed to being surrounded by apolitical, uninformed, and indifferent females and found it distasteful. However, prison deepened her understanding of the complicated, multifaceted aspects of human behavior. She read hundreds of non-Left, British and American classics. She had time to contemplate and experience life in the lower depths. The damaging effects of poverty, and especially of emotional neglect, became apparent to her; she realized that not only the environment and the system had to change, but also human nature. She gained a new respect for the family and felt psychological conditions could not merely be ignored. She left prison a confirmed Communist, but more humble and open to new ideas.

December 2, 1955

My Dear Friend,

Received your very nice and welcome letter of Nov. 25th starting with the good advice to watch the calorie line. I am very glad to hear you had a jolly Thanksgiving with your family. I was surprised that I did not go up in weight and now stand at 190. I'm heading for 160. John Abt, our very able and distinguished lawyer was here yesterday. We visited for several hours—all morning and afternoon. It was such a joy to see him, not only as a lawyer but as a friend, and brother of my dear friend Marion. He brought me news of all Smith Act cases and particularly the McCarran Act appeal before the U.S. Supreme Court, in which I am an interested party, as a National Committee member as of 1950. I was also one of two defense witnesses before the SAC Board, John Gates being the other one.[1] Mr. Abt is very cautious, as befits a good lawyer, but has some hopes of a favorable decision in this case. Too bad Vito Marcantonio did not live to participate in the arguments.[2] He told me of several indications of some *slight* changes in atmosphere. It was nice to see and talk to a *man*, and a charming good looking one, at that. I enjoyed the odor of his pipe tobacco. I am frankly very tired of an all woman's atmosphere. I have worked with men all my life and while I have many wonderful women friends, I do believe I understand men and get along better with them than with women. Of course the mental level is low and the emotional instability is high at this place, so it is not a good criterion. I feel in a vacuum, where companionship is concerned. . . . Providence was always on my schedules from the earliest days. It must be nearly fifty years since Kathie and I first went there and returned via the Old Fall River line. We had a good IWW textile union there, at Olneyville, in 1912 and thereafter. Once in the 1920s I was to speak at Brown University (is that the correct name?) with Roger Baldwin. He was allowed to speak but I was barred as "an agitator of the IWW." I have many pleasant recollections however of that city. I picked up a book here about Roger Williams—very interesting. How long have you lived there? . . . The good and sweet birds on the trees of West Va. should sing songs of me. I travelled all through this state, which is scenically very beautiful and has a thrilling labor history among the coal miners. My escort, who

[1] SAC was the Subversive Activities Control Board. John Gates was the editor of the *Daily Worker,* and a good friend. He left the Communist party in 1957.

[2] Vito Marcantonio was the congressman from East Harlem and an old friend of Flynn's. He said that the "Defense of the Communists is the first line of defense of the Bill of Rights" (Simon Gerson, *Pete: The Story of Peter V. Cacchione, New York's First Communist Councilman,* New York: International Publishers, 1976, 93).

arranged all the meetings, introduced me as chairman, sold the literature, and generally managed all my trips was John Lautner, of whom
you have undoubtedly heard before. I was a witness at his wedding
(one of them). He is now a star witness in Smith Act cases. I often wonder what those hundreds of fine honest miners to whom I spoke in
Miners' Union halls think about it all? I feel as if I had personally met
Judas and imagine they feel the same way and they probably do. Well
enough of that. Take care of yourself. I recall New England winters
are cold.

As ever, Your affectionate friend,
Elizabeth

Women's Rebellion (1947)

*ALTHOUGH Elizabeth Gurley Flynn was a rebel, in many ways her tastes were
conventional and low brow. She, like most Party members, did not go in for a
bohemian life-style or the avant-garde in art. Her home decoration was Vic-
torian and functional, part of her mother's lace-curtain Irish legacy; the chairs
and couches were covered with lace antimacassars. Her clothing was ladylike
and proper, even when she was young. Her mother, a skilled tailor, made most
of Flynn's clothes, in dark, rich, solid colors, with collars, which she wore with
wide-brimmed hats. After 1936, when she gained weight, she wore matronly,
flower-print dresses, nunlike shoes, and small tailored hats. When riding trains
she liked to ask people to guess her profession. Inevitably they would conjecture
teacher, librarian, or telephone operator. She loved to watch their faces sink
when she would reply, "Communist party official."*

MANY women readers of the *Worker* did not like the article "A Year
of Grace," and I am one of them. It is distinctly out of step with

the trends among the average American women, who are very definitely resisting "The New Look," as it is called.

The gist of the article is that the resisters will fail and by next year women, sheeplike, will accept the long skirts. The acceptance of short skirts in the 1930s is cited as an example. What is left out of account is that short skirts were a progressive trend, allowing greater freedom of motion, were adapted to athletics, shop work, bicycles, hiking, climbing on busses and street cars, and were better for housework, too, while the return of long skirts is retrogression, going in the direction of the past, not the future.

Low shoes, short skirts, tailor made suits, shirtwaists, sport clothes, slacks, shorts, abbreviated bathing suits, pajamas, not to mention modern underwear, and short hair, plain hats, or finally no hats at all, are all milestones in the progress of women and have accompanied their entrance into industry, the professions, and sports. Women have liked this greater freedom.

I have a picture of myself taken in 1906 with a skirt down to my ankles. I wouldn't be found dead in such a get-up today and no profit-hungry manufacturer or daffy designer will succeed in wrapping me up like a mummy. I can sew and will make my own, if need be.

I stood outside Marshall Field's windows in Chicago, where the dowdy, ugly looking museum pieces are on display. I have yet to see a woman, young or old, look at them with admiration or desire. Their faces expressed curiosity, dislike, even horror, I'd say. I notice Windy City skirts are usual. In fact I haven't seen long skirts appear anywhere I've been.

The present solid resistance is based primarily, as the article correctly states, on economic reasons. Such a drastic shift in styles is calculated to force women to discard all their present wardrobes, if they bow to fashion's dictates. But who can afford to do that? Only rich women, idle women, whose main diversion is style. It is unthinkable to the average woman, especially with the high cost of living straining the budget to the breaking point. Hold the line on prices and on hems, too—is their reaction.

It is also a rebellion against the tyranny of avaricious fashion makers, who have apparently gone back to *Godey's Ladies Book* this time and would make women into monstrosities. The pocketbook, progress, and a good appearance are all in conjunction in this revolt, which augurs well for its success.

How come such a defeatist note in our forward-looking paper? "By next year they'll feel out of place in their short skirts and gradually they'll give in"—is no way for us to discuss this subject. This growing buyers' strike of women against the new styles is a part of the struggle

against the high cost of living. We should encourage and help organize it, not capitulate to capitalist pressure campaigns. Even the dressmakers are a part of this revolt, as women and workers.

I interviewed a number of dressmakers at a Communist Party club
meeting in Chicago on this subject. There were ten women and one
man, a presser, present. They told me "The New Look" came from
French designers, caterers to the aristocrats and bourgeoisie, who are
trying to recapture their prewar control of styles through these extreme modes. . . .

The dressmakers don't like them, although they are beginning to
work on them. One woman said she saw one of the new dresses on the
figure and her first thought was: "The price committee will have to
fight for more money if we have to make those things!"

They require a lot more work than the simpler styles and the workers are not being paid for the extra work. Price committees are bat-
tling it out, but, as it stands now, the manufacturers will charge more
for the new styles while the garment workers are actually taking a cut.
The customer will pay five or six dollars more a dress but the workers
are not proportionately compensated for the extra work. . . .

The consensus was that this is a move to cut wages, boost prices, sell
more and make fools of American women. It's the old skin game, nobody profits but the boss!

SOURCE: *Sunday Worker,* Oct. 29, 1947.

Letter to Muriel Symington (1956)

*IN "Women's Rebellion," written in 1947, Flynn did not seem so offended by
slacks, or so-called antifemale attire, as she was in this letter written in 1956
from Alderson prison. Why then did slacks bother her so much in prison? Perhaps she associated them with a lesbian image, and in Alderson she became
nearly homophobic, commenting in letters and poems about lesbian behavior*

she considered offensive. She could not have been too offended by Marie Equi,
with whom she lived for ten years, nor by Muriel Symington, who was a les-
bian, a good friend, and the recipient of this letter. Was Flynn trying to deny
her own loving feelings toward women? Or did she simply believe lesbians
should not advertise their identities?

July 7, 1956

Dear Muriel,[1]
Your account of fishing is interesting though it never appealed to
me. I like to take it easy when I vacation. I guess I love creature comforts a lot. I agree with you that political leaders are very careless
about Pres. Eisenhower's health. In all his recent pictures he looks ill
and aging rapidly. The ferocity of the attacks on Justice Warren indicate some political malice behind them. I quite agree with you on the
subject of women but my peeve are slacks. Very few, and those young
and slender, look attractive in them, and they do belong to the beach,
picnics, hikes, etc. I hate to see women look like poor imitations of
men, and that's about it in most slacks. I have come to absolutely hate
them here. I prefer sunsuits, shorts, to slacks. They are more feminine. I deeply appreciate what is *womanly* as a result of some of the
attire here. Of course it's necessary for some types of work—farm,
dairy, shops, garden, paint group, etc. But when they wear black
shirts and brown khaki slacks to the movies, it sickens me. I stay away.
And they have some very nice dresses, pink, blue, green, red, gray,
etc. and well made. For Sunday dinner and church, dresses are com-
pulsory. I wish it could be true of movies, meals, and after work hours.
I may be wrong, but I think it would be better for the morale to limit
slacks to occupations only. It's a hangover of adolescence—"Dungaree Doll" psychology.[2] You'll laugh at my heat I fear. Such changes—

[1]Muriel Symington was a suffragist and socialist and did publicity work for
General Foods. When she was older, she typed for Elizabeth and W. E. B. DuBois.
She was from a wealthy family, and was related to Sen. Stuart Symington. Muriel
put up part of the bail for Elizabeth in her Smith Act case. She was an industrious
newspaper reader and correspondent and wrote letters to many of the progressive
papers, objecting to sexist and conservative articles and congratulating them on
progressive articles. She wore severe, tailored clothes and lived with a woman
named Julia. Symington wrote Flynn over four hundred letters at Alderson. After
Symington's death, Flynn wrote that "Muriel brought the outside world into my
cell" ("In Memory of Muriel Symington," *Daily Worker*, Sept. 1, 1963).
[2]"Dungaree Doll" was a hit tune at the time. Flynn hated these pop songs,
which the inmates played full blast. In fact, it drove her to learn something about
music. She took classical music appreciation courses, partly to imbibe some culture
and partly to escape the top forty tunes.

how will I know the world? Third Ave with trees,[3] and eggs without
shells . . .

> Warm regards—
> Affectionately your friend—
> Elizabeth

SOURCE: Flynn Papers, Tamiment.

Thoughts on a Fiftieth Birthday (1940)

*ELIZABETH Gurley Flynn resented the way many of the male Party leaders
treated her as a relic. She was not embarrassed about her age because she was
proud of her years of struggle.*

B Y the time you read this I shall have passed into what is considered
that fatal "bourne from which no traveler returns"—the second
half century. Already, after four days, I feel like those foreign celebrities coming up New York Harbor on the ships, who are asked by in-
quisitive reporters, "How do you like America?"

The retort of Pat who just came off the Ellis Island boat, "Sure, it'd
be a foine country if there weren't so many foreigners here!" occurs to
me. At least, even if I don't enjoy the new state too well, nobody can
say: "If you don't like it go back where you came from!"

Seriously speaking, I feel the same today as I did yesterday.
Change is fortunately gradual in the ageing process. I'm sure that my
arrival at the five-decade mark embarrasses my father a lot more than
it does me. He's convinced nobody ever takes him for a day over sixty-
five! Too bad, Pop, to have to give you away like this.

In capitalist countries, there's a lot of nonsense about women's

---

[3]The Third Avenue el came down while Flynn was in jail.

ages. A man at fifty is considered in the prime of life. But because of economic conditions women are forced to make too much of a fetish of grey hairs and lines. Clarence Darrow once said to a photographer, "Don't take the wrinkles out and make my face as smooth as a baby's bottom! I worked too hard to put them there!" In the Soviet Union, where economic security and freedom from personal worry abound, artificial concepts of beauty disappear and women, like men, grow old naturally and gracefully. They are too busy with important and interesting activities to give it undue attention, except as regards health.

What makes people suddenly old? Primarily grief and worry, living in the past, being compelled to think too much about themselves, having no hope of improvement, no plan of any better life for the future.

Collapse of personality and physique, which is really old age, can be caused by both overwork and unemployment; by a lack of self-confidence which comes from a sense of personal failure; by the desperate struggle to keep one's looks in order to hold a job. The mother grows old prematurely when her children are not properly fed, clothed, and housed. The nervous anxiety and excitement in the world as it is today of war and fascism, the menace to our children and to our freedom, are not conducive to remaining young.

Despite their hard work, serious purposes, risks and difficulties, Communists are the youngest-minded people I know. Life to them is not a "cold and barren vale between two eternities"—or "all sound and fury, signifying nothing." They do not relinquish it with relief. They know the infinite possibilities of a happy human existence, and glory in the struggle to sweep capitalism from the face of the earth.

When I first began to work in the labor movement, the remark that "Socialism is just around the corner!" was usually greeted by a facetious comment on the size of the corner. In the intervening thirty-four years, however, we turned the corner. Socialism was just around it, and is now here, achieved on one-sixth of the earth's surface. I am happy to have been so fortunate as to have lived in just these past years, which are beyond all doubt the most important that history will record. I hope to now enter the period when the mopping up of capitalism takes place. That's worthwhile waiting for! I congratulate myself for being here.

My present ideals of womanly beauty, worth emulating, are Mother Bloor, Madame Sun Yat-sen, La Pasionaria, Helen Keller, Anita Whitney. Inside of each are all the selves that they have ever been: the child at play, the young girl, the young mother, the militant fighter—the continuity of an ever growing and expanding self, which learns more, fights better, and never gives up.

In greeting my second half century of triumphant socialism, I hope I can say:

> Grow old along with me
> The best is yet to be—
> The last of life, for which the first was made.

SOURCE: *Sunday Worker,* Aug. 11, 1940.

Letter to Dorothy Healy (1964)

DOROTHY Healy (1914–) was one of the most militant organizers in the California Communist party, which she joined at age fourteen, organizing cannery workers and working for civil rights and peace. (She left the Party in 1973.) Healy challenged the Party orthodoxy more frequently than Flynn, so Flynn felt both inspired by her and scared for her. Flynn treated her like a younger sister.

This letter was one of the last that Flynn wrote.

Aug. 15, 1964

In Kremlin Hospital

Moscow—USSR

Dear Dorothy,

I feel I should communicate to you what I have learned from the Drs here in consultation with my N.Y. Dr.—Epstein—who is here with his wife. When he examined me on July 21st there was no sugar in my blood or urine. When I was examined here, by Drs from the Clinic on Aug 11th—they found sugar in both—three times the normal amount. So they put me in the hospital and I am here now for the fourth day. Dr. E. was shocked and so was I. They say the symptoms of regular diabetes are excessive appetite, excessive thirst, and desire for sweets. I have none of these, and it struck me that you do not have them either. They call what I have and the Dr also had after a mild stroke—is tension or tense diabetes. They attribute it to extreme tension, overwork, anxiety, etc. Certainly I have my full measure of all that. They prescribe *rest*—plenty of it, and relief from all tension. Getting ready to leave, getting all my stuff into storage, meetings, visitors, and very hot weather—all got me down. I was exhausted, leaving NYC. On arrival here, in spite of advice from G, the first week was a work out, interviews, visitors, two birthday parties, it was too much. Dr. E advised that I should go somewhere for a complete rest. The examination ensued and here I am. But they assure me I can be cured, and I have said, "Take all the time you need, I'm in no hurry." But I wonder, Dorothy dear, if you do not need the same? What do your doctors say? Why not come here, not for tours around or political missions *but for a complete rest?* I'm sure all here and there would agree if you ask for it.

I was shocked to hear of Togliatti's *serious* illness, a few days after his arrival.[1] I did not realize he is 70. He was visiting a pioneers' camp. He should have been in a rest home or sanitorium. I do not think they fully realize the stress and strain of capitalist countries, which is entirely lacking here. It's another world. Since 8 A.M. (it is now 9:30) nine women have come to do things to me or the room. They are so quiet and kind. All the doctors, technicians, etc. are women. Only "the Head" is a man, of course. It dies hard. I'm beginning to feel rested.

Love to you and all dear friends,
Elizabeth

Source: From FBI, DOJ, CIA (CA-82-8736) Sanitized Documents. This letter is also in the California State, Long Beach, Special Collection; it was brought to the author's attention by Charlot Holzkamper.

[1] Palmiro Togliatti was the head of the Italian Communist party who advocated greater independence of national Communist parties from Soviet control. Although he established a liberal line, he never broke with Moscow.

Conclusion

Elizabeth Gurley Flynn holding nine-month-old Fred,
May 19, 1910

Pioneer or Aunt Tom? Elizabeth Gurley Flynn's Feminism

How does Elizabeth Gurley Flynn measure up as a revolutionary and model for women today? Elizabeth Gurley Flynn, the rebel girl, larger than life, worshiped and reviled, was also an ordinary mortal—a lonely single mother, often estranged from her child, alienated from her comrades, sometimes extremely brave, and occasionally even cowardly. One expects clarity and consistency from a revolutionary. In this search for an ideal, when one recognizes shortcomings one becomes disillusioned, and demotes and diminishes the blemished hero. But in spite of the contradictions and inconsistencies, the heroism and bravery remain and should not be forgotten in the search for divine right or perfection. Flynn, then, remains extraordinary, but flawed.

The perfect Bolshevik is a selfless, resourceful man of action. The model revolutionary is predicated on the labor of a wife, mother, and female comrades to minister to daily and mundane needs. Or, the iron-willed hero must forgo the traditional domestic pleasures of children, companionship, comfort, and beauty. A revolutionary life requires unbounded energy and is associated with youth. Most revolutionaries die young, or they burn out, grow middle aged and conservative; if lucky they become bureaucratic heads of state. Though female, Flynn thought of herself as a life-long rebel. She considered the Communist party the heir of the IWW and had no regrets. As she wrote to her sister Kathie from Alderson Reformatory, "If I had my life to live over again, I would do the same thing again."[1]

Judging Flynn is complex because as a revolutionary she demanded from herself that she set an example for others; she wanted to represent a vanguard and sacrifice the ordinary everyday creature comforts for the creation of a better world. As a female Party leader, she often had to set herself above other women— and other men too. Yet this is a contradiction; how to represent the people while outranking them? Flynn solved this problem in part by taking pride in her ability to talk to and get on with common folk. She had a homey, personal, and forceful manner, which encouraged militance. She also saw herself as addressing "the woman question" through personal action and living the life of a liberated woman, a role to be emulated. This exemplary role model strategy for change was rejected by the early radicals of the contemporary women's liberation movement as, at best, insufficient and, at worst, as embodying the dangers of tokenism.

Flynn's life was different from that of most women of her period and of ours too. Her leadership and speaking ability inspired and stretched the boundaries of what was possible for all women. In one sense, then, she paved the path for today's female activists. In fact her courage was tested in ways the feminist vanguard of today has not been.

Yet in another way Flynn was a token, providing the window dressing for male leadership. Because she was female, the IWW and the Communist party could parade Flynn as representative and avoid the accusation of being a male club. Although she periodically brought up the fact that she was the only female on the Party's national board, she did not organize other women for fundamental change, nor did she dare bring up the matter formally. Perhaps she sensed that outright confrontation was futile. Most of her griping about being a token was playful. For example, writing from the Soviet Union, she sent a photo of herself, autographed, "for the Board Room, where no woman's presence adorns the walls, at present. Got to remind you guys I'll be back eventually." [2]

Of the thousands of columns she wrote, only five concerned male chauvinism within the Communist party and two of those were written in 1964, inspired by the Kennedy Commission and such feminist literature as Betty Friedan's *Feminine Mystique* and Eleanor Flexner's *Century of Struggle*. In the last year of her life she felt that women's options were shrinking, and she was embarrassed that she had not acted sooner. However, she died before she got a second chance.

Flynn was a much more successful role model in her Wobbly period. In the IWW she used her skills to organize female strikers, strikers' wives, society women, and Socialist party women. She wrote and lectured on birth control, cooperative housekeeping, and the benefits of small families. She organized a women's issue of the IWW paper, and generally was responsible for the Wobbly line on women. It may not seem that she particularly encouraged women's activity, but her speeches, writings, and example no doubt inspired others.

In the Communist party, however, Flynn did not oppose Party policy or educate others about female issues. She wrote only one column on birth control, which stated that "abortions are forbidden unless medically necessary. Soviet experience agrees with all good gynecologists that continued abortions are dangerous and are not a good substitute for birth control."[3] Her shift on birth control, which in her Wobbly period she wrote and spoke about as a most important issue for women, was apparently inspired by changes in the Soviet Union. In 1936 Stalin became worried about the declining Russian population and changed Lenin's earlier policy of free abortion on demand. Stalin outlawed abortion for women who had less than four children and rewarded women for producing large families. This policy was not rescinded until many years after World War II, and Flynn went along with it. But to be fair, no feminist movement supported abortion at this time, though many fought and wrote about birth control and the advantage of small families. Flynn never wrote about birth control after she joined the Communist party. Perhaps her concern about these issues was not great enough to battle the Party line, or perhaps after her son's death her conviction about small families shifted. She only campaigned for day care during World War II, and during a period when not only the Communist party thought it was necessary; the U.S. Congress had appropriated funds for it— hardly a risky issue.

As Flynn grew older, she resented that she was always given tasks concerning women. She knew that female issues were not regarded as the important ones, and she wanted to be at the center of power, not ghettoized with the weaker sex. The readers of her column even complained of her indifference to women's issues. One wrote, "Now look here Elizabeth, are you doing your duty by women? You never write what's supposed to be Women's Page

stuff." She replied, "I have always assumed that our women readers are interested in everything, not just recipes, and advice to the
lovelorn and how to make leftover foods and clothing—but in
politics, trade unionism, the international situation as well."[4] Flynn
did not seem to understand that any topic could be treated from a
female perspective; instead she interpreted her female critics as
desiring domestic drivel. But perhaps her critics did want her to
write about feminine, not feminist, issues. Perhaps this was Flynn's
way of rebelling against the narrowing of her sphere.

Flynn's early Wobbly articles and speeches as well as her early
Communist party articles focused on women.[5] This topic did not
represent her preference, but rather what the organizations assumed was her forte. As she grew more seasoned she selected subjects more to her liking, such as defense and labor. She felt she was
moving out of the ghetto, into mainstream policy issues. This was
her form of feminist struggle—a rather liberal, individualist approach for one so committed to a collectivist orientation on other
issues. She would not have approved a worker wanting to join
management, yet she aspired to the male dominion.

The need to deny relegation to femaleness and all alone to establish oneself as a universal is a perennial strain of the feminist
tradition. Emma Goldman and other radical women of the 1920s
and 1930s chose to live as equals in a man's world. Some of these
women revolted against the narrow definitions of femininity by
smoking, others by choosing careers, and Flynn by committing
herself to the IWW and then the Communist party. She never
called herself a feminist, although she acknowledged the feminist
cause and defended the suffrage legacy. In her youth there was an
active suffrage movement and she chose not to identify with it, although she often made alliances with suffragists and the existence
of the women's movement opened doors for her. As a member of
the IWW, her priority was overthrowing the capitalist wage labor
system rather than reforming it.

Women were the majority of workers in the IWW eastern textile
strikes, but they were organized mainly as workers rather than as
women. Special appeals were made to the wives of workers and
issues concerning them were highlighted, much in the same way
foreign workers were spoken to in their native tongue, as a way of
facilitating their participation in the universal class struggle. Male

chauvinism was considered a secondary contradiction that would vanish with the ascendance of socialism.

Flynn did not try to promote women to leadership positions within the IWW or push the IWW to emphasize female issues. In fact, Flynn enjoyed her special token status. She liked being surrounded by admiring males and did not welcome competitors to her turf. While waiting to be executed in a Salt Lake City jail in 1915, Joe Hill, the IWW agitator, wrote this song, which aptly described Flynn's position,

> The Rebel Girl, The Rebel Girl,
> To the working class, she's a precious pearl,
> She brings pride and joy to the fighting rebel boy . . .
> And the grafters in terror are trembling
> When her spite and defiance she'll hurl,
> For the only thoroughbred lady, is the Rebel Girl.

The rough-hewn Wobblies treated Flynn, the young beauty, as a special prize. She had grown up in a predominantly female household and relished being surrounded by brawny, fun-seeking men. She herself loved drinking and could outdrink the best of them. Her tastes were plebian, or "barbarian" as she put it, and she had a keen sharp wit.[6]

Flynn talked freely about preferring male company. As she wrote to her sister from prison, "I confess I long to talk to men. The minds of women are hard to fathom. Many never read a paper, tedious conversation and shallow love songs on the radio suffice."[7] Her sister Kathie was more of a feminist, and she often teased Elizabeth about her preference for men. In a letter to Kathie from prison Elizabeth wrote her that Peter, their nephew, "would only need to write when the spirit moves him and not regularly, as you girls do. Ha Ha I can hear you say—weakness for the male species. Special privileges. But don't forget I'm smothered with women here."[8] In this respect she resembled the professional career women of her day; the only difference was that she was a radical and presumably committed to advancing the masses. Her attitude, then, could be said to be hypocritical. But there were no men or women committed to a militant mass approach to women's liberation at that time.

In spite of Flynn's preference for men, in her IWW period she developed a close friendship with Mary Heaton Vorse. They saw each other frequently, cried on each others shoulders, and worked together. After Flynn joined the Communist party, they drifted apart but remained in touch, ready to help each other when needed. Flynn's friendship with Marie Equi is less decipherable. Were they lovers? Equi was an obvious lesbian; Flynn's family believed they were lovers and plotted to free Flynn. Equi seemed not to have wanted her to leave and warned that Flynn would die if she left. It is difficult to tell if Equi was giving medical or personal advice. After Flynn left the two did not stay in touch; Flynn later regarded the ten years she spent with Equi as the most difficult and trying of her life. While in Alderson, Flynn thought often of Portland and seemed to use it as a yardstick of misery, with jail being preferable. Flynn's relationship with Equi, although first providing Flynn a shelter in a storm, turned out to be a prison.

In her Communist party years Flynn had several female friends, Clara Bodian and Muriel Symington, who, like Flynn's sister Kathie, often served as her secretary, but Flynn did not consider them political equals. In fact in letters to them her tone was often impatient and condescending. One former Party organizer said that the women who surrounded her were "sychopants." Another interpretation is that she preferred action-oriented, earthy, working-class women to female intellectuals and leaders.[9] Marion Bachrach, and Claudia Jones, a West Indian Party organizer who was in Alderson with Flynn, were her close friends, but not as close as Mary Heaton Vorse, with whom all life's joys and sorrows were shared. Flynn's letters to them are chatty and newsy rather than intimate and vulnerable. Dorothy Healy, the gutsy nonconformist from Los Angeles, and Peggy Dennis, a Party activist and wife of the man Flynn called her best friend, Gene Dennis, were also her friends, but Flynn saw her mission with them as that of a mother hen keeping the unruly children in line. She appreciated their energy and spirit, but tried to keep them, especially Healy, along the CP, doctrinaire path.

Some Communist party women have said that Flynn was known for fighting male supremacy within the party. When Betty Mallard worked on the *New Masses*, a Party cultural magazine, Flynn asked her and Joe North, the editor, why Mallard's name was not on the masthead. Mallard said this got her thinking about male chauvinism and made a big difference in her life.[10] Martha Stone, who was the New Jersey State Party chairman, also said that Flynn had a reputation for fighting male chauvinism. Once in the 1950s Flynn talked to Martha Stone about a Party insurance organizer who bought a gift of falsies for a flat-chested worker. Flynn thought this behavior was antifemale and was surprised when Stone saw it as inoffensive and good fun. However, it seems Stone convinced Flynn that the female worker thought it humorous and in good taste, and it was left at that. In evaluating the situation Stone said that "Flynn tried to be all things to all people and there wasn't much consistency there."[11] Most people have said that although Flynn was concerned about women, it was in an abstract way. They could not remember examples of her feminist consciousness, but could provide detailed examples of Flynn preferring male company and going out after Friday meetings to drink with the men, while the other women scurried home to their kids and domestic duties.

Many former Party people noted that Flynn had two personalities, one public and one private. In private she was often quiet, warm, and had a great capacity for cheer and a fine-tuned humor. She always remembered birthdays, inquired about the children, and visited the ailing. Peggy Dennis said Flynn was the only Party official who visited her dying husband and offered help after he died. Steve Nelson, a leader of the unemployed and Spanish Civil War hero, reported that she was the only Party member to talk to him after he left the Party. She broke Party ranks for the sake of friendship. However, this warmth and humanity did not prevent her from being icy in public and carrying out brutal orders against friends if Party policy ordered it.[12]

In her Wobbly period Flynn was a nonconformist in her personal life, especially in relation to nineteenth-century standards. She refused to settle down, give up organizing, and become a housewife. Even though she loved Carlo Tresca, her work always came first. She had a strong sense of herself as an important person and was not willing to take a subordinate place.

Flynn's later ideas about sex seemed to have been formed by her youthful anarchist contacts; her sex life remained free and unfettered by official Party prudery. She had affairs with various Party officials and young working-class men because she liked sex, or as she put it, "the passions of the flesh," and because she was lonely and needed male companions. Perhaps she found that men listened better in bed. Male politicos used sex to recruit new members and establish a loyal cadre, so why couldn't she? She was never a puritan or a prude, and in this way she rebelled against public Party morality. Once a Communist Youth official, Danny Rubin, complained to her that the switchboard operator at Party headquarters was sleeping around and should be chastised. Flynn fired back, "Do you know that I have slept with almost every man in the party starting with William Foster and if you have a free afternoon, I'll tell you about it."[13] In 1960, at age seventy, weighing over 270 pounds, Flynn forgot protocol and had an affair with her Hungarian guide. They drank tokay, "wine after which there is no better," went to "an open air dancing garden and to the highest mountain to see the city all lit up." She did not seem to hide or squash her sexual passion and wrote several letters to her family and friends about her newest Hungarian flame.[14]

The Communist party was against homosexuality. It pushed obviously gay people to leave the Party and purposely ignored less openly gay people, especially wealthy women. During the McCarthy years the Party believed gays would be more vulnerable to investigation and bribery and therefore should not be members. Flynn, by contrast, was proud of her lesbian niece. When Party people tried to fix her up with men, repressing the fact that she was gay, Flynn replied that she was happy as she was.[15]

Flynn, however, never tried to change or interfere with the Communist party's official position on homosexuality. In *The Alderson Story: My Life as a Political Prisoner,* Flynn had written a chapter on lesbians, which in itself was daring, but the chapter assumed that lesbians in prison were abnormal and suggested that the problem might be solved with correspondence courses, such as existed in men's prisons, and conjugal visits, like those allowed in Mexican and Latin American prisons. She chastised the prison administration for ignoring the problem, suggesting "squeamish puritanism" as the cause.[16] Flynn was upset that the Russian translation of her book eliminated the lesbian chapter. First, she wrote, she was displeased as they had not consulted her; "secondly they're acting in a *puritanical* manner." After all, she wrote, "I am showing the degeneracy of the capitalist system, that's an important part of the book."[17] This is hardly a strong defense of homosexuality and one might have expected a stronger one from Flynn, especially in lieu of her own relationship with Equi and her family background.

Most of Flynn's family were bohemians. Her sister Bina had a female lover for a time; sister Kathie had a child without being married or having a relationship with the father. Flynn's nephew, Peter Martin, together with Allen Ginsberg, started City Lights Bookstore in San Francisco, which went on to publish the Beats and become the center for Beat culture in the 1950s. Martin later became the owner of the New Yorker bookstore. With a family such as this, Flynn must have found the Communist party, especially its New York City officials, stodgy and dull. Brendan Behan, the rakish Irish playwright, whom she got to know while living at the Chelsea Hotel, where she preferred to live during the last years of her life, was a welcome relief. After her mother died, Flynn lived on Twelfth Street and Second Avenue, in the middle of the Lower East Side, the center of seedy bohemia and Beat culture. Even when she lived with her mother in the Bronx she hung out in old anarchist bars and restaurants.

Although Flynn lived in an independent and unconventional manner, never putting any man's career or child's future ahead of her political work, she gave the woman question less attention than recent feminist activists. And even though the Communist party gave women's emancipation low priority, the Party played an important part in keeping the goal of women's political activism alive during the 1920s through the 1950s. A number of the women's liberation movement activists of the late 1960s were red diaper babies, grew up with such terms as "male chauvinism" and the "woman question," and heard frequent gossip about which Party families were backward about women. The "woman question" was a radical nineteenth-century term, and only the Communist party continued its use.

Flynn was not a feminist, but she inspired many women. Half a dozen people now in their late thirties and forties were named after her. There are at least two recent feminist songs about her. Women who heard her speak were inspired to become political activists. She herself wanted to be taken seriously as a revolutionary and resented being appointed to stereotypical female positions, like heading the Women's Commission or giving fund-raising talks.

If she sounded antiwoman on occasion, it was the result of the kind of women's liberation strategy she was attempting. In order to assert her equality in a political culture that assumed women were inferior, Flynn was forced to assert her atypical superiority, much in the same manner as Emma Goldman and Margaret Sanger had. Without a feminist movement, and feminist consciousness, an exceptional woman is a token, a rebel and not a revolutionary. Flynn believed she could not excel if she identified with women, so she had no choice but to try and make herself one of the men. This task was impossible since the men around her saw women as subordinate. Her life shows both the possibilities and inherent limitations of trying to make it in a man's world without the backup of a feminist movement that could stress accountability and collective strength.

Notes

ACKNOWLEDGMENTS

1. Sarah Eisenstein, although dying of cancer, talked to me a great deal about the Flynn project. She was extremely thoughtful and made me think about the larger issues. Her thesis, which she was researching at the time of our study group, was published posthumously as *Give Us Bread but Give Us Roses: Working Women's Consciousness in the United States, 1890 to the First World War* (Boston: Routledge and Kegan Paul, 1983). At the time of the study group, Meredith Tax was doing research that resulted in the following two books: *The Rising of the Women: Feminist Solidarity and Class Conflict, 1880–1917* (New York: Monthly Review Press, 1980); *Rivington Street* (New York: William Morrow and Co., 1982).

2. A. P. Olmstead, "Agitator on the Left: The Speechmaking of Elizabeth Gurley Flynn, 1904–64," Ph.D. diss., University of Indiana, Aug. 1971. I talked to Olmstead as well.

3. My correspondence with International Publishers is in the Flynn Papers, Tamiment.

4. Dee Garrison, *Rebel Pen: The Writing of Mary Heaton Vorse* (New York: Monthly Review, 1985).

5. Peter Carlson, *Roughneck: The Life and Times of Big Bill Haywood* (New York: W. W. Norton Co., 1983).

6. Nancy Krieger, "Queen of the Bolsheviks: The Hidden History of Dr. Marie Equi," *Radical America*, Jan. 1984, 55–73.

7. Rosalyn Baxandall, "Elizabeth Gurley Flynn: The Early Years," *Radical America*, Jan.–Feb. 1975, 97–115.

INTRODUCTION

As noted in the acknowledgments, most of Flynn's papers have been found, although a few are missing, mainly those from her Oregon years and a criticism of the Communist party. Fortunately I possess copies of many of these lost papers. I will refer to the papers at New York University as EGF Papers, Tamiment. The epigraph was written by EGF, in a letter to her sister Anna K. Flynn (Kathie), written Aug. 6, 1955, while EGF was in Alderson prison. EGF Papers, Tamiment.

1. EGF's mother and later EGF saved and clipped momentos and news

items, both favorable and unfavorable. Many of them are deteriorated and undated. Much of my unfootnoted background material is drawn from this source, as here. EGF Papers, Tamiment.

2. Adolf Wolff, *Songs of Rebellion, Songs of Life, Songs of Love* (New York: Albert and Charles Boni, 1914), 32.

3. *New York World*, Aug. 23, 1906.

4. "Hoarse," *New Yorker*, Oct. 26, 1946, 25. *Los Angeles Times*, Mar. 15, 1908.

5. Richard O. Boyer, "How Elizabeth Gurley Flynn Became a Communist," *Daily Worker [DW]*, Apr. 28, 1952.

6. Joe Doyle, "Elizabeth Gurley Flynn," part 1 *Ais Eiri* 2 (1979): 12–18.

7. *Sunday Worker [SW]*, Mar. 15, 1959.

8. Thomas Flynn to Professor Fletcher, Sept. 2, 1915, Dartmouth College Library, Hanover, N.H. Peter Martin, EGF's nephew, gave me copies of these poems.

9. *DW*, May 13, 1945; *SW*, Sept. 20, 1942; *DW* Oct. 29, 1948.

10. *DW*, Apr. 29, 1949.

11. EGF to Mary Heaton Vorse, May 16, 1930, in Mary Heaton Vorse Papers, Wayne State University, Detroit, Mich. This remark should not be taken as anti-Semitism. In the *DW* Flynn wrote at least twelve columns condemning and analyzing anti-Semitism. Her mother, Annie Flynn, believed that the Irish might have been one of the lost tribes of Israel because her grandfather celebrated the Sabbath on Saturday and adopted the Jewish method of killing animals and processing meat.

12. *DW*, Apr. 29, 1949.

13. EGF, *Rebel Girl: An Autobiography, My First Life, 1906–1926* (New York: International Publishers, 1973), 23. The first edition of this autobiography is called *I Speak My Own Piece* (New York: Masses and Mainstream, 1955).

14. Carl Reeve and Ann Barton Reeve, *James Connolly and the United States* (Atlantic Highlands, N.J.: Humanities Press, 1978), 82. The Reeves quote from the Connolly Archives, Connolly to John Matheson, Oct. 28, 1907.

15. *SW*, Oct. 5, 1952.

16. EGF, "How I Became a Socialist Speaker," *Socialist Woman*, no. 3, Aug. 1907. In an interview in the *Daily Socialist of Chicago*, Sept. 17, 1907, Flynn was quoted, "My addresses have always been utopian, but never anarchistic. I am not an anarchist, but a thorough socialist." In the closing paragraph in *Rebel Girl*, she stated: "I saw LaGuardia then Mayor of New York City out at Flushing Meadows. He said, 'Elizabeth, I hear you joined the Communist Party,' and I said, 'Yes, Fiorello, don't you remember you told me to leave the Italian anarchists and get back where I belong?' He laughed his hearty, roaring laughter and said, 'Well, I rather see you with the Communists than with those freaks.' But I had not been able or willing to take his advice in 1924" (p. 335).

17. From various torn clippings, EGF Papers, Tamiment, marked 1904, 1905, Apr. 11, 1906, Aug. 23, 24, 1906, from the *New York Globe, New York Evening Journal, New York American, New York Times, New York Sun, New York Tribune, New York World, The People, Morning Star*, and *Philadelphia Record*.

18. *DW*, Feb. 2, 1959.

19. EGF, *Memories of the Industrial Workers of the World*, Occasional Paper no. 24 (New York: AIMS, 1977). From a speech of EGF's, Nov. 8, 1952, Northern Illinois University, DeKalb, 3.

20. EGF, *Rebel Girl*, 15. *DW*, Jan. 29, 1952. In this account, contrary to the account in *Rebel Girl*, she recalled it was the Socialist Labor party that paid her. Both recollections may be correct as the Socialist Labor party was affiliated with the IWW at the time.

21. Untitled manuscript, EGF Papers, Tamiment. This is an article or speech about the IWW, first written in 1920, revised in 1941, and then in 1943.

22. EGF, "I Have No Regrets: A Chapter from American Labor History," *Women Today*, Apr. 1937. Microfilm, Tamiment.

23. These observations come from Charlot Holzenkamper, who shared them with the author in a letter dated June 18, 1984. Holzenkamper wrote a manuscript titled "Rebel Girl."

24. For accounts of these organizing drives, see *Solidarity*, Apr. 19, 1910, May 9, 1914, Dec. 9, 1916, Jan. 2, 1913. Microfilm, Tamiment. Later, when she became a Communist, she forgot this aspect of the IWW and said, "Now their attitudes towards what we call white collar workers was not good. Not good at all, because they just considered that they didn't belong to the working class. You had to wear overalls, be muscular, you had to work. If you were a pen pusher, you were not a worker according to the IWW. . . . In other words, what they would call today a very sectarian organization." EGF, *Memories of the IWW*, 29.

25. Harbor Allen, "The Flynn," *American Mercury*, Dec. 1926, 428; *SW*, Aug. 7, 1955. Interview with Art Shields, Feb. 16, 1984.

26. *St. Petersburg Florida Times*, Sept. 6, 1964.

27. Joseph Conlin, *Big Bill Haywood and the Radical Union Movement* (Syracuse, N.Y.: Syracuse University Press, 1969), 103. In the Department of Justice Files, National Archives, Washington, D.C., I noticed many of the agents were interpreters.

28. Elizabeth Ewen, *Immigrant Women in the Land of Dollars* (New York: Monthly Review Press, 1985), 166–183.

29. EGF, *Rebel Girl*, 87–88.

30. Ibid., 76.

31. Fred Thompson, *The IWW: Its First Seventy Years* (Chicago, Ill.: IWW Publishing Co., 1976), 49.

32. George A. Venn, "The Wobblies and Montana's Garden City," *Montana: The Magazine of Western History*, Oct. 1971. EGF, *Rebel Girl*, 104.

33. FBI File, U.S. Parole Commission, No. 100-1697-349, Mar. 24, 1955, lists her various names; Mrs. John Jones, Elizabeth Gurley Flynn Jones, Elizabeth Jones, Mrs. John Archibald Jones, Mrs. EG Jones, and Mrs. E. G. Jones are included. FBI File No. 100-1693-693, Apr. 2, 1949, states that Fred Flynn's birth certificate says that he was born Frederick Vincent Jones.

34. EGF, *Rebel Girl*, 322–323.

35. Albert Parry, *Garrets and Pretenders: A History of Bohemianism in America* (New York: Dover, 1933), 200–209; and undated newsclipping in EGF Papers, Tamiment. "Jack Jones," Sherwood Anderson, *The Dil Pickler, Chicago Daily News*, June 18, 1919. Roger Bruns sent me a copy of *The Dil Pickler;* other copies are in the Newberry Library, Chicago, Ill., which is across the street from where the Club and Tookers Alley used to be. Bruns has written a biography of Ben Reitman, who was a habitué of the club. *The Damnedest Radical* (Urbana: University of Illinois Press, 1987), 230–245.

36. Interview with Peter Martin, Feb. 9, 1982.

37. EGF Papers, Tamiment. Several of these invitations over the period 1912—1926 are pasted in notebooks. Judith Schwarz, *Radical Feminists of Heterodoxy* (Lebanon, N.H.: New Victoria Publishers, 1982), 1.

38. EGF Papers, Tamiment. From a list of her speeches on women and from announcements in the IWW press of her speeches, which she clipped. In a speech outlined she noted before the title of a speech, "Birth Control," "the most fundamental of all the claims made by women."

39. Dr. Elizabeth Shapleigh, "Occupational Diseases in the Textile Industry," *New York Call,* Dec. 29, 1912. Located in New York Public Library, Annex.

40. EGF, "Figures and Facts and Contract Slavery in the Paterson Silk Mills," *Pageant of the Paterson Strike,* (New York: Success Press, 1913).

41. Ardis Cameron, "Bread and Roses Revisited: Women's Culture and Working Class Activism in the Lawrence Strike of 1912," in *Women, Work, and Protest: A Century of U.S. Labor History,* ed. Ruth Milkman (Boston: Routledge and Kegan Paul, 1985), 44. The article quotes *Lawrence Evening Tribune,* Feb. 23, 26, 28, 1912; *Lawrence Sun,* Feb. 2, 1912.

42. Cameron, "Bread and Roses Revisited," 51, quotes *Lawrence Evening Tribune,* Feb. 12, 19, 24, 26, 1912.

43. EGF, *Rebel Girl,* 122.

44. *Paterson Press,* Apr. 4, 1913. This article was brought to my attention by Peter Carlson.

45. Vera Buch Weisbord, *A Radical Life* (Bloomington: Indiana University Press, 1977), 113—123. Phone interview with Sophie Melvin Gerson, Feb. 2, 1982; and Anne Fishhel, "Women in Textile Organizing," interview with Sophie Melvin Gerson, *Radical History Review,* Spring/Summer 1977, 113.

46. Mary Heaton Vorse, *Footnote to Folly* (New York: Farrar and Rinehart, 1935).

47. Mary Heaton Vorse, "Elizabeth Gurley Flynn," *The Nation,* Feb. 17, 1926, 175—176.

48. EGF, *Rebel Girl,* 125—126.

49. *Industrial Worker* (Spokane), Feb. 22, 1912. Microfilm, Tamiment.

50. Joyce Kornbluh, ed., *Rebel Voices* (Ann Arbor: University of Michigan, 1964), 162.

51. Haywood Trial Papers, vol. 1, no. 188032, National Archives, Washington, D.C.; and Conlin, *Big Bill Haywood,* 162.

52. Fred Thompson and Patrick Murfin, *The IWW: Its First Seventy Years, 1905—1975* (Chicago, Ill.: IWW, 1976), 76.

53. Carlo Tresca Autobiography, Manuscript Division, New York Public Library. This autobiography hardly mentions EGF as it was translated by Margaret de Silver, Tresca's wife.

54. EGF, *Rebel Girl,* 324. Max Eastman, *Heroes I Have Known* (New York: Simon and Schuster, 1942), 17—18, 37.

55. EGF, *Rebel Girl,* 208.

56. Information supplied to me by Peter Martin, in many interviews; he is the son of Bina and Tresca. None of this information is in Tresca's autobiography. Interviews on Oct. 10, 1979, Feb. 9, 1982, Sept. 30, 1982, and several informal chats during 1976—1980.

57. Peter Martin interview, Feb. 9, 1982; interview with Jane Bobba, Oct. 24, 1972; and FBI Files, NYC, No. 100-1696, filed Aug. 5, 1952. Old German Files, OG 5400-5699, Reel 62A, National Archives, and interviews with Peter Martin.

58. Joe Doyle, "Clear the Way for Elizabeth Gurley Flynn, Fag An Bealach?" part 2, *Ais Eiri*, 1979.

59. *Elizabeth Gurley Flynn Speaks to the Court*, pamphlet (New York: New Century Publishers, 1952), 7.

60. Philip Foner, ed., *Fellow Workers and Friends: IWW Free-Speech Fights as Told by Participants* (Westport, Conn.: Greenwood Press, 1981), 17.

61. EGF, *Rebel Girl*, 236. She calls Tresca her husband here.

62. Art Shields, "She Was the Soul of the Workers' Struggles," *SW*, Aug. 7, 1955.

63. For these cases, and the files of many labor defendants, see the Workers Defense Union Papers, Wisconsin Historical Society, Madison, Wis. EGF gave this collection to the society in 1958. Tamiment has a microfilm of the collection.

64. Workers Defense Union Papers, File No. 20, Mollie Steimer to Agnes Smedley, published in the *New York Call*, May 9, 1920. Steimer still lives in Mexico.

65. Naval and Old Army Office Files, NNMO, Box 108, MID, National Archives, Washington, D.C.

66. Old German Files, OG 188032-47, National Archives, Washington, D.C.

67. Old German Files, OG 5400-5699, Reel 62A, National Archives, Washington, D.C. *Solidarity*, Nov. 1, 1913. Microfilm, Tamiment.

68. Melvin Dubofsky, *We Shall Be All: A History of the IWW* (Chicago: Quadrangle Books, 1969), 425–426.

69. Haywood Trial Papers, File 146, National Archives, Washington, D.C. Nunzio Percione brought this to my attention. Letter to President Wilson, Jan. 10, 1918, National Archives.

70. Peter Carlson, *Roughneck: The Life and Times of Big Bill Haywood* (New York: Norton, 1983), 256–257.

71. File No. 3, No. 188032-250-349, National Archives, states that EGF's and Tresca's case was severed on Oct. 31, 1922.

72. EGF, *Haywood, Debs, and Ruthenberg* (New York: Workers Publishing, 1939). Interview with Steve Nelson, Nov. 24, 1981, Truro, Mass.

73. Scrapbook of this 1926 dinner, EGF Papers, Tamiment. In 1983 the Communist party gave some of EGF's papers to the Tamiment, mainly official documents and ceremonial notebooks. They are now being recataloged.

74. Mary Heaton Vorse Papers, Box 79, Folder 1926, "Daily Notes," Archives of Labor History and Urban Affairs, Wayne State University, Detroit, Mich. This diary entry was brought to my attention by Dee Garrison, who is writing a biography of Mary Heaton Vorse, and has edited a collection of her writings, *Rebel Pen* (New York: Monthly Review Press, 1985).

75. "San Quentin Girl Prisoner," *World*, Sept. 10, no year in manuscript. Division of Library of Congress, Washington, D.C.

76. Interview with Jane Bobba, Oct. 24, 1972. The FBI was bewildered by Flynn and Equi's relationship. A lesbian lawyer from Chicago, Rene Hanover, told me in a telephone interview, Mar. 31, 1982, that Flynn said she had come

out in the *Alderson Story,* but that the Communist party had censored the chapter and instead substituted an antigay chapter. This seems unlikely as Flynn was a leading CP executive and the Party disapproved of lesbians. In the Margaret Sanger Papers, Sophia Smith Collection, Northampton, Mass., there are many love letters from Equi to Sanger. Linda Gordon brought these to my attention. There is no evidence that Sanger reciprocated.

77. From an envelope marked personal 1916, Margaret Sanger Files, Sophia Smith Collection. A letter from Equi to Sanger, undated except for Saturday, closes, "My arms are around you—I kiss your sweet mouth in absolute surrender." In Flynn's photo albums there were pictures of Dr. Equi's adopted daughter in an aviator's helmet in front of an airplane. These pictures have vanished with all the Equi material. EGF Papers, Tamiment.

78. Nancy Krieger, "Queen of the Bolsheviks: The Hidden History of Dr. Marie Equi," *Radical America,* Jan. 1984; *Solidarity,* July 21, 1917, 8.

79. Robert Tyler, *Rebel of the Woods: The IWW in the Pacific Northwest* (Portland: University of Oregon, 1967), 139–140. Tyler quotes *Albers v. U.S. Dept. of Justice,* Nov. 22, 1918.

80. Blanche Wiesen Cook, "Female Support Networks and Political Activism: Lillian Wald, Crystal Eastman, Emma Goldman," *Chrysalis,* no. 3 (1977): 43–61.

81. Letter to Kathie Flynn, Aug. 6, 1955, EGF Papers, Tamiment.

82. EGF Papers, Tamiment. Jotted on a piece of paper and kept in one of her scrapbooks for these years.

83. Letter to Kathie Flynn, Jan. 29, 1955, EGF Papers, Tamiment.

84. EGF to Agnes Inglis, Sept. 10, 1936, Labadie Collection, University of Michigan, Ann Arbor. The librarian Dione Miles, who was writing a biography of Inglis, made these letters available to me.

85. Interviews with Peter Martin, June 6, 1982, Feb. 9, 1982.

86. Interview with Dorothy Healy, July 12, 1982. Fred Flynn to EGF, May 7 and 23, 1924, EGF Papers, Tamiment.

87. "To My Mother—September 19, 1938," spiral notebook of poems, EGF Papers, Tamiment.

88. Scrapbook of poems dated June 1939, West Virginia, EGF Papers, Tamiment.

89. *Elizabeth Gurley Flynn Speaks to the Court,* 10–11.

90. "It Didn't Take the First Time," draft manuscript for her book, EGF Papers, Tamiment. The FBI Files, Jan. 2, 1952, state, "On May 16, 1951 confidential informant [name blacked out] of known reliability, advised that the subject applied for membership in the Communist Party during the 1920s through James P. Cannon, but that Cannon kept stalling the acceptance because of factionalism." (James Cannon was the national secretary of the Socialist Workers party.) "In the fall of 1920 C.E.R. [Charles E. Ruthenberg] took Elizabeth Gurley Flynn's first application to join the Communist party, but it was decided she would postpone it because she was in the ILD. Jim Cannon says Sam D'Arcy's wife, C.E.R.'s secretary, took Elizabeth Gurley Flynn's application out of the files and pocketed it" (Charles E. Ruthenberg Collection, Reel 4, Box 5, Folder 4, Ohio Historical Society, Columbus, Ohio). These are Oakley Johnson's notes and were brought to my attention by Jeff Perry.

Interview with Emma D'Arcy, July 26, 1984, in Harvey Cedars, N.J. She did not remember the incident at all, but thought it might be possible. Charlotte Stern, a Communist party member who was living in Seattle, and working for the Centralia Defense Committee and the International Labor Defense League, told me on June 22, 1982, that she talked to Flynn about joining the Party in 1928 and that Earl Browder and William Foster visited EGF in Portland to convince her to join. In *Elizabeth Gurley Flynn Speaks to the Court* Flynn said she thought her membership was misplaced because Ruthenberg, then secretary of the Communist party, died suddenly in 1926 (p. 11). Everyone seems to take the credit for Flynn's joining the Party or for sabotaging her joining. Albert Weisbord said he converted her at Passaic (interview, Apr. 18, 1970, in Chicago); also Vera Weisbord, *A Radical Life,* 114. Perhaps all these stories are apocryphal and covered up Flynn's embarrassment about joining the Party so late, or perhaps people projected their ideas onto EGF.

91. Diary, 1937, EGF Papers, Tamiment. Flynn at about this time relinquished her IWW membership. She wrote, "I ceased to be a Wobbly the first time I voted for Mayor LaGuardia." Of course there were rumors that she had been kicked out of the IWW much earlier, but these are probably untrue; see Flynn's letter printed in *Solidarity,* Aug. 25, 1917.

92. Interview with Jane Bobba, Oct. 24, 1972; interview with Peter Martin, Feb. 9, 1982. However, there is no written evidence in the Roosevelt papers of a correspondence between Eleanor Roosevelt and EGF about her joining the Communist party.

93. In the United States at this time (1928–1935) there were three major factions, each tied with Moscow in some way: the Foster group was loyal to Stalin, the Cannon group to Trotsky, and the Lovestone group to Bukharin. There were other small non-Moscow-aligned groups headed by the Weisbords, Muste, Mattick, and DeLeon. By 1935 the Communist party emerged as the largest, most prestigious group in the United States.

94. EGF to Mary Heaton Vorse, May 16, 1930, Labor Archives, Wayne State University. EGF told Charlotte Stern in 1928 in Seattle that she could not join because she respected Gitlow and Lovestone, and the Comintern had discredited them; she did not know who was right or what to do. Interview with Charlotte Stern, June 22, 1982.

95. Fernando Claudin, *The Communist Movement: From Comintern to Cominform* (New York: Monthly Review Press, 1975), 126–242; and Al Richmond, *A Long View from the Left* (Boston: Houghton Mifflin, 1973), 226–241.

96. *Elizabeth Gurley Flynn Speaks to the Court,* 11–12.

97. Richard Boyer and Herbert Morais, *Labor's Untold Story* (New York: United Electrical Radio and Machine Workers of America, 1955), 295. Saul Alinsky, *John L. Lewis: An Unauthorized Biography* (New York: Vintage Books, 1949). Art Preis, *Labor's Giant Step* (New York: Pathfinder Press, 1972), 44–94.

98. Barrington Moore, Jr., "American Government and Politics: The CPUSA, An Analysis of a Social Movement," *American Political Science Review* (Feb. 1945): 31–41; and Richmond, *Long View from the Left,* 131–158; Theodore Draper, *American Communism and the Soviet Union* (New York: Viking, 1963), 234–441.

99. Earl Browder, "Building the Mass Communist Party," *Party Organizer,* July 1938; also EGF, "Why I Joined the Communist Party," text of a speech given at Mecca Temple, Apr. 24, 1947, EGF Papers, Tamiment.

100. EGF, "Speech to the National Committee," *Political Affairs,* July 1945, 613−614.

101. *DW,* July 16, 1944. *Earl Browder: The Man from Kansas* was published in 1940 by Workers Library, New York.

102. Interviews with Joe Starobin and Annette Rubinstein, Aug. 6, 1971. Interview with Gurley Turner, June 22, 1982. All interviews occurred in New York City unless specifically located.

103. *The Trial of Elizabeth Gurley Flynn by the American Civil Liberties Union,* ed. Corliss Lamont (Monthly Review Press, 1968), 98−99, 105.

104. Ibid., 15, as quoted from Lucille Milner, *Education of an American Liberal* (New York: Horizon Press, 1954), 282. Interview with Peter Gessner, July 3, 1982, San Francisco, Calif., and interview with Peter Martin, Nov. 13, 1983. Margaret de Silver erased Flynn from Tresca's autobiography. In fact there is one mention of her, as a Lawrence strike leader. Roger Baldwin refused to talk to me. He said EGF was one subject he did not care to discuss. He did however talk with Helen Camp, for her Ph.D. diss., "Gurley: A Biography of Elizabeth Gurley Flynn, 1890−1964," Columbia, 1980, but she did not ask him about their relationship.

105. *Trial of Elizabeth Gurley Flynn by the American Civil Liberties Union,* 25.

106. Theoretically this constitution is a model of democracy. However, in practice this was the period of the Stalinist purges.

107. *Trial of Elizabeth Gurley Flynn by the American Civil Liberties Union,* 104.

108. *New York Times,* June 22, 1976.

109. EGF to Mary Heaton Vorse, from Portland, Ore., Mar. 22, 1929, Mary Heaton Vorse Papers, Wayne State University Library.

110. EGF to Agnes Inglis, May 2, 1930, and July 11, 1934, Labadie Collection, University of Michigan, Ann Arbor, Mich.

111. *Five Years of the International Workers Order, 1930−35,* published by National Executive Committee of IWO, 1935. Lent to me by Josh Freeman. The papers of the IWO are in the Tamiment.

112. *Trial of Elizabeth Gurley Flynn by the American Civil Liberties Union,* 126. In EGF Papers, Tamiment, there are ALP voting ballots with Fred Flynn's name as delegate. His date and address books with Communist party contacts are there as well. Interview with Manie Eisenhandler, friend of Fred Flynn, Jan. 18, 1985.

113. Poems to Dennis and Nelson in EGF Papers, Tamiment. Peter Martin gave me a copy of Flynn's will and told me also of her affection for Nelson and Dennis. Peter Martin also told me of a long affair she had with Jimmy, a fireman. Party members were upset at this tempestuous affair (1946−1947). Interview with Peter Martin, June 7, 1982. Jimmy wrote to EGF while she was in Alderson, and Kathie reported it to her. "Nice that Jimmy remembered it. He is improving with age—he must be forty-one now." Aug. 8, 1946, letter no. 101, EGF Files, Tamiment.

114. EGF Poetry Scrapbooks, Tamiment.

115. EGF, *I Speak My Own Piece,* 1.

116. Interview with Peter Martin, June 7, 1982; interview with Roberta Bobba, June 13, 1982.

117. *New York Times*, Feb. 20, 1977, an obituary of Carmine Galante, it stated, "What made his reputation in the syndicate, according to police sources was the widely held belief in the underworld that he [Galante] was linked with the killing of Carlo Tresca, the editor of an anarchist newspaper in New York in 1943. The murder, which made international headlines, was believed to have been ordered by Vito Genovese, who wanted to eliminate a political enemy of his friend, Italy's Fascist leader, Benito Mussolini. Mr. Galante, whose car was found abandoned two blocks from the scene, was held for questioning in the case but was released for lack of evidence." The lack of sufficient evidence was confirmed in an April 16, 1987 interview with Eleazar Lipsky, assistant district attorney at the time.

118. *DW*, Nov. 18, 1945.

119. EGF Papers, Tamiment; in the notebook the poem is dated Spring 1943 and written to C—.

120. *DW*, Oct. 3, 1937, Mar. 16, 1940, Oct. 6, 1940, June 29, 1958, July 19, 1957; FBI Report, June 12, 1943, No. 1006261; *DW*, May 5, 1945.

121. Maurice Isserman, *Which Side Were You On? The American Communist Party during the Second World War* (Middleton, Conn.: Wesleyan University Press, 1982), 148.

122. Ibid., 141. Isserman quoted from the Browder papers, 111–357, EGF to Browder, undated manuscript; EGF, *Women and War* (New York: New Century Publishers, 1942); and *DW*, Dec. 14, 1941, Feb. 22, 1942, Aug. 9, 1942, Nov. 22, 1942, May 23, 1943, May 30, 1943, June 13, 1943, June 27, 1943, Sept. 5, 1943, Jan. 21, 1945.

123. *DW*, Dec. 6, 1942.

124. *SW*, Jan. 3, 1943; *DW*, Jan. 11, 1943, May 23, 1943, July 18, 1943, Jan. 21, 1945.

125. *DW*, Mar. 26, 1939, "I had a secret admiration for that man" (referring to John L. Lewis). FBI Report, May 26, 1942, reported Flynn's activities in Pittsburgh. EGF wrote a pamphlet titled *Coal Miners and the War* (New York: Workers Library, 1942), 12.

126. *DW*, Dec. 26, 1947, July 19, 1964.

127. The Women's Commission was reinstated in 1969 when the women's liberation movement grew and women again became politically important. Flynn was head of the commission for the whole of its life.

128. *Elizabeth Gurley Flynn Speaks to the Court*, 13–14.

129. *DW*, Mar. 1, 1948, and Nov. 20, 1953.

130. Kathy Moos Campbell, paper on Congress of American Women; tapes, interviews, and papers of Charlotte Todes Stern, now at Tamiment Library, New York University, done by author.

131. Interview with Edythe Lutzker, Feb. 20, 1973.

132. *Trial of Elizabeth Gurley Flynn by the American Civil Liberties Union*, 123.

133. Joseph R. Starobin, *American Communism in Crisis: 1943–57* (Cambridge: Harvard University Press, 1972), 273, n. 30. Interview with Starobin, Truro, Mass. July 24, 26, 1972.

134. EGF, "Speech to National Committee," *Political Affairs*, July 1945, 615.

135. *DW,* Aug. 13, 1944. Flynn complimented Eleanor Roosevelt in a column, again in *DW,* Dec. 13, 1959, for not visiting Spain. Reported as overheard by FBI agent, July 5, 1941, for period May—July; report made by CVM Internal Security R and C, No. EL360. EGF wrote anti—Eleanor Roosevelt columns in *DW,* Jan. 19, 1949, and Mar. 1, 1961, complaining about Eleanor Roosevelt's opinions about the Soviet Union.

136. Interviews with Charlotte Todes Stern and Vera Buch Weisbord (Chicago) during 1977—1982; both women have become friends so it is difficult to document the dates of the interviews in which EGF was discussed. Interview with Sam D'Arcy, Harvey Cedars, N.J., July 26, 1984.

137. Overheard Jan. 3, 1961; FBI Report made Nov. 27, 1961, New York, No. 100-1696. Overheard Oct. 1, 1958; FBI Report filed Nov. 7, 1958, New York, No. 100-1696. Overheard Oct. 29, 1958; FBI Report filed Nov. 7, 1958, New York, No. 100-1696.

138. The FBI seized a letter EGF sent to the New York City office, written on May 26, 1947, from Chicago, describing her quelling of the dissident Inman faction in San Francisco. The FBI Report was filed on June 17, 1946, New York, No. 100-1696. The FBI further reported another trip Flynn made to Philadelphia to criticize Samuel D'Arcy on behalf of the Communist party for "causing difficulty" and "going haywire" and "suffering from wild cat leadership"; as a result D'Arcy was dropped from the Central Committee. EGF stated that "she was doubtful if he was aware of his removal from this body and further, that his continued presence in the Pennsylvania district was a matter of doubt as he had in fact been supplanted by Frank Caestone. She [Flynn] expressed a hope that D'Arcy would come out of his difficulty 'OK' eventually." Report filed May 30, 1944, No. BU 1009242.

139. It is Stalin rather than Lenin who consolidated these tendencies and made the rigid policy, but the tendencies were there in Leninism.

140. Earl Browder, *DW,* July 24, 1945.

141. Report filed by New York agent, Aug. 28, 1951. Report filed by Agent Donald E. Harnett (usually the agent's name is blacked out), Dec. 6, 1960. Interview with Dorothy Healy, Los Angeles, July 12, 1982, and Washington, D.C., Apr. 19, 1985. Dorothy Healy told me that the Soviet officials would quiz U.S. Communist party officials visiting Russia about other American Party officials.

142. The articles and reviews are in the *DW* and span Mar. 16, 1941, to Sept. 4, 1961.

143. Lawrence Lader, *Power on the Left: American Radical Movements Since 1946* (New York: W. W. Norton, 1979), xi.

144. David Shannon, *The Decline of American Communism: A History of the CPUSA Since 1945* (New York: Harcourt Brace, 1978), 185; and Gil Green, *Cold War Fugitive* (New York: International Publishers, 1984).

145. Lader, *Power on the Left,* 82. Harry Haywood, *Black Bolshevik: Autobiography of an African Communist* (Chicago, Ill.: Liberator Press, 1973), 583—604.

146. Starobin, *American Communism in Crisis,* 306—307.

147. EGF, *Communists and the People* (New York: New Century Publishers, 1953), 11. Idem, *The Plot to Gag America* (New York: New Century Publishers, 1950), 11.

148. EGF, *The Alderson Story* (New York: International Publishers, 1963), 12.

149. FBI Reports, June 27, 1949, May 2, 1949, June 23, 1949, from San Francisco. "Well, they started very well, our first difficulty, frankly, came from their men and not the women, especially after what happened to Bob Thompson's kid. There was a little resistance to them leaving the home, leaving the children, all kinds of problems, and then Gene's proposal was that we should wait 'til a little later on, maybe that wasn't just the right time, we mapped out tours and everything. Well, we've worked the men down on the question and with the cooperation of the women, because the more the women went to court the more the women got indignant, excited and anxious to do something and we finally got a committee of the wives, headed by Mrs. Winston. We arranged a reception at the trial, we didn't make it a mass display because the women were very timid about speaking, some women haven't spoken for years it was just like pulling teeth. At first we had two, by the time we had the affair we had five out of ten women present, we had five speak and found out afterward that Lil Green had a speech in her pocket and didn't tell us, so we could have had six. We thought that was a real accomplishment. We made it an invitational affair of Comrades of both the Party, the IWO and the Congress of American Women, and we had over 800 women there. The place was jammed to capacity. We're figuring now that we're going to get Madison Square Garden and have these ten women speak at that meeting."

150. *DW*, Apr. 19, 1949.

151. In a report dated Mar. 28, 1961, Seattle, the FBI bragged about getting close to one hundred anticommunists to disrupt a public meeting in Seattle on Mar. 24, 1961. The FBI began planning this disruption on Feb. 9, 1961.

152. Interview with Martha Stone, West Orange, N.J., Apr. 16, 1985. Green, in *Cold War Fugitive*, stated, "Two members of the National Board argued that all should surrender" (p. 5). Martha Stone told the author that perhaps a few others voted against the policy at an underground meeting, but she and EGF were the only ones above ground.

153. EGF, *Communists and the People*, 31–32, 39.

154. George Charney, *A Long Journey* (Chicago, Ill.: Quadrangle Books, 1969), 225. Charney was on trial with Flynn. *DW*, Sept. 1, 1948, Feb. 11, 1949, Nov. 18, 1949, Oct. 17, 1950, Mar. 1, 1951, Jan. 24, 1952, July 21, 1953, Jan. 21, 1962.

155. *DW*, Dec. 8, 1950.

156. EGF, "Statement before Sentencing," in *Thirteen Communists Speak to the Court* (New York: New Century Publishers, 1953), 13. Haywood and Reed chose to go to the Soviet Union rather than risk jail in the United States. Flynn disapproved of them and felt they deserted. They did not wait for an official order; they fled.

157. EGF to Muriel Symington, Dec. 8, 1956, EGF Papers, Tamiment.

158. *DW*, June 28, 1959, an article EGF wrote on his death.

159. EGF to Clemens France, Mar. 23, 1957, EGF Papers, Tamiment.

160. Interviews with John Gates and George Charney, Jan. 24, 1985, and Oct. 31, 1972. Gates told the author that World War II had a similar effect on Communist party members.

161. Isserman, *Which Side Were You On?*

162. EGF, from Alderson, to Kathie Flynn (I numbered them): No. 80, Feb. 24, 1956; No. 93, June 6, 1956; No. 101, Aug. 18, 1956; No. 144, Nov. 17,

1956; No. 116, Dec. 2, 1956; No. 19, Dec. 23, 1956; No. 19, Dec. 23, 1956, to Clemens France; No. 24, Mar. 30, 1956; No. 47, Nov. 17, 1956; No. 49, Dec. 2, 1956; No. 51, Dec. 16, 1956; No. 52, Dec. 23, 1956, to Muriel Symington; No. 49, Mar. 24, 1956; No. 54, May 12, 1956; No. 60, June 30, 1956; No. 79, Dec. 2, 1956; No. 96, Mar. 29, 1957. EGF Papers, Tamiment.

163. EGF to Clemens France, June 23, 1953, EGF Papers, Tamiment.

164. Phone conversation with Rene Hanover, Mar. 1982. Most of Flynn's friends in the Party, especially Peggy Dennis and Dorothy Healy, do not believe Flynn could have written such a chapter as she knew she would be back in leadership and such an admission would have challenged her ability to be a spokesperson for the Party.

165. EGF, *Alderson Story*, chap. 18, and 211—212.

166. Betty Gannett, another codefendant in the Smith Act case, was in Alderson at the same time, but quartered in another section, so they saw each other infrequently, except at music appreciation classes. As EGF could not get down on her hands and knees and wax her floor because she was too heavy and old, Betty Gannett, who suffered from a heart condition, volunteered to do this for her. EGF, *Alderson Story*, 33.

167. EGF, "A Friend to Claudia," in *Alderson Story*, 118, 212.

168. EGF to Clemens France, June 23, 1953, EGF Papers, Tamiment.

169. Interviews with Evelyn Wiener, Dec. 9, 1981; Annette Rubinstein, Nov. 2, 1981; and Peter Martin, Feb. 9, 1982. *Virginian Pilot*, Norfolk, Va., Sept. 6, 1964.

170. EGF, *Alderson Story*, 186.

171. Interview with Sam D'Arcy, Harvey Cedars, N.J., July 26, 1984. D'Arcy said, "Flynn was always on God's side. She was all things to all people."

172. Maurice Isserman, "The Half-Swept House: American Communism, 1956," *Socialist Review*, Jan.—Feb. 1982, 361.

173. EGF to Clemens France, Nov. 22, 1946, Dec. 3, 1956, EGF Files, Tamiment.

174. Letter to Muriel Symington, Sept. 4, 1956, EGF Files, Tamiment.

175. Letter to Muriel Symington, Dec. 16, 1956, EGF Files, Tamiment.

176. Interviews with John Gates, Oct. 19, 1971, and Jan. 24, 1985; George Charney, Sept. 23, 1972; Dorothy Rose Blumberg and Al Blumberg, May 22, 1972; Steve Nelson, Aug. 18, and Nov. 24, 1981, Truro, Mass.; Evelyn Weiner, Dec. 11, 1981; Annette Rubinstein, Nov. 2, 1981; Gil Green, Mar. 16, 1981; Abraham Isserman, Oct. 22, 1981; Oakley Johnson, Dec. 6, 1971; Walter Lowenfels, June 9, 1972. Telephone interview with William Weinstone, June 6, 1982. Interviews with Al Richmond, San Francisco, July 5, 1982; Peggy Dennis, San Francisco, July 1, 1982; Dorothy Healy, Los Angeles, July 12, 1982. This list has disappeared from Tamiment. However, I have a xerox of the note in EGF's handwriting, which I xeroxed at AIMS.

177. List undated. I believe it was written in 1957 or 1958.

178. Many people associated the Gates faction with the now discredited Browder. This association was one of the problems the Gates group had.

179. Al Richmond to Rosalyn Baxandall, Mar. 23, 1985. Richmond knew EGF when she was seventy-three years old. Richmond's letter says sixty-seven years old, but the same criteria apply.

180. Isserman, *Which Side Are You On?* 1–18. Theodore Draper, "The Popular Front Revisited," *New York Review of Books,* May 30, 1985, 45.

181. During this period the *DW* came out only on Sunday and mid-week.

182. *DW,* Dec. 31, 1961.

183. Notebook on Soviet Union, EGF Papers, Tamiment.

184. EGF to Betty Gannett, Apr. 22, 1961, EGF to Betty Gannett, Aug. 8, 1960, Sept. 2, 1960, Sept. 25, 1960, Oct. 8, 1960. Betty Gannett Papers, Microfilm, Tamiment. The original Gannett papers are at the University of Wisconsin Historical Society. *DW,* Nov. 15, 19, 26, 1961; Dec. 10, 1961.

185. Peggy Dennis to Rosalyn Baxandall, Aug. 20, 1982.

186. Flynn FBI Files, filed on Nov. 21, 1961, by Stanley Reed of *Seattle Post Intelligencer; Los Angeles Examiner,* Art Berman, filed on Nov. 20, 1961; *Los Angeles Mirror,* Walter Scratch, assistant to editor, filed Nov. 20, 1961; *Citizen News,* Hollywood, Calif., Hadley Roff, staff writer, filed Nov. 22, 1961; *San Francisco Chronicle,* Art Hope, editorial writer, Nov. 22, 1961; *San Francisco Chronicle,* Dan Frishman, staff writer, Nov. 22, 1961; *San Francisco Examiner,* Nov. 21, 1961; Dick Leonard, staff reporter for Columbia Broadcasting Company, Nov. 22, 1961; Radio Station KCBS filed Nov. 22, 1961; Vic Reed, director of KGO-TV and KGO News Press Room, San Francisco, Nov. 22, 1961; Marshall H. Newton, of *New York Times,* city editor, filed Nov. 27, 1961; Louise Huger of *New York Times,* letter editor, Nov. 27, 1961; George Miller, Associated Press, Mar. 14, 1961, was interviewed by FBI and talked to them about Flynn's appearances.

187. Interview with Jane Bobba, Nov. 20, 1972. Jane Bobba has been unwilling to talk to me for several years.

188. *DW,* May 12, 1963. Interview with Elizabeth Ewen, member of Young Communist League at the time, Aug. 8, 1985.

189. FBI Files, Agent Report, June 14, 1962, San Francisco.

190. *DW,* Aug. 23, 1964. The notes and papers for this part of EGF's biography were left in the Soviet Union. In spite of many inquiries by mail and in person by James Allen, director of International Publishers, the Communist party press, and other Communist party officials, these papers could not be located in the Soviet Union. A few draft chapters exist in EGF Papers, Tamiment.

191. An acute gastroenterocolitis, an inflammation of the lining of the stomach and intestines, aggravated by a thromboembolism of the lung. Art Shields to Betty Gannett, Sept. 27, 1964, Betty Gannett Papers, Tamiment. "Esther and I had no idea there was anything seriously the matter when we saw her for the last time. That was in the hospital where she was taken with some blood sugar. She was sitting in a big chair and chatting with her usual spirit. We went on to Osetia in the Caucasus with a group of correspondents. When we returned a week later, we were told that she could not be seen. Then several days later, we were advised to send the paper a wire, saying her condition was serious. . . . For a while there seemed hope. She rallied, but her heart could not stand the strain."

192. *Los Angeles Times,* Sept. 13, 1964. *Evening Star Telegram* (Fort Worth, Tex.), Sept. 8, 1964. *Star Gazette* (Elmira, N.Y.), Sept. 9, 1964. *Time,* Sept. 11, 1964. *Shreveport Louisiana Times,* Sept. 9, 1964. *Rocky Mountain News* (Denver,

Colo.), Sept. 9, 1964. *Springfield Ohio Sun,* Sept. 10, 1964. *Herald News* (Passaic, N.J.), Sept. 10, 1964.

193. Interview with Martin Popper, May 16, 1985. Popper is an American progressive lawyer who was in Moscow when Flynn died; he attended the funeral. He told me that he found it sad and inappropriate. The pomp and ceremony were totally Russian, and her hardy American roots and spirit were not captured by the ornate formality.

CONCLUSION

1. EGF to A. K. Flynn, Aug. 6, 1955, EGF Papers, Tamiment.

2. Letter that FBI opened dated Aug. 18, 1960, from FBI, CIA DOJ CA-82-8736 Sanitized Document. I have them in my possession.

3. *DW,* Nov. 7, 1937.

4. *SW,* Nov. 30, 1941.

5. The first series of columns EGF wrote for the *DW,* during 1937–1947, was called "The Feminine Ferment"; in 1947–1950 the column was called "Life of the Party"; from 1950 to her death, "A Better World."

6. EGF to Muriel Symington, from Alderson, Apr. 21, 1956, EGF Papers, Tamiment.

7. EGF to A. K. Flynn, June 16, 1955, EGF Papers, Tamiment.

8. EGF to A. K. Flynn, June 3, 1955, EGF Papers, Tamiment.

9. Interview with Charlotte Stern, CP union organizer and labor writer, Apr. 9, 1979. Dorothy Healy offered this interpretation in an interview, more like a visit, Apr. 19, 1985.

10. Phone conversation with Betty Mallard, Jan. 30, 1985.

11. Interview with Martha Stone Ascher, Apr. 16, 1985.

12. Interviews with Peggy Dennis, July 2, 1982; Steve Nelson, May 31, 1983; Herbert Aptheker, Dec. 1971.

13. Interview with Dorothy Healy, July 15, 1982.

14. FBI, CIA DOJ CA-82-8736, Sanitized Documents, Letter no. 77, Aug. 10, 1960. EGF also wrote about him in Letter no. 85, Aug. 13, 1960; Letter no. 86, Aug. 14, 1960; Letter no. 91, Aug. 18, 1960; Letter no. 94, Aug. 21, 1960; Letter no. 95, Aug. 22, 1960, where she wrote him to say her temptation is great to return to Hungary, but she cannot. The FBI crossed out the names to whom the letters were written, so I do not know to whom she wrote.

15. Interview with Roberta Bobba, July 12, 1982.

16. EGF, *Alderson Story,* 164.

17. Sanitized Documents, No. 294, Nov. 10, 1964. The return address is the Chelsea Hotel. As she wrote "Dear Folks," my guess is that she was writing to American Party officials visiting the Soviet Union.

Index